How It Works®

Science and Technology

Third Edition

Marshall Cavendish
99 White Plains Road
Tarrytown, NY 10591

Website: www.marshallcavendish.com

Third edition updated by Brown Reference Group plc.

Library of Congress Cataloging-in-Publication Data
How it works: science and technology.—3rd ed.
p. cm.
Includes index.
ISBN 0-7614-7314-9 (set)   ISBN 0-7614-7320-3 (Vol. 6)
1. Technology—Encyclopedias. 2. Science—Encyclopedias.
[1. Technology—Encyclopedias. 2. Science—Encyclopedias.]
T9 .H738 2003
603—dc21   2001028771

Consultant: Donald R. Franceschetti, Ph.D., University of Memphis

Brown Reference Group
Editor: Wendy Horobin
Associate Editors: Paul Thompson, Martin Clowes, Lis Stedman
Managing Editor: Tim Cooke
Design: Alison Gardner
Picture Research: Becky Cox
Illustrations: Mark Walker

Marshall Cavendish
Project Editor: Peter Mavrikis
Production Manager: Alan Tsai
Editorial Director: Paul Bernabeo

Printed in Malaysia
Bound in the United States of America
08 07 06 05 04   6 5 4 3 2

Title picture: Gaining energy from the wind, see *Energy Resources*

How It Works®

Science and Technology

Volume 6

Electricity

Firefighting

Marshall Cavendish

New York • London • Toronto • Sydney

Contents

Volume 6

Electricity

Electricity is the name given to phenomena caused by the accumulation or motion of electrically charged particles. The effects resulting from the accumulation of positive or negative charge are termed "static electricity," while the effects resulting from the motion of charged particles are termed "current electricity."

Lightning is an electrical phenomenon that has occurred on Earth ever since the planet acquired an atmosphere. It consists of spectacular current discharges between regions of positive and negative charge formed by atmospheric convection, such as occurs in storm clouds and around erupting volcanoes.

Early experiments

The first recorded observations of electrical phenomena occurred more than 2,500 years ago: in ancient Greece, Thales of Miletus noted that certain substances, when rubbed with cloth, were able to attract lightweight objects. One such substance is amber, a natural resin whose Greek name—*elektron*—is the root of the word *electricity*. The form of electricity generated by rubbing surfaces together is called triboelectricity. The Greeks associated triboelectricity with magnetism, which they had observed in the properties of magnetite ore, since both phenomena give rise to attractive and repulsive forces between objects that are not in physical contact.

In the mid-16th century, the Italian physician Jerome Cardan studied the relationship between magnetic and electrostatic forces. In 1551, he proposed that electricity was a type of fluid. In 1600, William Gilbert, an English physician investigating electromagnetic phenomena, conducted extensive research into triboelectrification. He classified substances as good or poor electrifiers—classifications that correspond to modern insulators and conductors, respectively. The theory of electrical fluid was further developed by the French scientist Charles du Fay. In 1733, du Fay proposed that there were two types of electrical fluid, and the phenomena of static electricity occurred when the two are out of balance.

In 1747, Benjamin Franklin, known for his celebrated experiments with kites flown during thunderstorms and with an early type of capacitor called a Leyden jar, proposed that there was only one electrical fluid that moved through conductors. According to this theory, it is buildup or depletion of this fluid beyond that normally found in an object that caused the effects of positive or negative charge.

Static electricity

The distinction between positive and negative electricity came about because some pairs of electrified substances attract one another, while others exert mutual repulsion. This behavior mirrors that of magnets: the north pole of a magnet will repel another magnet's north pole, just as two south poles repel one another, but a north pole and a south pole will attract one another.

The quantitative study of static electricity began in the second half of the 18th century when two scientists independently discovered a relationship between the electrostatic force between two charged objects, the size of their charges, and the distance between them. The discovery was made in 1767 by Joseph Priestley, a British chemist and physicist, then in 1785 by Charles Coulomb, a French physicist. The mathematical expression of the relationship became known as Coulomb's law and the standard unit of electrical charge the coulomb.

Coulomb and Priestley found that the force between two charged objects varies with the reciprocal of the square of the distance between the objects. The formula has stood essentially unchanged to this day—a tribute to the experimental precision of both scientists.

Current electricity

Before the 19th century, scientists generated electricity by triboelectric methods, and the only means of storing electrical charge were devices called electroscopes and Leyden jars. Both types of devices discharged too rapidly for scientists to study the flow of electrical current.

▲ Lightning is a dramatic discharge of atmospheric static electricity. At any time, there are around 1,800 thunderstorms occurring worldwide. The intense heat generated by lightning strokes may have played a role in the primordial formation of amino acids—the building blocks of proteins. Lightning continues to make soil fertile by converting atmospheric nitrogen and oxygen into nitrogen oxides, which form nitric acid with moisture and then nitrate salts, which are plant nutrients.

In 1800, a detailed study of current electricity was made possible by the invention of the voltaic pile, named for its Italian inventor, Alessandro Volta. A forerunner of the modern battery, the voltaic pile was the first reliable source of continuous current. It generated current by a similar process to that of some modern batteries—the electrolytic action of an acid on a metal. The unit of potential difference—the property of a power supply that makes it able to drive current in an electrical circuit—is named the volt in honor of Volta's contribution to the study of electricity.

One aspect of the study of current electricity is resistance—a property of materials that hinders the flow of electrical current. Georg Ohm, a German physicist, studied the flow of currents in circuits and devised a mathematical description, now called Ohm's law, that relates the current that flows through a circuit to the potential difference across the circuit and the resistance of the circuit. Ohm's law states that the potential difference is the product of the current and resistance in a circuit so that the current is inversely proportional to the resistance for a given voltage.

Ohm's research would not have happened had he been unable to measure the sizes of currents and voltages in different circuits. The devices that enabled him to make such measurements functioned by exploiting the relationship between electrical currents and magnetic fields.

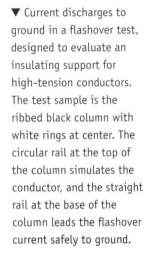

▼ Current discharges to ground in a flashover test, designed to evaluate an insulating support for high-tension conductors. The test sample is the ribbed black column with white rings at center. The circular rail at the top of the column simulates the conductor, and the straight rail at the base of the column leads the flashover current safely to ground.

Electromagnetism

The first observation of the direct relationship between magnetism and an electrical current was made in 1820 when a Danish physicist, Hans Oersted, watched a magnetized needle align itself at right angles to a current-carrying wire. The needle was reacting to a magnetic field caused by the movement of charge through the wire. Then, André Ampère—the French physicist for whom the unit of current is named—studied the force that arises between two current-carrying wires when their magnetic fields interact. Ampère also used a current-carrying coil as the basis for a device to measure the strength of current—an instrument that would help Ohm's studies.

In 1831, the British physicist Michael Faraday demonstrated that the variation of a magnetic field passing through a loop of conducting wire causes a current to circulate in the loop—the converse result of earlier experiments, which had shown that a pulse of current in a coil causes a fluctuation in the magnetic field around the loop. Interconnected variations of electrical currents and magnetic fields are the basis of inductance, the mechanism by which transformers function. In 1873, the British physicist James Clerk Maxwell published a theory of electromagnetism whose equations mathematically described the connections between variations in electrical currents and magnetic fields.

The electron

Remarkably, the early researchers of electricity and magnetism achieved striking success in describing electromagnetic phenomena without even knowing of the electron. The concept of the electron developed with the emergence of modern atomic theory in the late 19th century. In 1897, the British physicist J. J. Thomson provided the first positive demonstration of the existence of the electron. By unfortunate coincidence, the electron—the principal charge carrier in electrical circuits—turned out to have a negative charge according to the equations and conventions that had developed by the time it was discovered. One of the consequences of the electron's negative charge is that the flow of electrons in a circuit is in the opposite sense to the direction of conventional current, which flows from positive to negative.

In 1926, the Austrian physicist Erwin Schrödinger developed an equation describing the motion of an electron in a hydrogen atom. Further developments of the equation have since helped relate electrical resistance, semiconductivity, superconductivity, the photoelectric effect, and the thermoelectric effect to the electronic structures of molecules and crystalline materials.

Back to basics

The simplest electrical system consists of two infinitely small charged particles. An electrostatic force acts between the two charges, and the strength of that force is inversely proportional to the square of the distance between them—if the distance doubles, the force between the charges diminishes to a quarter of its previous value. This relationship forms part of Coulomb's law. As the distance increases, the force continues to diminish until it becomes negligible. If the two charges are of opposite signs—one positive and one negative—the force is an attraction that tends to pull the charged objects closer together. If the charges have the same sign, the force is a repulsion.

Electrostatic forces arise from interactions between the electrical fields that permeate the space around charges. In electrically neutral matter, each positive charge is matched by a negative charge—there is a proton for every electron, for example. The fields of negative charges counteract the fields of positive charges so that an object with no overall charge projects no net electrical field. When two objects are brought into contact, however, a repulsion builds between the electrons that orbit the nuclei of atoms in the two surfaces; this repulsion is the force that prevents one solid object from being able to pass through another.

A charged object has unequal numbers of electrons and protons, and the size of the charge depends on the difference between the numbers of electrons and protons. A negative charge indicates an electron excess, and a positive charge indicates a proton excess. In either case, it is impossible to identify individual electrons or protons as being responsible for the excess, so the charge is attributed to the object as a whole.

Triboelectricity

Triboelectricity is the separation of electrical charges by friction. For example, it is the mechanism by which a party balloon, when rubbed against a sweater, becomes charged and sticks to the sweater until the charge dissipates.

Any atom or molecule can be made to lose an electron by the input of a certain amount of energy, called its ionization energy. Similarly, an atom or molecule can accept a free electron in its vicinity, and the quantity of energy evolved when it does is called its electron affinity.

When two substances are rubbed together, electrons transfer from the substance with the lesser ionization energy to the substance with the greater electron affinity. The former material becomes positively charged, while the latter becomes negatively charged. Provided there is no conducting path to ground, the charge separation

persists, and the two substances are mutually attracted by the electrostatic force between their opposite charges. After a while, the charges dissipate—typically through a conductive surface layer of moisture from the atmosphere—and the attraction between the two objects fades.

Current electricity and cells

Because of the repulsion between like charges, electrons tend to flow from areas where there is a high concentration of electrons to areas where there are fewer electrons. Current electricity is this flow of electrons channeled through conductors in an orderly manner.

Electrochemical cells are a source of current electricity. They have two electrodes: one where an electrochemical reaction causes a surfeit of electrons and one where a different electrochemical reaction causes a deficit of electrons. The two reactions convert chemical energy into electrical energy if electrons flow through a circuit from the negative electrode to the positive electrode.

The electrons at the negative electrode have a greater electrical potential energy than those at the positive electrode, and this potential difference is called the electromotive force (emf) of the cell, measured in volts. A potential difference of one volt is equivalent to a change in electrical potential energy of one joule per coulomb of charge, or one joule per 6.24×10^{18} electrons.

The current that passes through an external circuit between the two electrodes is measured in amperes. One ampere is equivalent to one coulomb of charge per second passing through any section of the external circuit.

▲ The hair flying out from this wig demonstrates the repulsion that exists between like charges. The wig is on top of a van de Graaff generator—a device that accumulates charges at high voltage. The charges pass through a conductive layer of moisture on the fibers of the wig to collect at the tips of the fibers. The fibers then straighten to maximize the separation between like charges.

Resistance and resistivity

The resistance of a wire or other circuit component is its tendency to impede the flow of an electrical current. Resistance depends on the dimensions of the wire or component and the resistivity of the material of which it is made.

A wire of any given conducting material has twice the resistance of a similar wire with twice the cross-sectional area, since the latter provides more room for a current to flow; the same wire has half the resistance of a wire that is twice as long, since current has to travel farther through the conductor. For wires of different materials but the same dimensions, resistance is proportional to the resistivities of the different materials.

For most conductors, the current that flows is proportional to the potential difference, or voltage, that drives it—this is Ohm's law. The resistance in ohms is the potential difference in volts divided by the current in amperes. The equation that connects current (I), resistance (R), and potential difference (V) is written $V = I \times R$.

Superconductors and semiconductors

A few materials, called superconductors, have no electrical resistance below a characteristic temperature—the movement of their electrons is completely uninhibited. Such materials include certain ceramics and alloys of metals, and these substances lose their resistance only at extremely low temperatures.

Semiconductors, such as silicon, have few electrons that are free to move under the influence of an electrical field. As such, their resistance is greater than that of a metal, but much less than that of an insulator. The resistance of semiconductors becomes less at high temperatures, or if traces of certain impurities are added. Some semiconductors exhibit lowered resistance if they are exposed to light.

Resistance and power

When current flows through a circuit, the electrical energy expended in overcoming resistance becomes heat, which spreads through the conductor. As temperature increases, so does the resistivity of a material. Filament lamps and electric heaters operate in this way: when switched on, the temperature and resistance rapidly increase, while the current decreases until a stable condition is reached. At that point, the rate of heat loss from the resistor matches the rate at which heat is generated by the current flowing against resistance.

The rate at which electrical energy is used in a circuit is calculated from the potential difference across the circuit and the current that flows through it. Potential difference is the loss of elec-

▲ A Plexiglas sheet at the moment of discharge. An enormous triboelectric charge can be collected on such a sheet by rubbing it with cloth. The pattern seen above was formed by surface charges flooding toward a conducting ground lead placed at the edge of the sheet.

Conductors and insulators

The attraction between opposite charges means that electrons tend to move from regions of high electrical potential (electron excess) to regions of relatively low electrical potential. Whether they do so or not depends on how they are bound in a given substance. A static charge of many thousands of volts can build up in one part of an insulator, for example, while the same charge would spread throughout a conductor.

Electrons in insulating solids are tightly bound within atoms or molecules. The individual atoms or molecules can become distorted in an electric field so that the solid becomes positively charged on the surface closest to the negative pole of the field and negatively charged on the opposite surface. Nevertheless, electrons do not flow through an insulating solid unless the electric field becomes strong enough to disrupt the chemical bonds of the insulator and release electrons—a condition called breakdown.

Electrons in conducting solids are free to move, so that a current of electrons starts to flow toward the positive pole of the field. In a typical conductor, interactions between electrons and protons impedes the motion of electrons, a phenomenon called electrical resistance.

Liquids are generally molecular, so they tend to be good insulators. Exceptions are liquids that contain ions—atoms or groups of atoms that have unequal proton and electron counts. Such liquids conduct by their positive ions moving toward the negative pole of a field, while their negative ions move toward the positive pole.

◀ This testing ground for photovoltaic cells occupies the site of a deactivated nuclear power plant at Rancho Seco, California. The 1950s belief that nuclear energy would provide endless low cost electricity has been undermined by the great cost of decommissioning such plants, whereas solar energy is now proving to be a viable source of low cost renewable energy.

trical potential energy per coulomb of charge, while the current is the number of coulombs of charge flowing through the circuit in one second. The rate at which energy is used—the power (P)—is therefore calculated by multiplying potential difference by current to gave a value in joules per second, a unit better known as the watt. The equation is written $P = I \times V$.

Current and power loss

The equations already described for current, power, resistance, and potential difference (V) are $V = I \times R$ and $P = I \times V$. Using the first equation to replace V in the second equation gives a third equation: $P = I^2 \times R$. This equation reveals that the power lost in overcoming resistance increases in proportion to the square of current. The relationship between current and power loss explains why long-distance power lines operate at extremely high voltages: the power loss in the line can be kept to a minimum by using the highest possible voltages to deliver enormous amounts of power using as little current as possible.

Induction and alternating current

Induction is the effect whereby changes in the strength of a magnetic field cause currents to flow in conductors. The coupling between electric and magnetic fields is of phenomenal importance in the power-supply industry since it underlies the operation of generators and transformers.

A simple case of induction occurs when two coils of cable are placed side by side. When cur-

rent flows around a coil, it sets up a magnetic field along the axis around which the coil is wound. If a pulse of current passes through one of the coils, the field strength grows and collapses. As it does so, the second coil experiences a momentary pulse of magnetic field. As the field collapses, some of the energy stored in the magnetic field creates a pulse of current in the second coil.

An alternating-current generator consists of a coil of wire that rotates between the poles of an electromagnet such that the axis through the center of the coil faces first the north pole of the magnet then the south pole. The coil experiences a magnetic field that grows to a peak value in one direction along its axis, falls to zero, rises to a peak in the opposite direction, then falls to zero again.

If the ends of the generator coil are connected through an external circuit, the fluctuations in the magnetic field drive a current back and forth in the coil and through that circuit. This type of current is called an alternating current, or AC. The energy expended in overcoming resistance in the circuit translates to a mechanical resistance to the rotation of the coil. In a power station, a turbine provides the mechanical drive that turns the coil.

Transformer

A transformer is essentially a sophisticated pair of induction coils. One coil—the primary coil—is connected to an AC power supply. As the current switches back and forth, so does the magnetic field it creates along the central axis of the coil. The alternating magnetic field passes through a secondary coil, where it has the same effect as the magnetic field experienced by a rotating coil in a generator: the fluctuations induce an alternating potential that can be tapped to feed an AC circuit.

In effect, the primary coil of a transformer puts energy into the growing magnetic field, and the secondary coil collects it as the field collapses. The efficiency of a transformer is boosted by focusing the magnetic field through the coils using a soft iron core, which is easily magnetized.

The ratio of the output voltage to the input voltage is equal to the ratio of the numbers of turns in the two coils. For example, a transformer with a 24-turn primary coil and a 48-turn secondary coil will produce a 220-volt AC output from a 110-volt AC input, or a 12-volt output from a 6-volt input. It will produce no output voltage if a direct-current input is used, however.

Large step-up transformers are used to increase the voltage of a power supply for transmission over long distances. Step-down transformers, which have fewer turns in their secondary coils than in their primary coils, are used to reduce the voltage for local distribution.

Capacitor

A capacitor is a device for storing charge and energy consisting of conducting plates separated by an insulating layer. When the two plates are connected to a DC (direct current) supply, electrons flood into the negative plate and out of the positive plate. The strong electric field between the two plates stores energy, and there is a potential difference between the two plates even when disconnected from the charging source.

Simple capacitors are used as power sources for flashguns and other devices that require a quick burst of energy. The capacitor is first connected to a battery, from which it draws charge until the voltage between its plates matches the emf of the battery. Connecting the capacitor to a device then drains all the charge in a short burst.

Variable capacitors play an important role in tuning circuits, where they provide the electrical resonance that enables the circuit to select desired frequencies from signals. They typically have fixed semicircular plates interspersed by a second set of plates on a movable spindle. Altering the overlap between the plates varies the capacitance.

◄ This repair team works on a live power-supply line with little risk of electrocution. A safety cable, draped against the right-hand worker's tool in this picture, ensures that the cradle is always at the same potential as the line. Consequently, no current can flow if the workers come into contact with the high-tension cable.

FACT FILE

- At least 500 species of fish have specialized organs for emitting electrical discharges. Electric eels are the best known, but others include skates and rays, the African elephant nose fish, and the electric catfish. Electric eels stun their prey with almost 600 V. The electric catfish, on the other hand, creates an electric detection field all around itself that helps it find its way in murky waters.

- The first deliberate use of electricity to execute a person occurred in 1890, when William Kemmler, a convicted murderer, was put to death by electric chair at Auburn, New York. In the electric chair, a 5-amp current is administered using 2,000-volt shocks. After the first shock, the supply is reduced to 500 volts then raised to 2,000 volts three times. Death takes less than three minutes.

- For many years, the only domestic use of electricity was for lighting. The electric light industry was established by Thomas Edison, a self-educated inventor who registered over 1,000 patents to his name, starting with an electrical vote recorder that he conceived and designed in 1868.

Photovoltaic cells

Photovoltaic cells convert light into electricity. The simplest photovoltaic cell consists of a wafer of silicon, one side of which has been doped with boron to make p-type silicon, the other with phosphorus to make n-type silicon.

When light strikes a photovoltaic cell, some photons are absorbed, and their energy kicks electrons from the p-type silicon to the n-type silicon. A wire attached to the surface of the n-type silicon collects the extra electrons, while another wire on the reverse of the cell supplies electrons to replace those that have been driven into the n-type silicon by the photovoltaic effect. The two wires therefore act in a similar way to the electrodes in an electrochemical cell, and there is a potential difference between them that can drive a current if they are connected through a circuit.

Photovoltaic cells convert less than 25 percent of the energy in sunlight into electricity—mainly because most of the photons in sunlight have too little energy to cause the photovoltaic effect. The manufacture of photovoltaic cells is costly, but their fuel source—sunlight—is free. Photovoltaic cells are useful sources of power in remote sun-drenched locations, such as deserts and even outer space, and they are also providing an increasing contribution to network electricity.

SEE ALSO:	ATOMIC STRUCTURE • BATTERY • ELECTROMAGNETISM • PHOTOELECTRIC CELL AND PHOTOMETRY • QUANTUM THEORY

Electric Motor

An electric motor is more properly described as an electric machine, for the same piece of apparatus can be used either as a motor or as a generator of electricity. There is no type of machine that can convert electrical energy into mechanical energy that cannot be used equally well to convert in the opposite direction if so required.

All types of electric motor use the principles of electromagnetism in which either electric currents flowing in wires situated in a magnetic field experience mechanical force or in which electromagnets apply force to a ferromagnetic (intrinsically highly magnetic) material. The electric current used by motors can be either direct current (DC), as obtained from a battery, or alternating current (AC), which is generally more convenient to use, mainly because the supply voltage can be raised or lowered effectively by static transformers.

Controls

The speed of some types of AC motors can be easily and efficiently controlled by using a form of thyristor called a triac. Triacs are electronic switches that remain off until triggered by a short pulse of current, after which time they turn on and remain on until the voltage across them falls to zero (which occurs twice in each current cycle). There are two main control techniques for using triacs. Phase control (also called conduction angle control) alters the power fed to the motor by adjusting the point in each half cycle when the trigger pulse is applied—early for high power, late for low power. It is simple to implement but can generate a lot of electromagnetic interference at mid power, when there is a high voltage across the triac immediately before it switches. Burst firing control triggers the triac only near the beginning of half cycles and so is less prone to producing interference.

In many applications, the speed or position of a motor shaft must be measured in order to allow accurate adjustments to be made. The transducer used for making these measurements is called a shaft encoder, which, in its most basic form, consists of a light shining through radial slots in a disk attached to the motor shaft. When the motor is turning, flashes of light are produced that can be detected by a photocell and used to calculate the motor speed. For increased accuracy, the shaft encoder may be connected to the motor through gearing so that it produces pulses at a higher rate. If one of the slots is made significantly wider than all of the others, the resultant long pulse of light

can be distinguished and the motor shaft position calculated by counting subsequent pulses.

For reversible motors, a second photocell slightly offset from the original is used to determine direction of rotation by detecting which photocell is illuminated first by each slot. Alternatively, a bank of photocells can be used in conjunction with a complex pattern of slots to give a unique light pattern for every position of the shaft. If a normal binary code is used for the pattern sequence, some shaft movements would result in changes at more than one photocell. If the photocells were read during the transition, an incorrect result might be obtained. To overcome this problem, a sequence called Gray code is used that has the property that only one bit changes between consecutive counts. Special integrated circuits are available to translate between Gray and binary if required.

Magnets and electromagnets

Electric motors usually produce rotational motion, which is directly applicable to mechanical systems with wheels. The various types of motor can be classified into two groups: electromagnetic machines and magnetic machines. The electromagnetic group includes induction, synchronous, DC, AC-polyphase commutator, single-phase AC commutator, and repulsion motors (the last are another form of single-phase AC commutator motor). Magnetic machines include reluctance and hysteresis motors, solenoids, and relays.

▲ A three-phase squirrel-cage rotor induction motor. Turning of the shaft is "induced" by an electric current. The field of the motor will rotate once with each cycle in the current; thus, in the United States, with a power supply of 60 Hz (Hertz, or cycles per second), the motor runs at around 3,600 rpm.

The classification into magnetic and electromagnetic machines is a comparatively recent concept and to some may seem artificial, since machines in both classes make use of electromagnets. But the difference between the two classes is of fundamental importance in appreciating the different uses to which motors of each class are put. Electromagnetic machines have a performance that improves naturally as they are made bigger. Magnetic machines, on the other hand, improve as they are scaled down to smaller sizes. The applications of reluctance and hysteresis motors are therefore restricted to such things as tape recorders, record players, and electric clocks. Electromagnetic machines, in contrast, supply the needs of both heavy and light industry alike, since they are effective down to the size of motor needed for washing machines and even hair dryers.

One unusual form of electric motor is the linear induction motor. This is little more than a rotary machine that has been split along a radial plane and "unrolled" (with minor subsequent modifications). There are as many possible types of linear motor as there are rotary types listed above.

Induction motors

When a magnet is moved across the face of an electrically conducting sheet, it induces eddy currents in the sheet and produces a force tending to drag the sheet along with the magnet. This fact is less well known than the fact that a magnet will attract pieces of iron and steel, because the conducting sheet of the induction device can (and usually does) consist of copper or aluminum, which is classed as nonmagnetic. This fact alone is an indication that magnetic things are very effective in small sizes, while induction devices (which are electromagnetic) are not very efficient in small sizes. So, while the principle of the induction motor cannot be illustrated by putting a small coin on a table and sweeping a magnet over it from side to side, such

an arrangement does produce a very small force on the coin, and if the experiment were to be repeated with a copper disk 12 in. (30 cm) in diameter and a large magnet, a large force would be obtained.

Yet such a system cannot be described as a "motor" because mechanical force (on the magnet) is needed to provide mechanical force on the sheet. It is, at best, a clutch. To make an induction motor, the moving magnet must be replaced by a system of fixed electromagnets, which are fed with currents that change in such a way as to produce the same effect as if a permanent magnet system had moved.

For an explanation of how such a thing is possible, imagine a ring of electric light bulbs that are being switched on and off one at a time in sequence around the ring. If this is done fairly rapidly, the effect is as if a spot of light is traveling around the ring, yet it is obvious from the physical structure that nothing actually moves. Now suppose instead only bulb numbers 1, 4, 7, 10, and so on, are switched on for a fraction of a second, then, as they are switched off, numbers 2, 5, 8, 11 are switched on, then 3, 6, 9, 12, and so on, a pattern of alternate light and dark patches will appear to rotate around the ring. The rotating magnetic field of the induction motor is produced in this way by arranging a ring of magnets on the stationary part of the machine. The magnets are energized in sequence and a pattern of north and south poles appears to travel around the periphery; this field is just as capable of inducing currents in a conducting cylinder as would be a system of permanent magnets that actually moved.

Instead of switching the primary ring of electromagnets, they are simply fed from an AC supply, making the whole machine cheap to build (for it has no commutator or brushes as in a DC motor) and very robust, as the rotating member consists only of what is virtually a solid lump of metal. So desirable are the robust, reliable, and low-cost

▼ In a single-coil DC motor with external field magnets, the current is periodically reversed by the action of the commutator, thus maintaining the same direction of motive force.

Stator

Rotor

Brush

Commutator segment

Negative lead −

Positive lead +

Battery

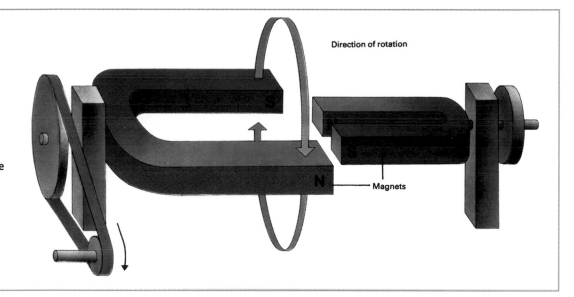

SYNCHRONOUS MOTORS

If the left-hand horseshoe magnet is rotated in the direction shown, it will pull the right-hand magnet with it. If the right-hand magnet has to do work, that is, if the shaft has to drive a load, it will rotate so that its poles are slightly behind the primary poles. Both magnets, however, will still revolve at the same speed.

Direction of rotation

Magnets

features of the induction motor that it is estimated that over 90 percent of the world's horsepower of electric motors consist of induction machines.

Synchronous motors

The production of induced current in an induction motor rotor depends on there being relative movement between the rotating field and the secondary conductor. In other words, the rotor never quite "catches" up with the field. If the rotor runs at 97 percent of the field speed, the 3 percent relative motion is referred to as the percentage slip. It is fairly obvious that the slip will increase with added load, and for some applications, such inability to maintain an exact speed is inadmissible. In such circumstances, a motor is used whose rotor consists of an arrangement of permanent magnets or of DC-fed electromagnets. The primary coils are, exactly as in the case of the induction motor, arranged to produce a rotating magnetic field, but this time the field locks with the field of the magnetized rotor. Thus, the rotor speed of the motor concerned cannot change with variations in load, and it is said to run in synchronism with the power supply.

If the system of primary coils is so arranged as to give the impression that one pair of poles, that is, a two-pole pattern (one north pole and one south pole), is contained in the full 360 degrees, the field will rotate one revolution in one complete cycle of the AC power supply. In Europe, the supply frequency is usually 50

▼ A squirrel-cage induction motor has a rotor consisting of copper or aluminum bars joined at their ends by thick rings of the same material. The conductor is on the left; the rotor on the right. A rotating magnetic field generated in the stator induces currents in the cage, producing a dragging force on the rotor and thereby causing it to revolve.

cycles per second (denoted 50 hertz). In the United States, the standard frequency is 60 hertz. Thus, a two-pole motor on 50 Hz supply has a field speed of 50 revolutions per second or 3,000 revolutions per minute (rpm). If the primary coils are arranged to give a four-pole pattern, the speed is halved, and so on, so the possible synchronous motor speeds in Europe are 3,000, 1,500, 1,000, 750, 600, and 500 rpm, and so on. Corresponding induction motor speeds are less than these values by the small amount of slip necessary to induce secondary current. A disadvantage of the synchronous motor is that it cannot self-start and the speed must be brought to within a very small percentage of synchronism before magnetic locking can take place. The synchronous machine is more commonly used as a generator or alternator, and almost all of the power stations in Britain presently employ machines of this type.

DC and AC commutator motors

There are two disadvantages common to both induction motors and synchronous motors. Neither is able to provide efficient speed variation over a wide range without a variable supply frequency. Neither is able to provide speeds over 3,000 rpm when fed directly from power supplies. Where high-speed or variable-speed electric drive is required for use from power supplies, a commutator motor is used. The action of a commutator is fairly complicated and more easily explained for the case of DC machines. In a DC machine, the stationary

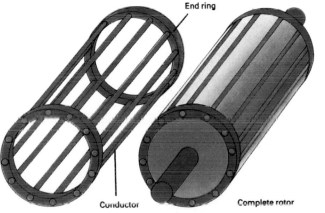

End ring

Conductor

Complete rotor

part (stator) consists of a ring of DC-fed field magnets. The rotor is, like the induction motor, a series of conducting wires or bars in slots in a steel core. In this case, however, they are insulated coils rather than solid-cast bars (and therefore more expensive to make), and each coil has its ends connected to a pair of conducting segments mounted on an insulating block on the rotor shaft at one end of the rotor. Connection to the rotor coils is made by carbon blocks or copper gauze brushes that make contact with pairs of commutator segments twice per cycle. In this way, current flowing in the appropriate direction can be fed to the rotor coils only when they are opposite the appropriate field pole (north or south).

The disadvantage of commutator motors is that sparking tends to occur between commutator segments and brushes, which eats away the metal of the segment. Even without sparks, the rubbing of brush on segments wears away both, and more maintenance is required than in the case of brushless machines. Power electronics have tended to increase the popularity of the DC machine, although the small single-phase AC commutator motor (generally known as a universal motor since it can also run on DC) is still the principal form of drive for household devices requiring high speed, such as vacuum cleaners and do-it-yourself power drills and similar tools.

Reluctance motors

A reluctance motor is simply a synchronous motor with the magnetized rotor replaced by an unmagnetized piece of steel shaped so that it has a number of preferred positions into which it will settle for any given primary field configuration. A preferred position is one in which the resistance of the magnetic circuit (which is called reluctance) is minimum, hence the name of this type of motor. Reluctance motors are used to drive electric clocks, their synchronous running being frequency-dependent only.

Hysteresis motor

A hysteresis motor is even simpler in construction than a clock motor, for the rotor can be a smooth cylinder. The steel used to make the rotor is, however, very similar to that used to make permanent magnets (unlike that of all other types of motor) so that, as the moving magnetic field passes over any point on the rotor (in induction motor language we should say "slips"), it leaves the part passed over permanently magnetized. This hysteretic lag produces force and tends to make the motor run more and more nearly as a synchronous motor as it speeds up, until finally it succeeds in locking in on the rotating field.

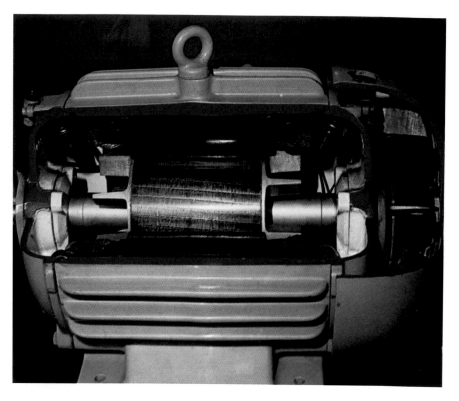

Unlike the reluctance motor, however, it is capable of driving loads at all speeds up to synchronism, but of course, synchronism is never guaranteed, as in the reluctance machine.

Stepping motors

Most of the motors discussed so far are optimized for use at one steady speed or range of speeds. Stepping motors are designed to allow them to rotate a precise number of revolutions or fractions of a revolution and then stop in one of a number of accurate and repeatable positions. The simplest form of stepping motor uses a permanent magnet as its rotor and two sets of coils placed at right angles to each other around the rotor as its stator. If a pulse of current is applied to one set of coils, the rotor will move to align itself with the resultant magnetic field. If a pulse of current is now applied to the second set of coils, the rotor will turn 90 degrees to realign itself with the magnetic field. By applying a series of pulses to each set of coils in turn, the motor can be driven forward or backward in quarter-turn increments. If the number of sets of coils (or poles) is increased to 12, the motor position can be controlled to within 15 degrees. Integrated circuits are now available to provide the necessary patterns of drive voltages. Stepping motors are used in a wide range of applications, including chart recorders, electric watches, and machine tools.

▲ A cutaway view of a three-phase motor. Turning of the shaft is induced by an electric current. The brushes can be seen on its side and the fan outside in front.

SEE ALSO: ELECTRICAL ENGINEERING • ELECTROMAGNETISM • INDUCTION • LINEAR MOTOR • MAGNETISM • STARTER MOTOR • THYRISTOR

Electrochemical Machining

Electrochemical machining and the related process of electrodischarge machining use the passage of an electrical current to remove material from the surfaces of metal workpieces. In the case of electrochemical machining (ECM), an electrolyte carries metal ions away from the workpiece; in the case of electrodischarge machining (EDM), heat generated by an electrical discharge vaporizes atoms from the surface of a metal workpiece.

Versus mechanical machining

ECM and EDM benefit by not suffering the limitations of more conventional mechanical machining techniques. Mechanical machining uses sharp-edged tools to form objects by cutting slivers of material from the surfaces of workpieces. The cutting edge of the tool must be harder than the surface being machined, which limits the availability of tool materials for machining extremely hard workpiece materials.

Mechanical machining subjects the workpiece to significant mechanical stress, which can cause defects in the finished object. Tools wear and become blunt with use, and there is a lower limit to the amount of metal that can be removed by a single cut. Below this limit, a tool simply skids across the surface of the workpiece without cutting into its surface.

Electrochemical machining

In electrochemical machining, a metal workpiece is connected to the positive terminal of a direct-current power supply and immersed in a suitable electrolyte, such as sodium chloride solution. The tool is a cathode, or negative electrode, which is also immersed in the electrolyte. It is held very close to the anode—at distances of a few hundredths of an inch (around 1 mm)—which minimizes power loss and ensures that the electrolytic action is confined to the part of the surface that is to be machined. Part of the cathode may be shielded with an insulator to the same effect.

When the electric current flows, the metal atoms at the anode's surface lose electrons and become transformed into positively charged metal ions, which dissolve in the electrolyte. Atoms close to the electrode are preferentially removed, so any spikes in the surface are dissolved away and a smooth surface results.

In some ECM applications, a shaped cathode acts as a die for the finished product: the workpiece erodes most quickly near ridges in the die, so it recedes until the profile of the workpiece

▲ An electrochemical machining device. The tank in the background at right is a reservoir of electrolyte solution, which is drawn through the hose visible in the wall of the tank.

surface matches that of the die, when the rate of erosion becomes uniform across the surface.

In some applications, electromechanical machining is used for shaping articles that must be finished to precise dimensions. The amount of metal removed from the surface obeys Faraday's laws, so it depends on the quantity of electric charge that passes through the workpiece, and the depth of the cut can be controlled accurately.

ECM is most useful for forming objects out of extremely hard metals. The electrolyte is pumped through the gap between the anode and cathode at high speed so as to rapidly remove the dissolved metal. This flushing action prevents sludge formation in the gap, which would cause uneven machining. Instead, the sludge forms subsequently, and it is removed by filtering before the electrolyte is recirculated through the gap.

In order to remove surface metal at a convenient rate, current densities as great as 50,000 amps per sq. ft. (around 500,000 amps per m²) are used. The great bulk and high cost of the equipment used to produce strong direct currents places a practical limit on the area that can be machined at any one time. Considerable heat develops as the current passes through the workpiece and tool, and the ability of associated cooling equipment to dissipate that heat also places a limit on the rate of machining.

A typical application of electrochemical machining is in the shaping of blades for gas turbines. Such components are typically made of hard, oxidation-resistant nickel-based alloys.

Electrochemical machining is sometimes used to smoothe or polish workpieces that have been roughly formed by mechanical machining. In such cases, strongly acidic electrolytes are used with typical current densities of around 500 amps per sq. ft. (5,000 amps per m²). An example of such a combination of techniques is sometimes used to produce gear wheels: ECM removes any burrs left by mechanical machining. Another example is in the finishing of stainless-steel drums for automatic washing machines. Electrochemical treatment gives a pleasing bright appearance as well as removing any ragged edges that would damage laundry items during wash cycles.

Electrodischarge machining

Electrodischarge machining—sometimes called spark erosion—is similar to electrochemical machining, except that an insulating gas fills the gap between the tool and the workpiece. When the voltage between the tool and workpiece exceeds a critical value, the insulating gas breaks down and an electric arc forms between the tool and the workpiece. A high-frequency alternating current supply maintains the arc, whose heat vaporizes metal atoms from the workpiece more rapidly and with better dimensional precision than occurs with electrochemical machining.

One application of EDM is in the machining of cavity dies. Typically, a tool with a complex surface profile is lowered into the workpiece. The arc vaporizes the metal surface to match the surface of the tool electrode as it sinks into the workpiece. The amount of material removed depends on the power of the arc: 1,000 watts is sufficient to remove around one cubic inch (16 cm³) of metal in an hour.

An alternative form of EDM uses a wire stretched between two spools as its tool electrode; the metal of the workpiece forms the other electrode. In operation, the workpiece moves across the wire, which cuts a fine line through it. The wire is slowly wound from one spool to the other so that the active section is always replaced before it is in any danger of breaking. This technique is particularly well suited for integration with computer-aided design, since the form of the finished article is determined completely by the movements of the workpiece—which can be computer-controlled with ease—rather than by specific tooling on the machine. Electrodischarge machining is used to produce articles that have complex shapes, such as precision punch tools.

THE ELECTROLYTE CYCLE IN AN ECM DEVICE

The diagram below is a schematic illustration of the flow of electrolyte through an electrochemical machining device. The positive charge in the metal workpiece encourages its surface atoms to lose electrons and form positive ions. These ions drift toward the negatively charged tool, where they regain electrons and form insoluble metal atoms.

The insulating sheath around the tool concentrates the current flow between the negative tool and the positive workpiece, and the constant flow of electrolyte carries the insoluble metal atoms away from the surface of the tool before they have a chance to form a layer of insoluble sludge. As the machining progresses, the surface of the workpiece erodes faster at the points closest to the tool. When the machining is complete, all parts of the workpiece surface erode at the same rate near the tool, so the profile of the surface ceases to change. According to Faraday's laws, the amount of metal removed from the surface depends on the amount of charge that passes through the circuit and hence on the current and duration of machining.

Later in the electrolyte circuit, the insoluble metal atoms coagulate and form a suspended solid. A series of filters of increasing fineness remove this sludge from the electrolyte flow, and the clean electrolyte then passes through a cooler, which removes heat generated by the machining process. A pump then returns the cool, clean electrolyte to the start of the cycle.

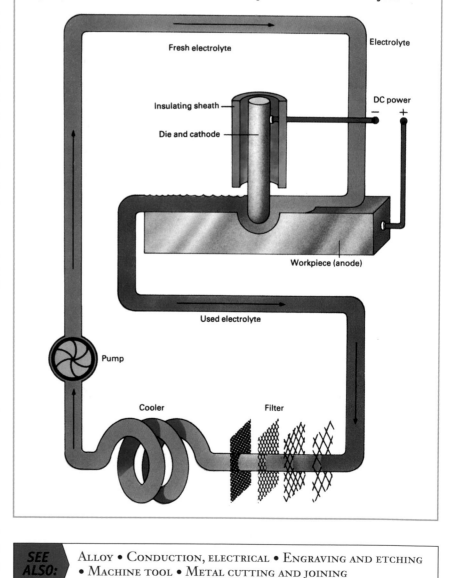

SEE ALSO: ALLOY • CONDUCTION, ELECTRICAL • ENGRAVING AND ETCHING • MACHINE TOOL • METAL CUTTING AND JOINING

Electrolysis

Electrolysis is a process whereby the passage of an electrical current through a liquid induces a chemical change. The liquid, or electrolyte, may be a pure molten salt, a molten mixture of salts, or a solution of one or more salts in a liquid solvent. Although electrolysis was discovered within months of the invention of the electric battery by the Italian physicist Alessandro Volta in 1800, some twenty years passed before the British chemist Michael Faraday formulated mathematical laws to describe electrolytic processes.

For a liquid to function as an electrolyte, it must contain electrically charged particles, called ions. When electrodes are dipped into an electrolyte, both types of ions are attracted to the oppositely charged electrodes: the positive ions drift toward the negative electrode, while the negative ions drift toward the positive electrode. In this way, both types of ions contribute to the passage of current as they move. When common salt (sodium chloride, NaCl) dissolves in water, for example, sodium ions (Na^+) and chloride ions (Cl^-) break free from the rigid structure of solid salt and become able to carry current. Molten sodium chloride also conducts electricity.

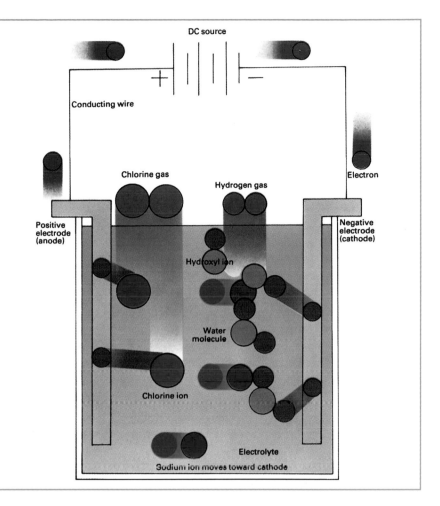

Electrolysis with inert electrodes

The chemical changes that occur in electrolysis happen when ions reach oppositely charged electrodes. When the electrodes are made of inert materials, such as graphite or platinum, their only function is to provide or accept electrons, depending on the charge of the electrode. In the electrolysis of sodium chloride solution, for example, the anode, or positive electrode, accepts one electron from each chloride ion that reaches it. The neutral chlorine atoms so formed immediately pair up to form chlorine molecules (Cl_2):

$$Cl^- \rightarrow \tfrac{1}{2}Cl_2 + e^-$$

The cathode reaction in the electrolysis of sodium chloride is slightly more complex. Instead of sodium ions accepting an electron each to form sodium atoms, water molecules accept the extra electrons, forming hydroxide ions (OH^-) and molecules of hydrogen gas (H_2):

$$H_2O + e^- \rightarrow \tfrac{1}{2}H_2 + OH^-$$

The overall reaction is obtained by combining the two electrode reactions. If sodium ions are added to both sides of the equation, it can be seen that the products of the electrolysis of brine, or sodium chloride solution, are hydrogen and chlorine gases and sodium hydroxide solution. This

▲ In the electrolysis of sodium chloride solution, chloride ions lose electrons at the anode, while water molecules gain electrons at the cathode. The products are chlorine, hydrogen, and sodium hydroxide solution.

process was one of the earliest adopted on a large scale by the heavy-chemicals industry, since its products are important raw materials for numerous products, such as bleach and plastics:

$$NaCl + H_2O \rightarrow NaOH + \tfrac{1}{2}H_2 + \tfrac{1}{2}Cl_2$$

Hydrogen gas collects over the cathode, while chlorine gas collects over the anode; at the same time, the concentration of sodium chloride gradually diminishes in the electrolyte, while the concentration of sodium hydroxide increases.

Faraday's laws

In the case of the electrolysis of brine, it is clear that one chloride ion is neutralized for each electron that passes through the solution. The connection between the charge passed and the extent of electrolysis is the basis for Faraday's laws.

Faraday's first law states that the amount of any substance produced (or consumed) by an electrolytic reaction is proportional to the amount of charge that passes through the electrolyte. Since current is the rate of flow of charge, that mass is proportional to the product of the current and the duration of the electrolysis.

Faraday's second law states that the mass of two substances produced (or consumed) by a given amount of charge in an electrolytic reaction

◀ Copper being refined by an electrolytic process. Impure copper is purified by passing an electric current through cells filled with the molten metal. The impurities collect at one electrode, and the pure copper that is deposited at the other electrode is run off to be collected for processing. This modern plant in Germany produces 190,000 tons (170,000 tonnes) of pure copper per year.

is proportional to the ratio of each substance's mass and valency. The electrolysis of molten calcium chloride illustrates this law:

$$Ca^{2+} + 2e^- \rightarrow Ca$$
$$2Cl^- \rightarrow Cl_2 + 2e^-$$

Calcium has a relative atomic mass of 40 and a valency of 2, so the charge that liberates 20 mass units of calcium will liberate 35 mass units of chlorine, which has a relative atomic mass of 35 and a valency of 1.

Electrolysis with reactive electrodes

Given an appropriate choice of electrolyte and electrode materials, the electrodes of an electrolysis cell can participate in the electrolytic process. An example is nickel plating, where a combination of a nickel anode and a nickel-sulfate electrolyte are used to deposit a thin decorative and protective layer of nickel on objects made of a cheaper metal or alloy, such as steel.

At the anode, electrons from nickel atoms in the surface of the electrode pass into the body of the metal and out through the supply cable. At the same time, those nickel atoms become nickel (II) ions (Ni^{2+}) and pass into solution. At the cathode, which is the object to be plated, nickel ions acquire electrons to become insoluble nickel atoms and add to the layer of nickel plate on the object. Since one nickel ion enters solution for every nickel atom deposited on the plated object, the concentration of nickel ions in the electrolyte never diminishes, but the anode wears away.

The Castner-Kellner cell

The Castner-Kellner cell is an example of how the course of an electrolysis can be influenced by the choice of electrodes. It also demonstrates how

technical problems can be overcome to develop an efficient industrial process.

As already mentioned, the electrolysis of brine was one of the first large-scale processes of the chemical industry. The problem with the straightforward electrolysis of brine is that the solution of sodium hydroxide obtained contains significant amounts of sodium chloride.

In a Castner-Kellner cell, the product of the cathode reaction is a liquid amalgam of sodium metal in mercury, rather than hydrogen gas, because it is difficult for hydrogen molecules to form on a mercury surface, while the stability of the amalgam of sodium in mercury promotes the formation of metallic sodium.

The mercury–sodium amalgam drains from the floor of the electrolysis cell to a second compartment, where the sodium reacts with water to form pure sodium hydroxide solution and hydrogen gas, which is a useful by-product.

Extraction of metals

A number of metals are such reactive elements that they are extremely difficult to extract from their compounds by chemical methods. Electrolysis is the only practical method for obtaining these metals from their ores.

Before the use of electrolysis, aluminum metal was produced from its ores by an expensive chemical process. The cost of its extraction excluded aluminum from general use, and it was considered a precious material. Napoleon III used it for dinner services and on military uniforms.

Metals such as aluminum cannot be obtained by electrolysis of solutions of their salts in water, since hydrogen ions from water would discharge at the cathode in preference to metal ions. Instead, they are produced from their molten salts. Production costs are reduced by adding salts that reduce the melting point of the metal salt, just as common salt reduced the melting point of ice. In the case of aluminum extraction, the addition of cryolite (Na_3AlF_6) allows the electrolysis to proceed at 1650°F (900°C); in magnesium extraction, the chloride salt is dissolved in a hot molten mixture of sodium and calcium chlorides.

Electrolysis also assists in the purification of metals obtained by chemical methods. Crude copper is purified by using it as the anode in a bath of copper sulfate. The copper in the anode gradually dissolves and deposits itself pure on the cathode, leaving behind impurities as a sludge in the bottom of the electrolysis cell.

SEE ALSO: ALUMINUM • CHEMICAL BONDING AND VALENCY • COPPER • ELECTROCHEMICAL MACHINING • METAL

Electromagnetic Radiation

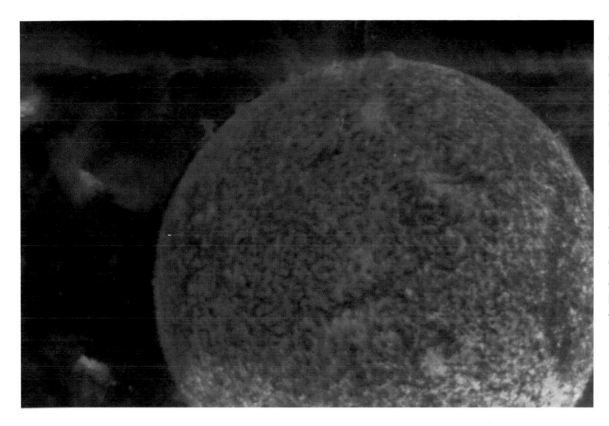

◀ The Sun is a seemingly inexhaustible source of energy, producing electromagnetic radiation of almost all wavelengths. Its peak wavelengths occur in the yellow part of the spectrum, characteristic of a body at around 10,800°F (6000°C). Some stars are much hotter and appear blue; others have a surface temperature of around 5400°F (3000°C), which is cooler than a light bulb, although they give off a lot of heat because of their size.

Many apparently unrelated phenomena, such as light, radio waves, and X rays are different examples of just one type of radiation, electromagnetic radiation. They are in fact waves of energy produced when an electric charge is accelerated.

Whenever a charged particle, such as an electron, changes velocity, an electromagnetic wave is produced. In an oscillating electric charge, for example, the changes of velocity at each end of the oscillation generate perpendicular electric and magnetic fields, and it is the combination of these fields that make up the electromagnetic wave. The speed at which the electromagnetic wave moves outward depends on the surrounding material; in a vacuum it is 186,282 miles (299,792 km) per second.

James Clerk Maxwell, a Scottish physicist, was the first to calculate that these electromagnetic disturbances could exist and would travel at this velocity. He noticed that this velocity was the same as the measured speed of light and suggested that light was a form of electromagnetic radiation.

Frequency and wavelength

To produce a steady wave of electromagnetic radiation, the charge must be vibrated up and down continuously. The number of vibrations of the charge in one second is called the frequency of the wave, and is measured in hertz (Hz), named for the German physicist Heinrich Hertz, who first produced and detected radio waves. The lowest frequencies of interest are around 150,000 Hz (150 kilohertz, or kHz), which are long-wave radio frequencies. VHF (very high frequency) radio uses radiation at about 100 million Hz (100 megahertz, or MHz), but light occurs at very much higher frequencies (600,000 gigahertz, or GHz) and X rays are higher still (3 billion GHz).

Another way of distinguishing types of electromagnetic radiation is by their wavelength, the distance between successive crests of the wave. For any type of wave, it must be true that the velocity of the wave = frequency x wavelength.

Electromagnetic radiation travels at different speeds in different materials, and so the wavelength must also vary according to the medium the wave is passing through—the frequency is always constant. The wavelength of a particular radiation usually means the wavelength it would have in a vacuum. For example, the yellow light emitted by a sodium lamp has a wavelength of 589.3 nanometers in a vacuum. (1 nanometer is one thousand millionth of a meter, abbreviated to nm. Wavelengths can also be given in angstroms; 589.3 nm = 5,893 Å). In air, the wavelength of the yellow light is reduced to 589.1 nm, and in glass it is only 388.6 nm.

The longest radio waves are more than 6 miles long (over 10,000 m), and the shortest waves (gamma rays) occur at wavelengths less than

0.001 nm, smaller than an atom. (Note that low frequencies correspond to long wavelengths and high frequencies to short wavelengths.) Atomic clocks rely on the constancy of frequencies emitted by excited atoms of particular elements for their accuracy.

Blackbody radiation

Unlike the elements in an atomic clock, most bodies when excited do not produce radiation that is of uniform frequency or wavelength. The way in which the intensity of emitted waves changes with increased temperature is shown in the diagram of two blackbody curves. The calculations for these curves are based on the behavior of a theoretical blackbody, which is capable of absorbing and emitting radiation of all frequencies. An electric heater emits most radiation at wavelengths over 1,000 nm, beyond the visible spectrum, in the infrared. A body as hot as the Sun, however, emits far more radiation than an electric heater, most of it at wavelengths around 520 nm, which is the wavelength of yellow-green light. As the temperature of the body increases, the intensity of wavelengths emitted shifts toward the shorter wavelengths of the spectrum.

Radio waves

Electromagnetic waves longer than 1 mm are known as radio waves. They are subdivided into groups, such as very high frequency (VHF) and ultra high frequency (UHF). The longest waves usually detectable are called VLF, for very low frequency, with wavelengths longer than 6 miles (10 km) and frequencies lower than 30,000 Hz. At this end of the scale, it becomes rather impractical to detect the signals, which are of very low energy.

▶ In this diagram, two blackbody curves have been superimposed, showing the intensity of wavelengths emitted by the Sun (the temperature of which is 10,832°F, or 6000°C) and a bar of an electric heater at 3632°F (2000°C). Radiation from the Sun peaks in the visible part of the spectrum, whereas the heater emits most radiation at infrared wavelengths.

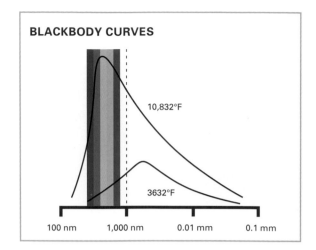

BLACKBODY CURVES

10,832°F

3632°F

100 nm   1,000 nm   0.01 mm   0.1 mm

Radio transmitters work on the principle of rapidly switching on and off an electric current. Whenever current is switched on, as in, for example, some domestic appliance, one pulse of electromagnetic radiation is produced. If the current is switched on and off at a high frequency, then electromagnetic radiation of that frequency will be produced. In principle, this is how radio transmitters work: electrons are forced to pulsate at the chosen frequency along the transmitting antenna, which should be carefully designed for efficient propagation of the chosen wavelength. One of the most popular designs for both transmitters and receivers is the half-wave dipole. This consists of a conductor whose length is half that of the chosen wavelength. Connection to it is normally made by either injecting current into its midpoint (for example, by winding a coil around it or by breaking it and feeding a signal across the two ends) or by injecting a voltage at one of the ends (the most common technique used for automobile antennas).

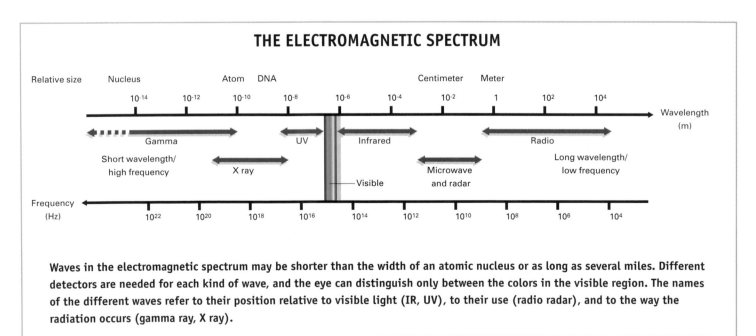

THE ELECTROMAGNETIC SPECTRUM

Relative size   Nucleus   Atom   DNA   Centimeter   Meter

10^{-14} 10^{-12} 10^{-10} 10^{-8} 10^{-6} 10^{-4} 10^{-2} 1 10^{2} 10^{4}

Wavelength (m)

Gamma   UV   Infrared   Radio

Short wavelength/ high frequency   X ray   Microwave and radar   Long wavelength/ low frequency

Visible

Frequency (Hz)

10^{22} 10^{20} 10^{18} 10^{16} 10^{14} 10^{12} 10^{10} 10^{8} 10^{6} 10^{4}

Waves in the electromagnetic spectrum may be shorter than the width of an atomic nucleus or as long as several miles. Different detectors are needed for each kind of wave, and the eye can distinguish only between the colors in the visible region. The names of the different waves refer to their position relative to visible light (IR, UV), to their use (radio radar), and to the way the radiation occurs (gamma ray, X ray).

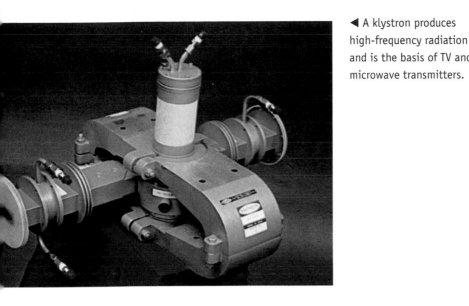

The electrons that constitute the current are accelerated as the current changes, and they radiate electromagnetic waves whose electric field is parallel to the transmitting antenna. If this antenna is vertical, only a vertical antenna will receive the radiation; it is said to be vertically polarized. Similarly a horizontal antenna will radiate horizontally polarized radiation, which can be detected only by a horizontal receiving antenna. (Polarization can be produced in all forms of electromagnetic radiation and has useful properties.) The electromagnetic wave produces currents in the receiving antenna that are amplified in the receiver to reproduce the transmitted message.

Microwaves

Microwaves have wavelengths between 1 and 300 mm, that is, they have frequencies between 1 GHz (10^9 Hz) and 300 GHz (3×10^{11} Hz). These wavelengths occur approximately midway between radio waves and infrared and share some of the properties of both. Infrared radiation, however, is normally produced by heat, while microwaves and radio waves are produced by electronic methods, because the highest frequency that can be produced electronically is about 3×10^{11} Hz—the upper limit of microwave frequencies—corresponding to a wavelength of 1 mm. Higher frequencies—such as those for infrared—can be reached by using the natural vibrations of the molecules in a solid. These molecules contain electrons that generate electromagnetic radiation as the molecules vibrate. The hotter the solid is, the more rapidly the molecules vibrate and the higher the frequency of the electromagnetic waves. Radiation produced in this way is normally unpolarized, because polarization due to electrons moving in different directions will tend to average out.

As with radio waves, microwave devices produce rapidly oscillating electron currents, the frequency of the oscillation being the same as that of the frequency of radiation desired. High-power microwave sources have been developed from the vacuum tube. These developments took place in the early 1920s to overcome the deficiencies of the more conventional radio valve in its various forms when used to produce high power at the higher frequencies demanded by the rapidly expanding communications industry and resulted in the magnetron, klystron, and traveling-wave tube. While the magnetron is a self-sustaining oscillator tube capable of producing pulses of power well in excess of a megawatt—in low-power applications a solid-state device—both the klystron and traveling-wave tube are essentially amplifying devices capable of producing output power of several kilowatts.

Perhaps the most distinctive feature of any microwave circuit is the array of conductors that carry or guide the signal between components. These conductors take the form of waveguides, which are pipelike structures having either rectangular or circular cross sections, usually constructed of material of high electric conductivity and to a very high degree of precision. The effects of capacitance and inductance are introduced into waveguide circuits by siting posts, stubs, annuli, and so on, in the waveguide. The physical dimensions of these devices and their positions in relation to the guided field structure determine the type of effect that they are to produce. Microwave antennas are usually also quite different from the

more conventional types in that, although they may have many different forms, most employ parabolic reflecting surfaces, which are irradiated from waveguide feeds at their foci to produce highly directional beams.

It was the development of radar that initiated the application of microwaves in a variety of widely differing areas. Radar systems have been developed to the point that the positions, speeds, and courses of targets, moving at very high speeds at considerable distances from a radar installation, may now be continually recorded to accuracies of a few meters. Microwaves are also used in aircraft landing systems and in communications.

Infrared

Two hundred years ago the spectrum of what we now call electromagnetic radiation was thought to be comprised only of the visible colors from violet to red. Then, in 1800, the British astronomer William Herschel discovered that the Sun radiates energy beyond the red end of the visible spectrum, and he made the first measurements at infrared wavelengths.

Herschel's detection of infrared radiation was made during a simple experiment. He passed sunlight through a slit and then a prism to produce a spectrum on a table top. Into the various colors of the spectrum, he inserted the blackened bulbs of thermometers. The blackening absorbed all colors equally, so the temperature to which the mercury rose indicated the amount of energy carried by the light of each color. The Sun emits most of its energy in the yellow-green area of the spectrum. A prism spreads out blue, green, and yellow light and bunches up the red, but Herschel found his thermometers read highest in red light. This finding prompted him to sample beyond the red and so to make his discovery.

▼ A radio telescope can receive electromagnetic rays of a very low frequency and long wavelength.

The radiation Herschel discovered had a wavelength of about 0.8 μm (0.8 x 10^{-6} m). Visible light covers the range 0.4 to 0.7 μm, and the infrared extends to 1,000 μm (1 mm). Infrared radiation is invisible to human eyes but can be sensed by our skin just as Herschel's thermometers detected it—by its heating properties. When an electric fire is switched on, we can feel its radiant heat, owing to infrared, before the element begins to glow red. Throughout the visible spectrum, the cooler an object is the redder it appears; a comparable relationship is found to apply in the infrared range also. Objects cooler than about 1650°F (900°C) emit essentially all their energy in the infrared. Room-temperature bodies emit most strongly at a wavelength of 10 μm.

Detecting infrared

The ability to see warm objects even in the dark is of obvious military value and has promoted much research into detection systems superior to thermometers. Most infrared detectors are of the single-element type: they do not produce two-dimensional pictures of a scene but merely measure the total amount of radiation falling on them. The most versatile of these detectors are the bolometers, which respond to radiation of any infrared wavelength.

Infrared detectors are used on guided missiles to direct the weapons at a warm target. Infrared imaging devices—vidicons—have also been developed: they respond to 10 μm radiation and display a room-temperature scene on a television screen. Some snakes have 10 μm vision, which enables them to catch their prey by night.

Photographic emulsions can be made sensitive to light no longer than 1.1 μm wavelength—the near infrared. These wavelengths are considerably longer than the diameters of air and dust molecules, so a photograph taken on infrared film will penetrate haze and mist much better than one taken on blue-sensitive film: blue light is easily scattered by the air. A certain type of infrared color film is available in which the colors of objects appear shifted in the spectrum—blue light does not show up at all, green objects appear blue, red objects appear green, and infrared objects appear red. This false-color film has proved useful in spotting from the air areas of vegetation with different infrared reflectivities.

Uses of infrared

Infrared radiation can be employed either to transmit heat to an object or to detect radiant heat from it. It heats directly by radiation rather than by conduction, so it can heat objects quickly; an infrared grill will cook a steak in two minutes.

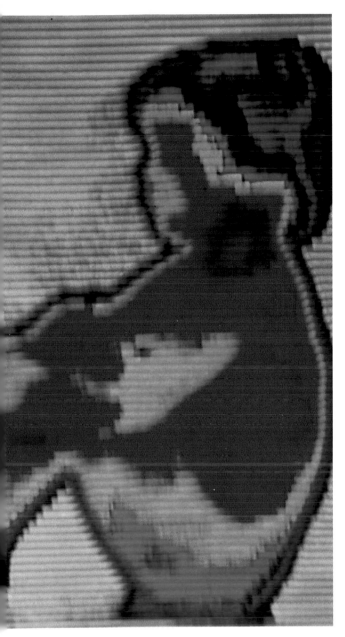

◀ A thermograph of a child sitting on a cold floor. The cold outer skin layers show up as green and the warmer inner body as red. After the child has been sitting on the floor for a while, another thermograph will show heat-building signals being stimulated.

windows. Conveniently, one of these occurs at 10 μm and allows distant viewing of room-temperature scenes. We can also examine objects outside our atmosphere. Infrared astronomy has led to the discovery of extensive clouds of dust in nebulas and around certain stars; some of these may represent the birth of stars and planetary systems.

Light

Visible light occurs at shorter wavelengths than infrared, from 390 to 750 nm. The eye sees different wavelengths as different colors: 680 nm is seen as red; 560 nm, yellow; 500 nm, green; 420 nm, blue; 400 nm, violet. The usual sources of light are hot bodies, such as the Sun or the filament of a tungsten lamp, and light can usually be detected by the human, animal, or insect eye, by a photographic plate, or by a photoelectric cell.

To understand why they respond to light but not to infrared radiation, it must be realized that electromagnetic radiation does not travel as a continuous flow of energy but in bursts of energy, called quanta (or photons). The energy of each quantum depends only on the frequency of the radiation: Energy (in joules) = $6.6 \times 10^{-34} \times$ frequency (in Hz). For comparison, a 100-watt lightbulb emits 100 joules of energy every second. The important thing to notice is that higher frequencies have photons of higher energy and that photons of light, therefore, have more energy than photons of infrared radiation.

Both infrared and visible light can be produced by exciting electrons under suitable conditions. Electrons gain discrete quanta of energy from the excitor, which they subsequently release as a photon, that is, a packet of light containing just one frequency. Typical environments producing these conditions include sodium lamps, neon

Just as human skin is slightly transparent to red light, it is even more transparent to light of longer wavelength. Infrared can therefore penetrate to some depth, and infrared lamps are used by physiotherapists in the heat treatment of muscles and tissues. Alternatively, 10 μm vidicons can be used to study the temperature of human skin, a process called thermography. Thermographs indicate areas of the body where the blood flow is abnormal and are therefore helpful in diagnosis.

Gaseous molecules have natural frequencies of vibration that occur in the infrared, so each type of molecule absorbs infrared radiation at different wave bands. Spectra of gases are therefore like fingerprints: by mapping the transmission at different wavelengths in a spectrophotometer, the composition of a sample of gas may be deduced.

Water vapor and carbon dioxide in Earth's atmosphere absorb infrared radiation at all but a narrow selection of wave bands, the atmospheric

▶ A radiation photograph from the *Landsat D* satellite's Thematic Mapper, which can operate on several spectral bands. The dramatic color changes indicate a wide variety of mineral deposits.

◀ A parabolic microwave antenna—a type mainly used in communications relay. Clearly visible is the hook-shaped waveguide feed receptor, with its opening positioned at the focal point of the reflector. It transmits a highly directional beam.

signs, lasers, cathode-ray tubes, and light-emitting diodes. Unlike blackbody radiators, they can produce light energy without producing large amounts of heat energy.

At the frequency of visible light, the energy of a photon is only 4×10^{-19} joules, but this is enough to start some chemical reactions. In the eye, the reaction triggers a nerve cell, which transmits a message to the brain, whereas in a photographic film emulsion, some of the silver compound is changed into silver metal, and the developing process enhances this reaction to produce an image.

Ultraviolet

At wavelengths shorter than 390 nm is the ultraviolet region, which extends down to 1 nm. This radiation is emitted by extremely hot bodies, but the temperatures needed are higher than the boiling point of all substances, so ultraviolet is produced this way only in very hot stars.

On Earth, ultraviolet is produced in a different way. The electrons in atoms and molecules can have only certain energies, and when they move from one energy state to another, they emit the excess energy as electromagnetic radiation. This radiation will occur at particular frequencies corresponding to the energy changes in the atom. Many atoms will produce frequencies that are in the ultraviolet part of the spectrum, one

example being mercury, which is used in tanning ultraviolet lamps. Atoms can also produce wavelengths that lie in the visible spectrum by this process. The color of sodium street lights is due to an energy change in the sodium atom, which results in radiation whose wavelength corresponds to yellow light.

X rays

Higher frequencies still can be produced by suddenly decelerating a stream of electrons. In a typical apparatus, the electrons are suddenly stopped by hitting the metal anode. The wavelength of the radiation emitted can range from 10 nm down to 0.001 nm, depending on how fast the electrons are traveling. These waves are known as X rays.

X radiation is easily detected by a photographic plate: a hospital X-ray examination is recorded on ordinary photographic emulsion. If a picture is not needed, a particle detector such as a Geiger–Müller counter can be used.

Gamma rays

The wavelengths of gamma rays are the shortest in the electromagnetic spectrum (less than 0.01 nm, which can be compared with the figure of 550 nm for visible light), and so their energy is even greater than that of X rays. The most energetic gamma radiation is capable of penetrating thicknesses of many tens of inches of lead.

Gamma radiation is most commonly produced by the rearrangement of protons and neutrons in the atomic nucleus. In the nuclei of radioactive elements, a neutron will occasionally decay into a proton, an electron, and an antineutrino. These particles escape from the nucleus, but the nucleus is left with surplus energy, which it emits as a gamma-ray photon.

Gamma radiation is also produced when an electron and positron combine. The positron is the antiparticle of the electron, a sort of mirror image with positive rather than negative charge. The combined mass of the electron and positron is converted into the energy of two oppositely directed gamma-ray photons. This is known as annihilation radiation. In the reverse process, known as pair production, the energy of a gamma-ray photon is converted into matter. The effect occurs when a high-energy gamma ray passes near the nucleus of a heavy atom. The result is an electron–positron pair.

Gamma rays are most commonly detected using a Geiger–Müller counter. An alternative technique is the use of a photographic emulsion sensitive to gamma rays, often called a nuclear emulsion. Gamma rays are also detected when they impact on a material such as sodium iodide. Such a material is known as a scintillator because it emits minute flashes when a gamma ray passes through. The weak flashes are detected after amplification by a device known as a photomultiplier tube.

Ionization will also occur in body tissues if these are exposed to gamma rays and, if the radiation is sufficiently intense, can cause radiation burns, cancer, and even death. Gamma radiation is particularly dangerous as it can penetrate the body to reach the internal organs.

Gamma rays have also been detected from space. They originate in very violent astronomical objects, such as supernova remnants, left behind when a star explodes. Most intriguing of all is the annihilation radiation emanating from a compact source, called Sagittarius A, at the very heart of our Milky Way galaxy. Some astronomers believe that the radiation is generated by a black hole that is hidden from sight and may be more than a million times more massive than the Sun.

Uses of gamma rays

There are, however, many beneficial uses of gamma rays. In medicine, they are used to study disorders of the brain, thyroid, kidney, liver, and pancreas. These organs will preferentially absorb very small quantities of a gamma-ray-emitting isotope administered to the patient and can thus be photographed by a gamma-ray camera located outside the body. Concentrated gamma radiation is also used in medicine to destroy cancerous tissue in the body. Gamma rays are widely used in industry to examine castings and welds for flaws.

Hermetically sealed packs of food or surgical supplies are sterilized by intense gamma radiation, which kills the potentially harmful bacteria, and the packaging prevents reinfection. Gamma radiation is also used to strengthen polyethylene and other polymers, because it creates cross-linkages between the long-chain molecules that form the plastic. The plastic's properties can be varied by changing the amount of radiation.

Electromagnetic interference

If a source of electromagnetic radiation generates a sufficiently strong electric or magnetic field, it may cause unwanted side effects in other electronic equipment, a phenomenon called electromagnetic interference (EMI). The commutators of some small electric motors are a common source of EMI and may be responsible for effects such as white spots appearing on a television picture while a vacuum cleaner is in use or the crackling from a car radio while the windshield wipers are running. EMI can be produced by either the magnetic or the electric component of electromagnetic radiation. If a flat conductor is placed across a varying electric field, it will act as one plate of a capacitor and have a voltage induced in it that varies in sympathy with the external electric field. If a linear conductor is placed around a varying magnetic field, it will act like the secondary winding of a transformer and have a current

KLYSTRON

The generation and amplification of microwaves is achieved by various devices. This double-cavity klystron is used for amplifying high-frequency microwave signals. All sources of microwave energy require the use, in their design and construction, of electric circuit techniques that exploit both the electric and the magnetic field properties of the wave. These techniques are necessary since both the physical dimensions and the electric properties of the materials used in the construction of the more conventional electric circuit conductors (wires and cables), inductors, capacitors, and resistors are such that these components do not retain their basic electric properties when carrying alternating currents at microwave frequencies.

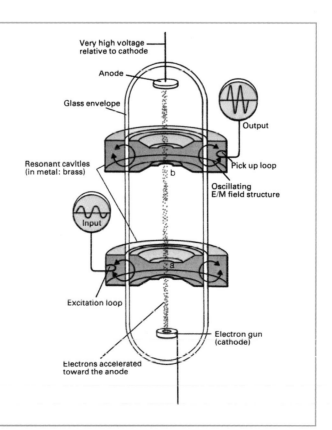

MICROWAVE COMMUNICATIONS

Microwaves are scattered (reflected and refracted) by the troposphere, the lower region of Earth's atmosphere. Clouds, air turbulence, water vapor, and constituent gases affect this scattering. Consequently, microwaves are useful for mapping and forecasting changes in the weather.

Although microwaves will generally pass through considerable distances of the troposphere, they cannot be reflected by the ionosphere (the outer part of the atmosphere), as are longer radio waves. For this reason, microwaves are used extensively in high-speed telecommunications using satellites and ground-based systems. They are also used in radar and to communicate with space probes.

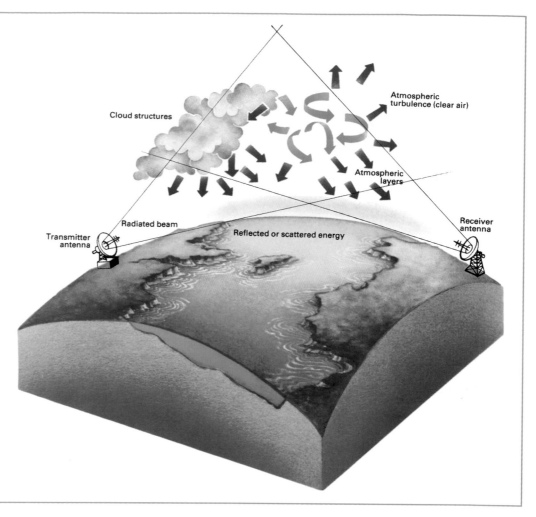

Cloud structures

Atmospheric turbulence (clear air)

Atmospheric layers

Radiated beam

Reflected or scattered energy

Receiver antenna

Transmitter antenna

---

induced in it that will vary in synchrony with the external magnetic field. A common example of this phenomenon is the hum that occurs in hi-fi equipment if the ground wiring is not satisfactory. Adding more ground wires may increase the number of loops created and hence make the problem worse. There are two main techniques for reducing EMI: screening and suppression. Screening attempts to stop radiation from traveling between the source and the susceptible equipment by placing a grounded barrier between them. Depending on the frequencies involved, the barrier will be either a solid metal plate or a wire mesh. Suppression attempts to prevent EMI by using capacitors and inductors to filter out the offending frequencies. Ideally, suppression and screening should take place at the source.

The most thorough form of screening involves placing the item to be screened within a sealed metal enclosure called a Faraday cage. Some sensitive measuring equipment needs to be used in Faraday cages with dimensions of several meters, in which case the metal screening material is normally hidden within the walls, floor, and ceiling so that the only indication that it is not a conventional room is the complex door-sealing arrangements.

Electromagnetic pulse energy

A massive meteorite impact or a powerful atomic detonation will produce a large uncontrolled burst of electromagnetic radiation called an electromagnetic pulse (EMP). This energy is distributed throughout most of the electromagnetic spectrum. Initially it travels radially from the source at just under the speed of light (because it is not in a vacuum). Individual wave bands will be reflected, defracted, or absorbed by materials that they encounter so that the spectral distribution of energy will vary from place to place.

At distances of more than a few miles from the source, the amounts of light and heat energy received may be insignificant while large amounts of energy are present in other parts of the electromagnetic spectrum. They can produce an extremely strong form of EMI that not only disrupts the operation of electronic circuits but may permanently destroy them.

SEE ALSO: ANTENNA • ASTRONOMY • ASTROPHYSICS • DIFFRACTION • DOPPLER EFFECT • ELECTRICITY • ELECTROMAGNETISM • GEIGER–MÜLLER TUBE • LASER AND MASER • LIGHT AND OPTICS • MAGNETISM • RADAR • RADIO • RADIO ASTRONOMY • TELECOMMUNICATIONS • WAVEGUIDE • X-RAY IMAGING

Electromagnetism

Throughout most of history, there has been much confusion about the relationship between electric and magnetic phenomena. In 1600, the English physician William Gilbert made a clear distinction between the attractive power achieved by rubbing a non-conducting substance, an electric phenomenon, and the lasting ability of the mineral lodestone to attract iron, a magnetic one. The distinction was not to last for in 1820, the Danish scientist Hans Oersted showed that the motion of electric charge is always accompanied by magnetic effects. Oersted's observation of electromagnetic effects was greatly enlarged by the subsequent work of the British physicist Michael Faraday in the first part of the 19th century.

One common manifestation of electromagnetism occurs when a current flowing in a wire produces a magnetic field—the operating principle of an electromagnet, and this effect can be harnessed to produce motion in electric motors through the attractive and repulsive forces of magnetic fields. When a magnet (either a permanent magnet or electromagnet) is moved near an electrical conductor, turbulent eddy currents are induced in the conductor, and it experiences a "dragging" force. This dragging force can be used to produce motion, and conversely, the eddy currents can be harnessed to produce a useful electric current (such as in alternators and dynamos). This is an example of a moving magnetic field producing an electric current.

A more complex example of electromagnetism is found in devices such as transformers, where a changing magnetic field produces a current. When two coils of wire are placed close together, a changing current (that is, changing in amplitude and/or direction) flows through one coil producing a changing magnetic field, which induces a voltage in the second coil. If this second coil is included in any kind of electric circuit, a current flows.

Understanding by analogy

A complete description of electromagnetic phenomena is provided by the set of four equations developed in the 19th century by the Scottish

▲ An electromagnet at work. This powerful electromagnetic hoist can lift up to 1 ton (0.9 tonnes) of shredded ferrous material, in this scrap-metal yard.

ELECTROMAGNETIC FIELDS

▼ In electromagnetic devices, the directions in which electric current, magnetic field, and mechanical force interact are all at right angles to each other.

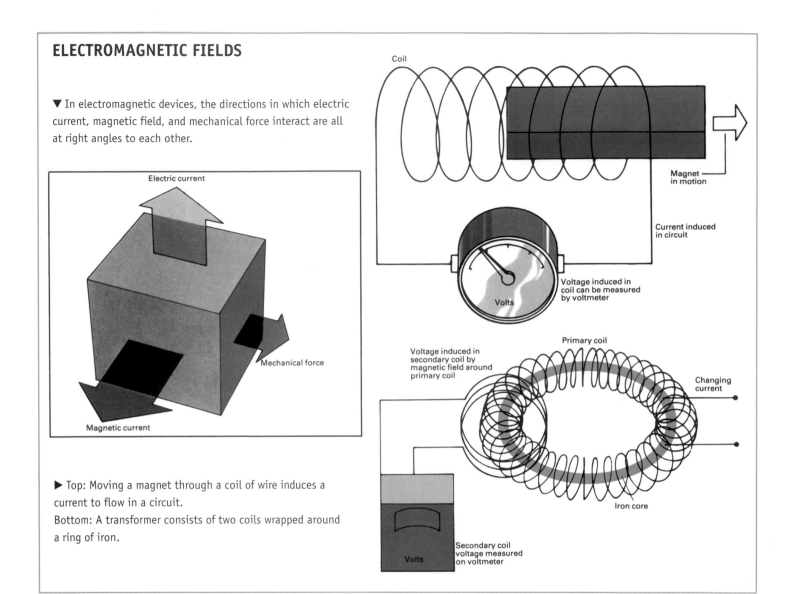

Electric current

Mechanical force

Magnetic current

Coil

Magnet in motion

Current induced in circuit

Voltage induced in coil can be measured by voltmeter

Volts

Voltage induced in secondary coil by magnetic field around primary coil

Primary coil

Changing current

Iron core

Secondary coil voltage measured on voltmeter

Volts

▶ Top: Moving a magnet through a coil of wire induces a current to flow in a circuit.
Bottom: A transformer consists of two coils wrapped around a ring of iron.

physicist James Clerk Maxwell. Solving Maxwell's equations requires advanced mathematics, however, and most people who work with electromagnetic devices make use of simpler mental models or analogs to understand how machines operate and to design new ones.

For electric circuits, it is helpful to compare the flow of electrons through a wire to the flow of water through a pipe. The rate of water flow depends on both the water pressure and the diameter of the pipe. The rate at which electrons move around a simple electrical circuit likewise depends on two quantities, the voltage, or electromotive force (emf) of the power supply, which is the analog of pressure, and the resistance, where a larger resistance corresponds to a lower diameter pipe. By another analogy, we sometimes think of a magnetic circuit in which the driving pressure is called the magnetomotive force (mmf) and the quantity analogous to the water flow is the magnetic flux.

Many authors and teachers declare that, despite its name, flux does not flow. The fact is

that flux does not exist, except as a human concept, and the only right or wrong about its flow is to be judged by whether the concept is useful to a particular individual. For some, it is more profitable to think of flux as merely being set up because it represents only stored energy and not a continuous loss of power, as is the case when electric current flows in a wire. For others, the analog is more profitable if flux is considered to be a more precise analog of electric current so that a magnetic circuit can be given the properties appropriate to those of inductance and capacitance in an electric circuit.

Linking electric and magnetic circuits

When discussing electric motors, generators, and transformers, it is essential to note that each machine includes at least one electric and one magnetic circuit. Since there is no simple equivalent in magnetic circuits to the insulating materials of electric circuits, it is usual to design a machine with only one magnetic circuit but two or more electric circuits. Indeed, the design of magnetic circuits has been likened to attempting to design an electric circuit that must work when immersed in seawater so that although most of the energy flows along the designated paths, an appreciable proportion will follow other routes. For the same reason, electric circuits in machines are usually multiturn coils of relatively thin, insulated wire. Magnetic circuits tend to be single-turn, short, and fat.

The subject of electromagnetism can therefore be expressed as the linking of electric and magnetic circuits. In such a linking the driving pressure from one circuit is seen to be derived from the flow in the other, and vice versa. For example, in a transformer an alternating voltage (emf) across the primary windings produces an alternating current in the windings and an alternating mmf in the magnetic circuit, which in turn creates an alternating flux. The alternating flux induces a voltage in the secondary windings, which, if connected in an electrical circuit, produces current.

Vector quantities

The commodity we seek to produce in an electric motor is force that arises as the result of multiplication of flux by current, but it is no ordinary multiplication, for the only quantities of flux and current that are effective are those that cross each other at right angles. Quantities that have both magnitude and direction are called vectors, and when determining the interactions of vectors with each other, the direction as well as the magnitude must be taken into account. In the above example, the force vector is the result of the multiplication of the flux and current vectors. Where the flux and current vectors are not at right angles to each other, they must be resolved into parallel and right-angular components, but it is always the right-angular components that produce the force vector. Furthermore, the force vector is always at right angles to both the flux and current vectors.

Vector multiplication and, more generally, vector mathematics are only a form of shorthand for handling quantities that have been shown experimentally to interact in this unusual way.

Electromagnetic radiation

The principles of electromagnetism are not limited to electric motor and generator design. Electromagnetic radiation is the name given to a variety of phenomena to which we give different names depending on the context in which we study them. Thus, gamma rays, X rays, ultraviolet radiation, visible light, infrared (heat radiation), and wireless (radio) waves are all of the same

nature and can all be expressed in terms of a continuous interchange of magnetic and electric energy, each of which pulsates in a plane at right angles to the direction of travel of the radiant waves. All travel at the same speed, about 186,000 miles per second (3×10^8 m/s). The two characteristics that distinguish one kind or radiation from another are the wavelength and frequency. The whole spectrum of radiation extends from very low frequencies with wavelengths of many miles to incredibly high frequencies of over 10^{22} Hz (1 Hz = 1 cycle/second) and wavelengths less than a millionth of a millionth of an inch.

The study of electromagnetism is therefore basic to the whole of physics, if not to the whole of science. Earth receives most of its energy from the Sun by electromagnetic radiation. The average private family house in the United States contains between 30 and 150 electromagnetic devices. (although the higher numbers generally occur where there are several children, each of whom has battery-powered toys). Electromagnetism is basic to the operation of radio and television sets, automobile ignition systems, radar, electron microscopes, electric motors and generators, telephones, and many other well-known inventions.

◀ Faraday's disk dynamo. Contact is made between the copper disk and the horseshoe electomagnet by means of "brushes." When the disk is rotated, a voltage is induced in the disk.

SEE ALSO: ELECTRICITY • ELECTRIC MOTOR • ELECTROMAGNETIC RADIATION • ENERGY STORAGE • GENERATOR • INDUCTION • MAGNETISM

Electronics

Electronics is the understanding, development, and application of devices that use the flow of electrons to store and manipulate data pertaining to images, sound, and other forms of information. On the theoretical level, electronics draws on knowledge developed in many other scientific disciplines, such as chemistry, condensed-matter physics, mathematics, quantum theory, and thermodynamics. As an applied science, electronics grew out of electrical engineering, which is concerned with every aspect of electricity: its generation, control, distribution, and applications.

Electrical and electronic circuits

Electrical circuits are designed for many purposes. They consist of components—typically capacitors, inductors, potentiometers, resistors, and switches—linked together by conductors, such as metal wires. Each component has specific electrical characteristics—resistance, capacitance, and inductance—that contribute to the characteristics of the circuit and govern its electrical behavior.

Electronic circuits are electrical circuits that include electronic components, such as vacuum tubes and semiconductor devices. The electrical characteristics of such components are more complex than those of electrical components. The resistance of a diode, for example, depends on the direction of current flow, being extremely high in one direction but negligible in the other.

Transducers and applications

In general, transducers are devices that convert energy from one form into another; in the context of electronics, one form of energy is electrical. As such, transducers form the interfaces between electronic circuits and their environments. The electrical energy can be the input or the output of the transducer. A microphone, for example, is a transducer that converts sound energy into electrical energy in the form of a signal that can be manipulated by an electronic circuit. A loudspeaker, on the other hand, is a transducer that converts the electrical output of an amplifier circuit into sound energy. Other types of transducers produce electrical signals in response to stimuli such as heat, light, or pressure or convert electrical signals into light or motion, for example.

The expansion of electronics at the cost of mechanical devices has been intimately linked to the development of transducers for specific tasks. Just as the British inventor John Logie Baird's mechanical image-scanning system for television was rapidly superseded by an electronic scanning

system developed by EMI, so the development of compact analog and digital displays enabled electronic devices to dominate the wristwatch market.

Vacuum-tube diodes as rectifiers

A simple vacuum tube consists of two electrodes sealed within an evacuated glass tube. One electrode—the cathode—is constructed from an alkali metal, such as cesium. When such metals become hot, some of their electrons "boil off"— they leave the surface of the metal. This is known as the thermionic effect, and vacuum tubes are sometimes called thermionic valves. If the other electrode—the anode—is at a positive potential relative to the cathode, thermionic electrons are drawn from the cathode to the anode and an electrical current flows through the device. There are no thermionic electrons available around the anode. Consequently, if the potential difference is reversed, no current flows through the device.

This type of vacuum tube is called a diode because it has only two electrodes. The ability of such devices to conduct electricity in one direction but not the other makes them useful for rectifying alternating current. That is, they produce a direct current from an alternating current. This

▲ Engineers plan complex chip circuitry using computer-aided design. Chip technology has advanced so much that there can now be as many as one million circuits on a single chip.

action is similar to that of a nonreturn valve in a hydraulic system, which is why vacuum-tube diodes are called valves in some countries.

Because of the unique direction of electron flow through a diode, the cathode is sometimes called the emitter and the anode the collector. When the potential difference between the electrodes is favorable for current flow, the diode is in forward bias. If the cathode is positive relative to the anode, the diode is in reverse bias.

Vacuum-tube amplifiers

A triode is a vacuum-tube device that has a third electrode between the anode and the cathode. The third electrode is in the form of a mesh and is called the grid.

A triode operates with its cathode at a negative potential relative to its anode, and the potential of the grid relative to the cathode determines the strength of the electron flow from cathode to anode. A positive grid potential relative to the cathode promotes the cathode–anode electron flow, while a negative potential impedes it. Small variations in the grid potential cause large variations in the strength of the current that flows between the anode and cathode, which is how triodes function as signal amplifiers.

Some vacuum tubes have two or more grids that control the electron current. Such vacuum tubes are called tetrodes (two grids), pentodes (three grids), and so on. Along with diodes, triodes and multiple-grid vacuum tubes were key components of electronic circuits from their invention in the 1910s until the 1960s, when they were largely replaced by semiconductor devices.

Cathode-ray tubes

Cathode-ray tubes are vacuum tubes designed to produce a visual display. Electrons boil off a hot cathode at the back of the tube and accelerate toward an annular (ring-shaped) anode held at a positive potential. Some electrons pass through the ring anode to form a beam, which strikes a screen that forms the front of the tube.

A phosphor coating on the inside of the screen glows where it is struck by the electron beam. Charged plates deflect the beam, while a grid controls its intensity, which in turn determines the brightness of the spot on the screen.

Klystrons and magnetrons

Klystrons and magnetrons are vacuum-tube devices in which the oscillation of electrons generates radio- and microwave-frequency radiation. In a klystron, electrons are made to oscillate in an electric field at frequencies of up to 400 gigahertz. A magnetron has a wire cathode within a cylindrical anode; a magnetic field acts along the axis of the anode. Connected to appropriate circuits, magnetrons amplify very-high-frequency signals to great powers. Their main uses are as sources of radiation for microwave ovens and radar devices. For radar, the output is usually pulsed.

▲ A close-up view of the probes used to test integrated circuits on a silicon wafer. After testing, the wafer will be cut up into individual chips.

SILICON CHIPS

The upper diagram shows *p*-type silicon on which a layer of *n*-type silicon was grown. Oxide was formed over this layer, then etched. Diffusion of boron through the etchings formed strips of *p*-type silicon. Complex combinations of etchings, diffusions, and metallizations can produce various components in the surface of a chip, as shown in the lower diagram.

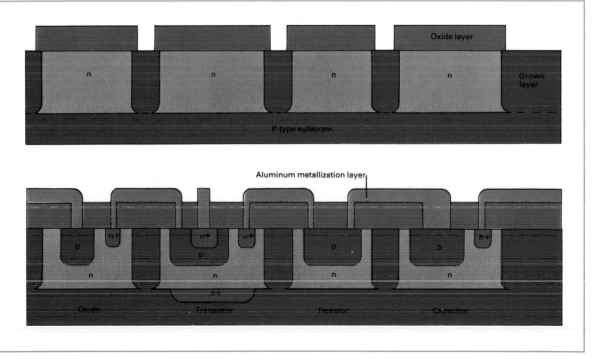

◀ The probes of this test rig automatically check each circuit of a silicon chip, which is barely visible at the center. The two devices above the test rig are ink guns used to mark defective chips.

History of semiconductor devices

Semiconductor devices, which are now the most common electronic devices, were also among the earliest. Crystals of semiconducting materials such as galena, a lead ore, were at the heart of early radio receivers, invented in 1901, called crystal sets. The point contact between the crystal and a "cat's whisker"—in fact, a fine metal wire—was the source of the semiconductor behavior. The precise characteristics of such a set depended acutely on the nature of the contact between the cat's whisker and the crystal, so a large proportion of listening time was spent adjusting and readjusting the contact to obtain reasonable reception.

Apart from being temperamental in use, crystal sets suffered from not being able to amplify the received signal, so they could only drive a single earpiece to any effect. For these reasons, crystal sets rapidly gave way to amplifying vacuum-tube radios in the 1920s and 1930s.

The use of semiconductors in electronic devices gained new impetus in the late 1940s, when methods became available for obtaining germanium of sufficient purity for the application (extreme purity is required, since even tiny amounts of impurities cause major changes in the electrical properties of semiconductors). The first of the new wave of semiconductor devices was a cat's-whisker device based on a crystal of germanium and point-contact electrodes.

Over the following years, however, silicon became the preferred material for semiconducting devices. The reasons for this are threefold: silicon is one of the most abundant elements in compounds on Earth, while germanium is rare; silicon retains its semiconducting properties over a wider temperature range than germanium, which starts to conduct above 185°F (85°C); and silicon forms an insulating layer of silicon dioxide when treated with oxygen at high temperature. This oxide layer adheres well to the surface of silicon, and its controlled formation is part of the manufacturing process for integrated circuits.

In 1947, a team of scientists at the Bell Telephone Laboratories, led by the U.S. physicist William Shockley, invented the transistor. This device was much more efficient than point-contact devices, because its electronic action occurred over the whole of the region between two forms of treated silicon, rather than over the minute area of a point contact.

Silicon and germanium diodes

The simplest type of semiconductor diode is made from a wafer-thin slice of pure silicon or germanium, for example, by diffusing different impurities, called dopants, into the two sides of the wafer. In the case of silicon, the dopants are boron, which has one electron per atom less than silicon, and phosphorus, which has one electron per atom more than silicon. The corresponding dopants for germanium are indium and antimony.

The two types of dopants create an excess or a deficiency of electrons when compared with the structures of the pure semiconductors. The side of the wafer that has an excess of electrons is called the n-type semiconductor (for negative); its extra electrons enable it to conduct better than pure semiconductor. The side of the wafer that has a deficiency of electrons is called the p-type semiconductor (for positive); its electron deficiencies, called holes, are free to move and carry positive charge, so they enable p-type to conduct better than pure semiconductor. At the junction between the n-type and p-type sections is the depletion layer, so called because neither of the charge-carrying species—holes and electrons—is present. The depletion layer therefore acts as a barrier to the flow of current.

The connections of a silicon diode are made by depositing vaporized aluminum on its surface and using the aluminum layer as an electrical contact to an outside circuit. If the contact of the n-type semiconductor is attached to a positive lead, its excess electrons drain through the contact and the depletion layer expands, increasing the resistance to current flow. If the p-type is connected to negative, electrons fill its holes, and its depletion layer also expands and increases resistance.

If the connections are reversed—n-type to negative and p-type to positive—the depletion layer contracts, the resistance falls, and a current starts to flow. Connected to an AC supply, current will flow for one part of the cycle but not for the other, when the polarity reverses. This is how a silicon diode rectifies alternating current.

Field-effect transistors

Transistors are the semiconductor equivalents of vacuum-tube triodes, since the electrical potential at a third electrode determines the strength of the current flowing between the principal electrodes and thus mimics how the grid voltage of a triode determines the cathode-anode electron flow. The transistor's equivalent of a grid is called its gate.

A field-effect transistor, or FET, consists of a bar of either *n*-type or *p*-type material, called the channel, with a connection at either end. These connections, called the source and drain terminals, are the equivalents of the emitter and collector of a triode. The gate electrode is close to but insulated from the channel.

If the channel is *n*-type and the gate is at positive potential, the electric field created by the gate potential attracts electrons from the channel and prevents them from moving, thus reducing the number of charge carriers in the channel and increasing its resistance to a current flowing between the source and drain. The channel is then said to be depleted. If the gate voltage is reversed, extra electrons are focused into the channel, which is then said to be enhanced. The source-drain resistance will then be reduced.

The reverse applies for a *p*-type channel. In such a device, a positive gate potential enhances the channel while a negative gate depletes it.

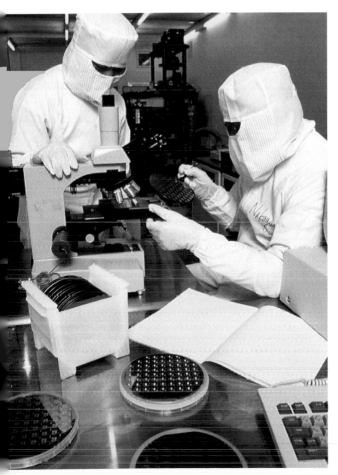

◀ Technicians perform quality-control tests on DRAM chips, which use capacitors to store data. Body suits and a clean environment protect the chips from contamination.

Bipolar-junction transistors

Like field-effect transistors, bipolar-junction transistors function by using a small potential to control the current between two electrodes. They are three-layer sandwiches of alternating semiconductor types, classified as *npn*-type or *pnp*-type transistors. The middle layer is the base; the outer layers are the collector and the emitter.

If the base is at neutral potential, a junction transistor behaves as if it were two diodes connected back-to-back. It will not allow current to flow in either direction, since at some point, electrons would have to flow from *p*-type to *n*-type semiconductor, which is the nonconducting direction of a simple silicon diode.

If the junction transistor is *npn* and the base layer is connected to a negative potential, the holes in the *p*-type base layer become filled and the barrier to electron flow is reduced, since the part of the transistor that acts as a diode in reverse bias is neutralized by the negative charges. Applying a positive potential to the base layer of a *pnp* transistor has the same effect.

A small current flows between the base and the emitter or collector, depending on the junction type, but that current is usually small in comparison to the current unleashed between the emitter and collector. This is the basis of the use of junction transistors to amplify signals: the signal provides the base potential, while the amplified output is the stronger current driven between the emitter and collector by an external power source. Since the resistance of the transistor varies in response to the signal current, so does the amplitude of the output current.

Thyristors

A thyristor consists of a *pnpn* sandwich and three external connections—anode, cathode, and gate. The anode connects to the outer layer of *p*-type material, the cathode to the outer *n*-type layer, and the gate to the inner *p*-type layer.

A pulse of current to the gate causes the whole assembly to behave like a simple *pn* junction diode so that half cycles of an AC supply can pass through the thyristor as long as the gate is triggered. Once the anode voltage falls below a critical value that is characteristic of the thyristor, the thyristor switches off until it is triggered again.

Since the voltage of an AC supply will fall below the cut-off value toward the end of each half cycle, the power supply can be moderated by delaying the trigger signal until well into the half cycle that can conduct. This type of behavior can be used to control and rectify the power supply for heavy-duty DC motors, such as those of railroad locomotives, using a weak signal current.

Gain and feedback

Gain is the factor by which the output signal of a transistor is greater than the input signal at the base. In an efficient *npn* transistor, 100 electrons pass from source to collector for every single electron that passes from the source to the base, so a nominal gain of 100 is possible.

Feedback is the use of the modified output of a transistor to control the base voltage of the same transistor. In the case of positive feedback, the boosted output signal boosts the base signal, so the current through the transistor could, in theory, continue to rise until the transistor melted. In the case of negative feedback, the output of the transistor acts to reduce the gain, so gain of the transistor is self limiting.

Oscillators

Positive feedback is used in oscillators, which can produce powerful AC signals of a given frequency. When an AC supply is connected to a resistor, the current through the resistor rises and falls in proportion to the voltage across the resistor. If an inductor and a capacitor are included in the circuit, they cause the current through the circuit to reach its maximum sometime after the maximum in voltage. The time shift between the maxima of current and voltage depends on the inductance and capacitance of the devices.

If part of the output of a transistor is fed through an inductor and a capacitor into its base, the timeshift between current and voltage means that a frequency exists where the rising base voltage—and therefore gain—matches the falling current, so the current starts to increase again. By the time the current is rising to its maximum, the base voltage is falling again, so the resistance of the transistor gain becomes less and the current starts to fall again. The frequency at which this stable oscillation of voltage and current occurs is usually controlled by a variable capacitor.

▲ A CD-ROM system uses electronics to combine still and moving images with text and sound.

◀ A widescreen high-definition television (HDTV) in testing. This system combines high-quality images with digital stereo or surround sound.

Electronics in computing

The use of transistors as signal amplifiers depends on the ability to vary the amount of current that passes between the emitter and collector by varying the voltage of the base. In computing, transistors operate outside the range where output responds to base-voltage changes.

If the base voltage falls below a certain value (near zero), the transistor acts as a diode in reverse bias: no current flows, and the transistor is said to be "cut off." At a base voltage above the amplifying range, increases in base voltage cause no further increase in the current that can flow from emitter to collector—the transistor is "saturated." These two states—cut off and saturated—are used to represent the zeros and ones of binary code, which is how computers store information.

Transistor circuits can be built to correspond to logical tests. These circuits are called logic gates. In an inverter gate, for example, the wiring is such that the input from a saturated transistor causes a second transistor to cut off, whereas if the first transistor is cut off, the second becomes saturated. Thus, if input is one, output is zero; if input is zero, output is one. Simple rules such is this might seem far removed from the familiar functions of computers, but they are the basis of any computer's operation.

Miniaturization and integration

The first electronic computer, built in the 1940s, consisted of more than 18,000 vacuum tubes, each with a hot filament. It used a great deal of energy in keeping the filaments hot, and the heat loss from the bulbs meant that they had to be well spaced and ventilated to avoid overheating.

The invention of the semiconducting transistor offered a means of vastly reducing the space occupied by computing, since a tiny transistor could replace each tube. Furthermore, since heavy currents and high voltages are unnecessary in the processing of information, transistorized computers had much lower rates of power consumption and dissipation compared with the demands of an equivalent vacuum-tube device.

The next great advance in the miniaturization of electronics came with the introduction of integrated circuits. Previously, electronic circuits had been constructed by soldering individual transistor components into circuit boards. Integrated circuits—silicon chips—have the same components created in the surface of a single silicon wafer by a series of etching, doping, and other operations—all in a minute space. Apart from being more convenient, the reduced scale of integrated circuits resulted in much higher operating speeds than were possible with earlier devices.

Continuous advances in the techniques for manufacturing integrated circuits have given rise to an explosive increase in the number of logic circuits that can be built on a single chip. The most advanced chips of 1967 had 20 to 200 circuits, each comprising between 10 and 100 transistors. This level of complexity became known as medium-scale integration, or MSI.

By the end of the 1970s, chips had grown through large-scale integration (LSI, 200–2,000 circuits per chip) to very-large-scale integration (VLSI, 2,000–20,000 circuits per chip). The era of ultra-large-scale integration (ULSI, more than 20,000 circuits per chip) started in 1989. By 2000, ULSI chips were approaching 10 million transistors, or 100,000 to 1 million circuits, per chip.

Since the early 1970s, computing power has also been enhanced by the use of field-effect transistors rather than bipolar-junction transistors. Field-effect transistors have a metal (aluminum) gate insulated from the semiconductor channel by a thin layer of silicon dioxide. This type of transistor is known as a CMOS (composite metal-oxide-semiconductor) transistor, or as a MOSFET (metal-oxide-semiconductor field-effect transistor). MOSFETs switch between states more rapidly than do bipolar junction transistors, making possible computing speeds of more than one billion operations per second.

Microprocessors and the digital era

The development of integrated circuits has increased the compactness and reduced the cost of data-handling devices to such an extent that electronics now control a wide range of appliances, from aircraft to toasters. The key components of the control systems of such devices are microprocessors—integrated circuits that are custom programmed for their appliances.

The availability of cheap, high-performance integrated circuits has also changed the way that electronics is applied: whereas devices of the 1960s and 1970s used electronics principally in analog tuning and amplification, modern electronic devices function using digital signals. A typical example of this trend is to be seen in stereo systems. Whereas a typical pre-1990s system had a record player as its principal source of prerecorded music, modern systems have a compact disc player. Record players used the continuously variable (analog) voltage from a piezoelectric stylus to generate sound, whereas compact disc players use pulses of digital information to describe the sound that is to be generated by the player and then amplified. The advantage of the digital system is that it is practically immune to noise caused by dust and electrical interference.

Error-correction circuits can eliminate signals owing to dust, and since the gaps between the distinct values of the digital signal are greater than the amplitude of any electrical noise, the device simply reads the correct signal through all but the most extreme interference. The result is a crystal-clear reproduction of the sound as recorded and mixed in the recording studio.

In contrast, the analog system of the record player is prone to any electrical interference or imperfection in the circuit that distorts the voltage, however slightly. Consequently, even the most advanced record players are prone to hiss.

Digital technology is also overtaking analog technology in many other fields. Digital television is much clearer than the traditional system and offers the scope for interference-free viewing, a choice of camera angles, and views that include background information for the current program. Digital radio also gives clearer signals. Minidiscs and digital audio tapes are replacing analog compact cassettes as the most popular medium for recording music, and digital cameras and video recorders are also becoming popular. Telephone companies have long used digital techniques for transmitting calls through their networks, and many now offer digital connections in the home, permitting clearer calls and more rapid data transfer for Internet connections.

◀ In-car electronics can provide route and traffic information using satellite positioning signals and digital radio broadcasts.

Optoelectronics

Microprocessors have now become so rapid that their potential for further improvement is at risk of being limited by the speed at which electrons can carry signals between communicating chips. A potential solution of this problem is optoelectronics, in which a semiconductor laser converts digital signals into light pulses that pass through optical fibers between integrated circuits.

SEE ALSO: AUDIO AND VIDEO RECORDING • ELECTRICAL ENGINEERING • INTEGRATED CIRCUIT • SEMICONDUCTOR • SILICON

Electronics in Medicine

In response to the demand for improved knowledge and treatment of illness, an increasing amount of electronic apparatus is being used in medicine today. Electronic apparatus used in medical care and treatment must be electrically safe, reliable, easily serviced, and have good hygienic and ergonomic design. In addition, some components must be able to withstand sterilization. Some types of equipment need to be easily transportable and may need to use internal batteries as a power source. Other types of equipment performing vital functions may need to be connected to an uninterruptible power supply or incorporate fail-safe features so that they can never cause danger if they break down. It has been possible to meet most of these requirements since the introduction of the transistor and modern solid-state devices.

The bulk of electronic equipment is located in hospitals, where it is used to assist in the diagnosis and treatment of illness, to monitor the condition of patients, to communicate with and educate hospital staff, and to control automated processes. Electronic instruments in common use include a wide range of patient-monitoring machines that display and record such factors as heart rate, body temperature, blood pressure, and brain activity. The information from the monitoring equipment may be displayed at the patient's bedside or at a central nursing station, using a large-screen oscilloscope monitor, pen recorders, and sometimes multichannel tape recorders to record the instrument readings.

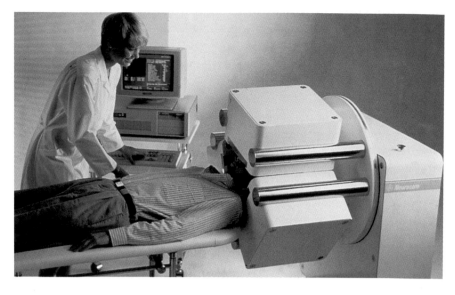

▲ A brain scan in progress. Hospitals now have a wide range of diagnostic tools available that can pinpoint the exact location of tumors or injuries and can monitor the patient's condition.

◀ A patient's heart signals being monitored by EKG. A number of disk electrodes have been attached to the arms and legs as well as the chest.

Electroencephalographs

The brain generates extremely small electrical currents which, when suitably amplified, produce distinctive traces that can be displayed on an oscilloscope screen or recorded on a pen recorder. The pattern of these brain waves depends on the activity of the brain, which in turn depends on the health of the patient and what he or she is doing. The general rhythms of the waveforms from a healthy brain are fairly consistent from one patient to another, and any irregularity or abnormality will show up as a distortion of the expected wave pattern.

The electric signals from the brain are very small, typically around 100 microvolts, but they can be detected by electrodes fixed to the scalp or, in some cases (such as during brain surgery), placed on the surface of the brain itself. These signals are then fed through high-gain amplifiers in an electroencephalograph (EEG) machine, and the output signals are recorded. The EEG machine is widely used both in the diagnosis and detection of brain damage or illness and in research into the functions of the different parts of the brain.

Electrocardiographs

The electrocardiograph (EKG) machine is related to the EEG machine, but its function is the monitoring of the electric signals given off by the muscles of the heart as they pump the blood around the body. When the EKG is used for monitoring the conditions of a patient in the hospital, a set of at least three metal disk electrodes covered on one face with a conductive saline gel are fixed to the patient's chest, gel face down, with adhesive tape. When sample EKG measurements are taken, as in an outpatient department, the electrodes may be attached to the chest with rubber suction cups, and readings may be taken from the arms and legs as well as the chest. A wire is connected to each electrode and plugged into the EKG amplifier. The signals obtained are in the order of one millivolt, and the resting rhythm of the heart is approximately 70 to 80 beats per minute. To protect the patient from any risk of electrocution, the part of the circuit closest to the body (the buffer or input amplifiers) is isolated electrically and mechanically from the rest of the circuitry and thus also from the power supply.

Optoisolators are often used to provide electric isolation. These consist of a light-emitting diode, which converts an electrical signal into light, placed in a black box with a phototransistor, which converts the light back into an electric signal. Because there is no electric connection between the phototransistor and the light-emitting diode, there is no possibility of transmitting an electric shock to the patient. Transformers can also be used to provide isolation.

The signal is displayed on a built-in oscilloscope monitor and can also be used to drive a pen recorder. The EKG apparatus also includes a device that counts the number of heartbeats and a meter to indicate the heart rate. EKG machines may be used to determine the condition of a person's heart during a medical checkup or if heart damage or disease is suspected, and they are also used to monitor the heart activity of a patient in the hospital following a heart attack, accident, serious illness, or surgery. In order to detect abnormalities in the EKG rhythm in such cases, the rate meter is fitted with alarm circuits that will trigger an audible or visible alarm to draw the nurse's attention to the change in the patient's condition. To assist the physician in deciding what abnormality has occurred, the alarm circuit also triggers a pen recorder, which will write out the EKG waveform.

Defibrillators

If the heart ceases to function (cardiac arrest), it may be due to fibrillation, where the individual muscle fibers of the heart do not contract in a coordinated manner as they should. No characteristic waveform or rhythm can be detected in the EKG, the heart is "shivering," and the patient's circulation is at a standstill. If undetected for more than five minutes, this condition will result in the patient's death, and so immediate remedial action must be taken by using a defibrillator. A portable battery-operated version of this instrument is also kept available in hospitals and increasingly in ambulances.

The purpose of the instrument is to induce the heart to restart its normal beating, and to achieve this end two large electrodes are held manually on the chest wall over the heart and a high-energy shock is given to the patient. Shock has the effect of contracting all the muscles in the chest, including the muscles of the heart, thus restarting the heart action. In some critical conditions, it may be necessary to apply the shock several times. The defibrillator contains large capacitors that are charged from a stable DC voltage source, which gives them a potential of several kilovolts and an energy content of up to 500 joules.

The capacitors are charged up, the electrodes applied to the chest wall, and the shock is triggered from a switch on the electrode handles. If the rhythm and waveform of the EKG are not completely absent, the defibrillator may be linked to the EKG machine so that the electrical shock is synchronized with the muscular contraction of the patient's heart.

Blood pressure monitors

It is often important to measure the patient's blood pressure, as this gives an indication of the heart's capability to maintain an adequate blood circulation. This measuring is normally done manually, but automated blood pressure monitors are in use in many hospitals. An inflatable rubber cuff is fitted around the patient's upper arm and inflated to a preset pressure by the monitor to cut off the blood flow in the lower arm. The monitor then actuates the pulse sound detectors and initiates a controlled leak of air from the cuff. The pressure in the cuff drops until it is equal to the peak pressure in the artery, and at this time, the blood is just able to pass underneath the cuff and a pulse can then be detected by the monitor. The pressure reading in the cuff, corresponding to the

▼ This automatic patient surveillance unit can be brought into the operating room. If a critical situation occurs during an operation, it can immediately be recognized, and emergency equipment, such as a defibrillator to restart the heart, can be brought into service. Much emergency equipment is easily portable or mobile so that it can be used anywhere in the hospital.

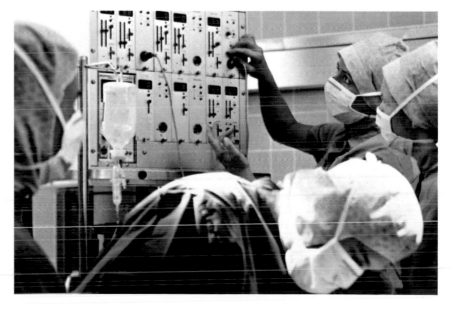

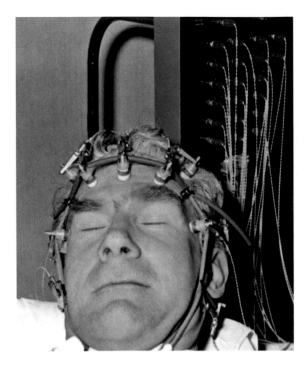

◀ Brain waves patterns can be monitored using an EEG machine. A number of electrodes are placed all over the head, and the signals picked up are displayed on an oscilloscope screen or traced onto paper by a pen recorder.

peak arterial pressure and called systolic pressure, is stored by the monitor and displayed on a meter. The pressure in the cuff continues to drop until sounds are detected, and again the pressure reading is stored and displayed. This reading corresponds to the minimum or trough pressure and is called the diastolic pressure.

The detection of peak pressure is easily made since it is the first pulse to arrive, but detection of the diastolic point is more difficult, and the various types of machine differ in how they achieve this measurement. The manual, semi-, and fully automatic cuff equipment all give erroneous readings both at very low (systolic below 80 mm of mercury) and high (systolic above 150 mm of mercury) pressures, so for a patient in a critical condition, it may be necessary to use a more direct and accurate method of measuring the blood pressure.

In this method a very fine catheter (a nylon tube) is inserted into an artery and connected to a pressure transducer. The dome of the transducer and the catheter itself are kept free from blood by keeping a saline (salt) solution in them, which keeps blood clotting from causing false readings. The transducer has a pressure-sensitive diaphragm, covered by an acrylic plastic dome, which usually has a four-arm strain gauge bridge bonded to it or incorporated in it, as in the case of semiconductor strain gauges.

The arterial pressure is displayed on an oscilloscope monitor and can be processed by peak and trough detection circuits to give the systolic and diastolic pressures. In some cases, the mean value of the pressure is measured to determine the mean arterial pressure.

Patient-monitoring systems

The EKG and the defibrillator may be used individually or, in the case of patients with more serious illnesses or injuries, such as those in intensive care units, they may be used in conjunction with other apparatus to provide a continuous monitoring of the patient's condition. Patient-monitoring systems may comprise several individual machines separately connected to the patient, or the machines may be physically combined into one main unit such as a multichannel physiological recorder (MCPR). In addition to providing the physician with information on the patient's condition, the monitoring systems also contain alarms that alert the nursing staff to any dangerous changes that require urgent attention.

A typical monitoring system might contain instruments to display and record the EKG waveform, the pulse rate and blood pressure, the body temperature, and the breathing rate, and some new systems are available that are connected to and supervised by a central computer system.

Other equipment

Modern operating rooms frequently use surgical diathermy apparatus. This equipment cuts tissue and coagulates bleeding vessels during surgery by passing a high-frequency current through a small electrode at the site to be treated. Many operating rooms also possess heart-lung and kidney machines in addition to X-ray machines, closed-circuit television, and other equipment.

Outpatient departments use a wide range of electronic equipment, which includes portable diathermy equipment, EKG, EEG, and EMG (electromyograph) machines, ultrasonic blood-flow-measuring apparatus and infrared temperature-scanning equipment. The EMG machine is used for investigating the electric activity of stimulated muscle and nerve fibers.

Laboratory support services use many forms of electronic apparatus, including blood-typing-and-clotting equipment, the automated biochemical machines that analyze urine and blood samples and serve to increase the speed with which sample analyses can be made.

Computerization has made a significant impact in the administration of hospitals, controlling such functions as medical records, stock control, central collation of patient's clinical data, and in medical research, such as the detailed analysis of abnormalities in EEG and EKG waveforms.

SEE ALSO: BODY SCANNER • ELECTRONICS • HEART SURGERY • OPERATING ROOM • OSCILLOSCOPE • PEN RECORDER • SURGERY • TRANSISTOR • X-RAY IMAGING

Electronic Surveillance

Until the introduction of telegraphy in the mid-19th century, investigators, spies, and petty eavesdroppers could only listen at keyholes or under windows. Since then, the developed world's growing dependence on electronic communications has provided ever increasing opportunities for those who are determined to "overhear" the exchanges of information between others.

Telephones can be tapped, and advances in electronics and computing have made it possible to listen in on conversations that take place within a room rather than by telephone and to screen other forms of communication, such as faxes and e-mails. At the start of the 21st century, the Internet is a major focus of attention for eavesdroppers and security forces alike.

The motives for electronic surveillance are many and varied. Government intelligence agencies monitor the communications of both enemy and friendly states as part of their routine activities, hoping that the information acquired might help forestall unwanted political developments or offer commercially useful information. Similar agencies monitor the communications of persons suspected of terrorist or subversive activities.

Police forces and security companies use electronic surveillance in the forms of telephone taps and closed-circuit television monitoring for the prevention and detection of crime. Private investigators use telephone taps and "bugs"— miniature microphones and cameras—in the hope of capturing information relevant to their investigations. The legality of such acts varies from state to state and from country to country.

Wiretapping

Telephone conversations are relatively easy to intercept, since they take the form of electrical signals that pass through wires for at least part of their transmission. In its simplest form, a telephone tap is nothing more than a secretly installed extension telephone. The tapping point might be in the basement of the building where the telephone is installed, at the local telephone exchange, or anywhere that the telephone lines are exposed so that the eavesdropper can make the connection with ease. The listening device might be a handset or recording device connected directly at the point of tapping or via a radio link or land line to a remote listening site.

The files of the now-defunct Stasi (Staats-sicherheitsdienst)—state security service of the former German Democratic Republic—reveal that some 5,000 telephone taps were permanently maintained in West Berlin. The taps were installed by Stasi agents and almost constantly monitored from Stasi headquarters in East Berlin until the reunification of Germany in 1990.

The computerization of telephone systems has done a great deal to simplify the work of legally authorized telephone tappers. Computerized exchanges can be programmed to monitor selected telephone lines and transmit conversations to a central listening station. With developments in voice recognition, it is possible in principle to monitor calls made by a given person on any telephone in a network, thus making it impossible to evading tapping by using public telephones.

Bugging devices

Listening in on conversations in a room presents more challenges than wiretapping, since the speakers cannot be relied on to stay within range of a hidden microphone as they can with a telephone tap. Moreover, microphones must be planted in a room by the eavesdropper, who therefore has to gain access in some manner.

Early bugging devices were simply microphones that were connected by wires to a listening station. They had the major disadvantage that their size and connecting wires made them easy to detect by a simple search unless the room was purpose built or modified for bugging purposes.

◀ The red components of this dismantled telephone are parts of a radio bug. The standard mouthpiece microphone has been replaced by one that also serves the bug. The red cylinder within the body of the telephone is the transmitter. The bug receives power from the telephone circuit.

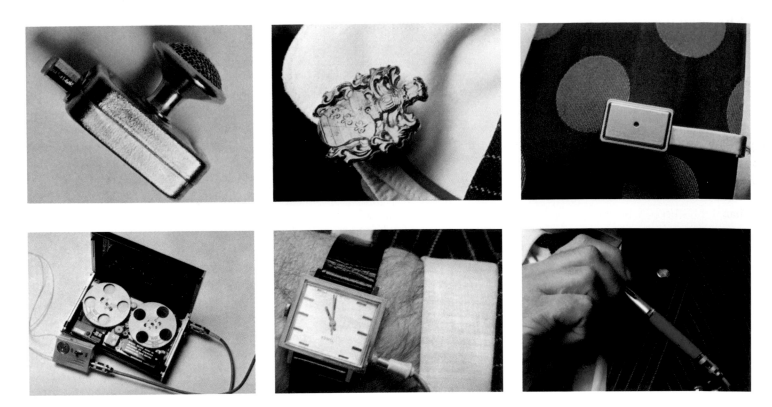

The first improvement in bugging technology came with high-sensitivity microphones, whose longer ranges meant that their location could be chosen for discretion and ease of installation, rather than for closeness to the likely locations of conversations. The wires of these devices made them still vulnerable to detection during more thorough searches, however.

Radio bugs

Wires continued to be a problem until the advent of the miniature radio bug—a device related to the cordless radio microphones used by stage performers and television presenters. Radio bugs consist of a miniature microphone and transmitter—each as small as 0.1 x 0.2 x 0.3 in. (3 x 5 x 8 mm)—with a power source and an antenna. The power source may be a lithium battery, the the device in which the microphone is concealed, or even a coil that converts radio waves from a nearby transmitter into usable power.

The smallest practical bug is the fountain pen transmitter, which encloses the bug in the space left by a shortened ink pod. A typical pen bug uses at least four miniature batteries, which give an operating period of seven hours, can pick up speech clearly at 10 to 16 ft. (3–5 m), and can transmit over 65 to 100 ft. (20–30 m) in normal conditions, just enough distance to reach listeners in a nearby parked car, for example. The pen can write, which helps avoid detection, but the noise of writing would "deafen" the microphone, so the pen must be planted where it is unlikely to be used by the person under surveillance.

▲ Miniature microphones in a variety of guises. Clockwise from top left, the microphones are disguised in a cuff link, a lapel badge, a tie clip, a pen, a watch, and a cigarette case. The bug in the cigarette case records conversations rather than transmitting them.

The operating time of a battery-powered radio bug is largely determined by the capacity of its battery, which depends on the physical size of the same. In many cases, an eavesdropper might choose to use a relatively large bug, which might be more difficult to hide but would operate for a much longer time. A typical unit would be a 3 x 2 x 1 in. (75 x 50 x 25 mm) casing—at least half of whose volume would be occupied by a 6-volt battery—with a 3 ft. (1 m) long antenna. Such a device could pick up speech within a 100 ft. (30 m) range, transmit over 1,300 ft. (400 m), and work for 25 days. Many devices of this type are fitted with an adhesive strip, so they can be attached to the underside of a desk, for example.

When radio transmitters are used to bug telephone calls, they can take their power from the telephone circuit. No batteries are needed, so the device can be very small. Some devices are merely telephone taps with radio transmitters, which can be hidden in a central terminal box either in the basement of a large building or on a telephone pole. It is quite common, however, to hide the transmitter in a telephone. One technique is to put the radio bug inside the telephone's mouthpiece, using the telephone line as an antenna.

Numerous other devices are used to conceal radio bugs. One example is a wall socket that resembles and functions as a normal power socket but uses the power circuit as a source of power and an antenna. Others include desktop clocks and mobile phones—items that are often given by sales representatives. These devices are used for industrial or commercial espionage.

The infinity transmitter

The most dramatic eavesdropping invention of the past few years is a device that uses the long-distance telephone as a bugging aid. It is called an infinity transmitter or harmonica bug. The device is a bug in that it picks up room conversations, but it is installed in a telephone.

In a typical scenario, the spy telephones the victim, then apologizes for getting a wrong number. The victim hangs up but the spy does not. Because the person who originates the call must hang up to break the connection, the line remains open. Next, the spy uses a small whistle to sound a particular note that activates the bug. Early devices reputedly responded to a note played on a harmonica, hence the name harmonica bug.

Conversations in the room are transmitted over the open line until the bug is automatically shut off when the spy hangs up. There are no time or distance restrictions—the spy can plant the bug and then ring weeks later from another continent, for example—and the bug can be activated an unlimited number of times.

Some countries' telephone systems have a delay between connection and the first ring, so the bug can be activated by calling the number and sounding the tone before the first ring. The bug "answers" the incoming call without the phone ringing. A more flexible device, which does not leave the line engaged, uses a second telephone line installed in parallel to the victim's line. In such cases, the spy simply calls the bug's own number, and the victim's line functions as usual.

Video bugs

Miniature CCD (charge-coupled device) cameras have made it possible to surreptitiously monitor and record images of conversations and actions within a room. Video bugs can also be used to capture the information and images on a computer monitor or video screen, for example.

As with audio bugs, the signal may be transmitted to a monitoring station at a typical distance of around 300 ft. (90 m), depending on the power of the transmitter. The camera may be placed behind a hole in the concealing object or, if it is possible to fit one, behind a one-way mirror.

Video bugs are somewhat larger than audio bugs, and they are typically concealed in ceiling-mounted smoke detectors or false walls. Portable video bugs can be built into desktop objects such as clocks, pencil sharpeners, and plant pots, or concealed in a bag or case. Fiber-optic leads add the option of viewing round corners. Body-worn video bugs consist of a tiny camera that can be stitched into a tie or buttonhole and a separate transmitter that fits in the pocket of a suit.

Detecting and preventing bugs

Radio bugs are relatively easy to detect, since their transmissions can be picked up by a broadband frequency scanner. Radio bugs that only transmit sporadically are less easy to detect: voice-activated bugs are an example.

Searches can detect bugs that have been hastily attached to furniture, for example, but are less effective in detecting bugs that have been installed in a wall socket or smoke detector or under plaster or in a ceiling tile. These bugs are often revealed by slight color differences between the bugged socket and existing sockets or by a discolored or uneven patch in the wall or ceiling. Since more sophisticated bugging devices are usually installed by bogus maintenance workers, security-conscious organizations often insist on using maintenance contractors whose employees have undergone a security clearance.

Telephone taps are less easy to detect than bugs. Unusual hissing and popping noises can be an indication that a line is being tapped, as can unusually frequent or long-term attendance of telephone company trucks in the vicinity. Harmonica bugs can sometimes cause short rings as their operators activate them. If this happens, they can be detected more conclusively by attaching an audio amplifier to the line to listen for signals while the telephone is on the hook.

High-security lines, such as those used by the military, are separate from telephone networks. They must first be inspected from one end to the other by a security-cleared operative checking every inch of the line for taps. Then, if the line has been cleared, any subsequent attempts to place a tap are revealed by changes in the electrical properties of the line.

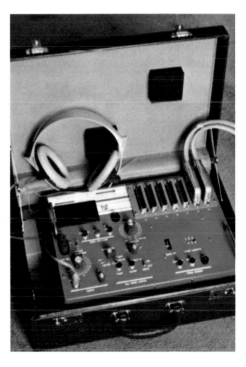

▼ This case contains all the equipment necessary to monitor conversations transmitted by a radio bug.

Data interception

The last two decades have seen a rapid growth in the amount of information transferred through telephone networks. It is estimated that billions of telephone calls, faxes, e-mails, and other data transmissions pass through the wires, fiber-optic cables, microwave, radio, and satellite links of the world's telecommunications networks every hour. Data interception can be done by tapping wires, breaking into optical cables, or collecting signals beamed from communications satellites or land-based microwave transmitters and relays.

◄ A handheld detector locates transmissions from a radio bug hidden in a wall clock.

▼ Turning the wall clock over reveals the bug, taped to the side of the clock and using the clock battery as a power source.

While it is relatively easy to intercept data signals by using appropriate equipment, it is less easy to decode the information they contain. Most data transmissions are protected by some form of encryption system. One such system, called DES (Data Encryption Standard), relies on the sender and authorized recipients being in possession of the same 56-bit key (a bit is a 0 or 1 of binary code). Since such a key has more than 7×10^{16} possible values, attempting to decode a message by using every possible key value is a lengthy but possible task for a powerful computer. Furthermore, once a key has been discovered, it is likely to remain valid for a considerable period of time, particularly if the message has been intercepted in an undetected manner.

A major disadvantage of single-key systems such as DES is that passwords have to be kept securely. A network of 30 users has 900 possible user pairs, for example, so there must be 900 keys in existence at any one time. If the 900 passwords are changed once a month to maintain security, then nearly 11,000 keys would have to be generated and kept securely each year.

To overcome the disadvantages of DES, researchers have been looking for more secure coding systems. One new class of systems is formed by the public-key cryptosystems (PKCs). These are coding systems that rely on two different passwords: a public password and a private password. A user who wishes to receive coded messages publishes his or her public password

widely—using a company notice board, e-mails, or an in-house journal, for example. Other users then employ this password to code messages. When these messages are received, the user must key in the private password, which nobody else knows, to decode the message. This system's security relies on the fact that only one user has to know the private password. There is no need to distribute it to other users and risk unauthorized disclosure. While PKCs were believed for a while to be infallible, they can nevertheless be broken by powerful computers.

As well as encryption, a number of other security methods also exist. The two most popular are high-speed transmission and frequency hopping. A shrill burst of radio traffic that suddenly interferes with your FM radio listening may well be a top-secret military communication—encoded, speeded up, and transmitted over a rapidly changing band of frequencies. The weakness of such a system is in the fact that the pattern of frequency changes must be known to both parties in the communication, so a suitably programmed tuner can accompany the frequency hops if that pattern is known.

Carnivore and Echelon

The Federal Bureau of Investigation now has an e-mail interception system that sifts through all the e-mail traffic of an Internet service provider, or ISP, to select and store e-mail communications between suspected criminals. Called Carnivore, the system works by examining the fragments of all e-mails as they pass through the ISP's server computer. When it locates address details—"to" and "from" names—that correspond to its targets, it forwards the associated e-mail to investigators. Just as with wiretapping, Carnivore may only be used once legal permission has been obtained.

If it exists, Echelon is believed to be a far more extensive and deeper-probing surveillance system than Carnivore. In September 2000, members of the committee of the European Union expressed concern that the United States, in cooperation with Australia, Canada, New Zealand, and the United Kingdom, is operating a screening system that intercepts satellite transmissions of billions of faxes, e-mails, and telephone calls every hour.

SEE ALSO: CHARGE-COUPLED DEVICE • COMPUTER NETWORK • CRYPTOLOGY • MICROPHONE • RADIO • VIDEO CAMERA

Element, Chemical

An element is any substance that cannot be split into simpler substances by chemical processes. Around 90 elements occur in nature, and they are numbered according to the number of protons in their nuclei. A few elements occur uncombined on Earth—notably, unreactive elements such as copper, gold, nitrogen, and platinum—but most occur naturally in chemical compounds.

The lightest element is hydrogen; its atoms consist of one proton and one electron. The heaviest naturally occurring element is generally considered to be uranium—atomic number 92—although in 1972, traces of plutonium (atomic number 94) were discovered.

Still heavier elements have been created artificially by bombarding heavy atoms with high-speed subatomic particles and light nuclei from particle accelerators. The heaviest such element, with an atomic number of 114 but no name as yet, was reported by Russian scientists in early 1999. The synthetic elements are all highly radioactive, often decomposing to form lighter elements within fractions of seconds after synthesis.

Early atomic theories

As long ago as the sixth century B.C.E., Greek philosophers developed theories of matter in terms of primary elements: water, air, fire, and earth. It was believed that all known substances could be formed by combining these elements.

In the 17th century, the Irish-born scientist Robert Boyle coined the word *element* for simple, pure substances. Then in 1789, the French scientist Antoine Lavoisier published a list of elements based on his findings that certain substances could not be decomposed. In fact, Lavoisier's list included some false elements, such as silica (silicon dioxide), that are now known to be extremely stable compounds.

In 1803, the British scientist John Dalton proposed a law of chemical composition, based on his observations that elements combine in simple weight ratios, that developed the concept of the chemical element. He found, for example, that eight parts by weight of oxygen combine with one part by weight of hydrogen to produce water.

Modern understanding of elements

Current understanding of elements, the atoms that compose them, and their chemical and physical properties owes much to the discoveries of the electron in 1897, the proton in 1918, and the neutron in 1932. These are the three particles of which all atoms of all elements consist.

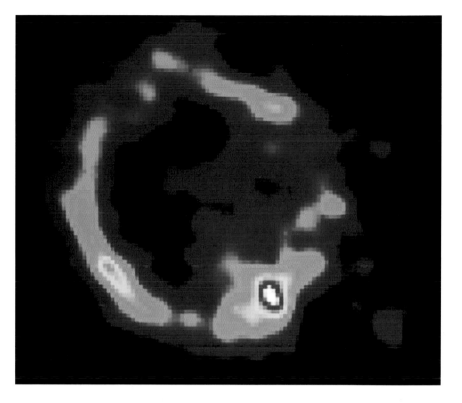

Atoms are often characterized by their atomic masses—measures of the quantity of matter in atoms. The mass of a hydrogen atom is around 0.04 million, million, million millionth of an ounce (4×10^{-26} oz.; 1×10^{-24} g). These are clumsy units, however, and it is easier to use relative atomic masses, which are numbers that represent the masses of atoms on a scale in which the most abundant type of carbon atom, which has six protons and six neutrons, is precisely 12.

Examples of relative atomic masses include hydrogen, 1.008; helium, 4.003; oxygen, 15.999; uranium, 238.03, and so on. As a guideline, the relative atomic mass is roughly the sum of the numbers of neutrons and protons in an atom. Until 1961, atomic weights were based on taking the oxygen atom as 16 rather than carbon as 12.

Isotopes

All atoms of any given element have the same number of protons; the number of electrons in neutral atoms of a given element is also fixed. The number of neutrons in atoms of a given element is rarely constrained to one value. Types of atoms of a given element that have different numbers of neutrons are called isotopes. Isotopes are denoted by the element name and isotopic mass, so the isotope of carbon that has six protons and six neutrons is carbon-12, whereas the carbon that has eight neutrons is carbon-14.

Different isotopes of an element all have essentially the same chemical properties, although they sometimes react with different degrees of vigor. The principal differences are

▲ Studies of supernovas provide useful information on the formation of the heavier elements needed to make planets. This image obtained by the Chandra X-ray Observatory reveals an expanding ring of oxygen and neon gas that is being heated to super-hot temperatures by the shock wave of the explosion. Most of the oxygen in the Universe is synthesized in the interior of a relatively few massive stars. When they explode, the newly manufactured elements are blasted into space to become the raw material for new stars and planets. Astronomers have estimated that this ring contains as much oxygen as could be found in many thousands of solar systems.

physical, resulting from the differences in masses, and these differences are exploited to separate isotopes. Uranium-235 hexafluoride (UF_6), for example, is a gas that diffuses through porous barriers slightly more rapidly than does uranium-238 hexafluoride (also UF_6). Since U-235 is radioactive and U-238 is not—another difference caused by the different numbers of neutrons—diffusion is a useful method for separating the isotopes.

For elements that have more than one stable natural isotope, relative atomic mass is calculated by taking an average of the different isotopic masses weighted for the relative abundance of each isotope. This type of calculation is meaningless for synthetic elements, however, since their isotopes decay at different rates, and so the mixture constantly changes composition.

Classifications

Of the total of 100 or so elements, some 65 are classified as metals, 15 as nonmetals and 6 as noble gases. The remainder are classified as semimetals or metalloids, showing some metallic and some nonmetallic properties; these include antimony, arsenic, germanium, and silicon.

Fortunately, the characteristics of the elements do not vary randomly. Distinct chemical and physical similarities exist among the members of such groups as the alkali metals (lithium, sodium, potassium, rubidium, and cesium) and the halogens (fluorine, chlorine, bromine, and iodine). When all the elements are listed in a table in order of atomic number, elements with similar characteristics (belonging to the same group) fall at regular intervals. The table is known as the periodic table of the elements.

Origins of natural elements

Unsurprisingly, the most abundant elements in the Universe are also the simplest—hydrogen, followed by helium. Generally, elements become less abundant as their atomic number increases, although the elements around iron are more abundant than this trend would predict.

Heavier elements form when huge clouds of hydrogen condense and become hot as they form stars, such as the Sun. At temperatures of 18 million°F to 36 million°F ($1-2 \times 10^7$°C), a chain of nuclear reactions occurs that converts four hydrogen nuclei, or protons, and two electrons into helium nuclei. This process, called hydrogen burning, is a form of nuclear fusion.

At higher temperatures—180 million°F to 360 million°F ($1-2 \times 10^8$°C)—groups of three or four helium nuclei join together to form carbon and oxygen atoms, respectively. This process is called helium burning. Higher temperatures—

900 million°F (5×10^8°C) and above—promote further nuclear fusions as well as nuclear reactions in which nuclei absorb successive neutrons to form heavier nuclei.

At temperatures around 7 billion 200 million°F (4×10^9°C), a vast complexity of nuclear reactions occurs and produces a mixture of elements that is governed by the relative amounts of binding energies that hold their nuclei together. Iron has the greatest binding energy per unit mass of all the elements, thus explaining its high abundance. Matter ejected by stars cools as dust and accumulates to form planets and other objects, so all the matter on Earth was once formed in the cores of stars much hotter than the Sun.

Transuranium elements

Some isotopes are so radioactive that, even if they were formed along with the matter that now makes up Earth, they would have decayed long ago. There are no stable isotopes for elements beyond uranium in the periodic table—the transuranium elements—and such elements only form from lighter elements by nuclear reactions.

In 1940, two U.S. nuclear physicists, Edwin McMillan and Philip Abelson, managed to produce the first synthetic element—neptunium—by bombarding uranium with neutrons. In one type of reaction, a neutron knocks one neutron from the uranium-238 nucleus to form uranium-237,

▶ A representation of the relative abundances of the elements on Earth. This distribution explains the prevalence of aluminosilicate minerals in the crust and magnesium silicates in the mantle. Note that oxygen and silicon are direct products of the fusion processes that occur in stars, and iron has the most stable nuclei of all the elements.

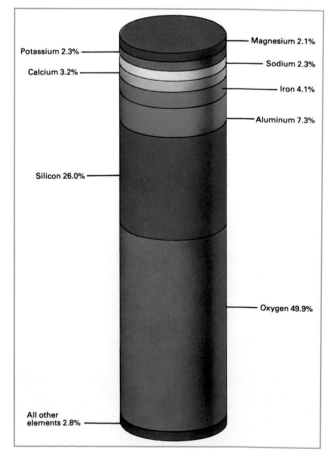

Potassium 2.3%

Calcium 3.2%

Magnesium 2.1%

Sodium 2.3%

Iron 4.1%

Aluminum 7.3%

Silicon 26.0%

Oxygen 49.9%

All other elements 2.8%

The synthesis of the first two transuranium elements by neutron bombardment was relatively simple as was the synthesis of the next four—americium (atomic number 95), curium (96), berkelium (97), and californium (98). The next two elements—einsteinium (99) and fermium (100)—were first isolated from the debris of a nuclear explosion at Los Alamos, New Mexico, in 1952. They were subsequently made under controlled conditions in a laboratory. The next three elements—mendelevium (101), nobelium (102), and lawrencium (103) were made by 1961. They completed a group of 14 elements, called the actinides, whose electronic structures mirror the naturally occurring lanthanides, as would be predicted by their position in the periodic table.

Transactinides

Once the actinides had all been synthesized, scientists continued attempts to produce yet heavier elements—the transactinides. The fact that the final actinide, lawrencium-260, already has 10 protons and 12 neutrons more than the heaviest natural isotope makes the scale of the task clear.

The first transactinides were produced by bombarding synthetic actinide atoms with neon ions, which have 10 protons and 10 neutrons. In 1969, rutherfordium (104) was made by bombarding plutonium atoms with a beam of fast-moving neon ions from a particle accelerator, while the same technique produced dubnium (105) from americium in the next year.

In 1974, U.S. scientists used a similar technique to produce seaborgium (106) from californium and oxygen ions (eight protons, eight neutrons), while Russian scientists produced the same element by bombarding lead (82) atoms with beams of chromium (24) ions.

an unstable isotope that has 92 protons and 145 neutrons. This isotope then loses an electron in a process called beta decay, which is accompanied by the conversion of a neutron into a proton. The resulting isotope has 93 protons, making it a different element from uranium, and 144 neutrons. Hence, the isotope is neptunium-237.

In a different process, a uranium-238 nucleus captures the bombarding neutron and sheds some of its kinetic energy as gamma radiation. The resulting uranium-239 then undergoes two beta decays to form neptunium-239 then plutonium-239, which has 94 protons and 145 neutrons. In this fashion, transuranium elements just above uranium can be created a step at a time.

▶ This plot shows nuclear stability (the "height" of the ridge) against the proton count on one axis and the neutron count on the other. Plots such as this have been used since the mid-1960s to predict the possibility of synthesizing superheavy elements that are relatively stable (the so-called magic ridge and mountain). The first such element was synthesized in 1999.

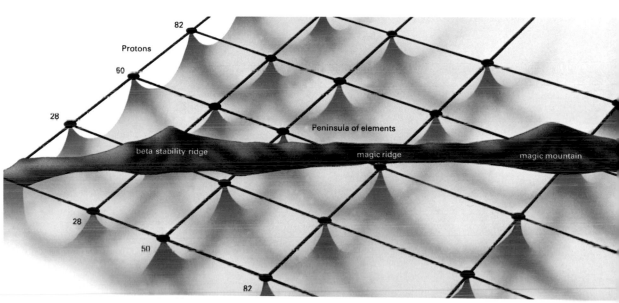

Heavy-ion bombardment

The Russians' use of a chromium-ion beam to synthesize seaborgium from lead was the first use of relatively heavy ions to form new heavy elements from stable, naturally occurring targets; as such, it had the advantage of not requiring a prior synthesis of starting materials. The approach was taken further by a German group, who produced bohrium (107), hassium (108), and meitnerium (109) between 1981 and 1984.

A barren decade followed the synthesis of meitnerium, to be broken only in 1994, when the German group synthesized element 110 by bombarding lead with ions of nickel (28)—an element yet heavier than chromium. In the same year, they used that same technique to make element 111 from bismuth (83), and in 1996, they produced element 112 by bombarding lead with zinc (30). Elements 110 and beyond are yet to be named.

The island of stability

The synthetic elements up to 112 are often extremely unstable, often having half-lives of fractions of seconds. In many cases, such elements can be detected only by observing their disintegration into lighter elements, and there is no chance of studying their chemical properties or producing samples large enough to measure their physical properties, such as melting points.

As early as 1966, theoretical physicists predicted the possibility of forming superheavy elements, heavier than the last actinides, that would have unusually stable nuclear structures.

▲ Elements can be synthesized in the laboratory by colliding beams of particles that have been accelerated in annular guides.

▶ Every stage in the manufacture and use of synthetic elements requires the ultimate in high technology. For example, the recovery of plutonium—which is the most important of the synthetic elements—from spent reactor fuel involves combining it with acids and forming a highly corrosive liquid.

They based this prediction on a model of the nucleus in which protons and neutrons occupy shells, just as do the electrons that orbit the nucleus. They predicted that a full nuclear shell would create nuclear stability, just as a filled shell of electrons creates chemical stability.

The numbers of neutrons or protons that make up a filled shell are called magic numbers. they are 2, 8, 20, 28, 50, 82, and 126. Doubly magic elements—those that have both a magic number of neutrons and a magic number of protons—are particularly stable.

A graph of the isotopes, plotted with their numbers of protons on one axis and their numbers of neutrons on the other, and with their stability plotted in the vertical dimension, reveals the stable nuclear configurations as forming a ridge of stability, often described as a peninsula of stability in a sea of instability. The most recently synthesized transactinide elements are close to the water's edge—at the tip of the peninsula. Out beyond, it is thought that there might be islands of stability, including a group of isotopes with atomic numbers around 114 that could have half-lives of millions of years—long enough to make stable samples for chemical analysis.

In 1998 and 1999, workers in Russia and the United States succeeded in making elements 114, 116, and 118. Of all the isotopes of these elements, that with 114 protons and 173 neutrons had an unusually high stability and long half-life, a result that some have taken to be the first "postcard" from the island of stability.

SEE ALSO: ATOMIC STRUCTURE • BINDING ENERGY • CHEMICAL BONDING AND VALENCY • FISSION • FUSION • METAL • PERIODIC TABLE • RADIOACTIVITY

Elementary Particle

Elementary particles are the building blocks of all types of matter, more fundamental even than the neutrons and protons that form the nuclei of atoms. They are also the entities that convey the four basic forces of nature: electromagnetism, gravity, and the strong and weak forces that act within nuclei. By developing theories based on the interactions of elementary particles, theoreticians hope to form a single model—the Theory of Everything, or TOE—that explains the four forces as different facets of a single force.

Particle physics is the study of elementary particles. To date, experimental particle physicists have found evidence for more than 200 elementary particles, most of which are combinations of a much smaller set of the most fundamental elementary particles. Proof of the existence of particles predicted by theoretical physicists plays an important role in the quest for the TOE.

Protons, neutrons, and electrons

Until the very end of the 19th century, atoms were thought to be the most fundamental form of matter, since they are immune to attempts to split them into simpler substances by chemical means. This view changed in 1897, when the British physicist Joseph Thomson announced his discovery that cathode "rays" were in fact streams of negatively charged particles: fragments of atoms, each with around $\frac{1}{2000}$ the mass of a hydrogen atom, that would become known as electrons.

In 1911, the New Zealand-born British physicist Ernest Rutherford discovered by experiment that each atom consists of an extremely dense positive core—the nucleus—surrounded by a diffuse cloud of negatively charged electrons. In 1919, Rutherford converted nitrogen atoms into oxygen atoms by bombarding them with alpha radiation, now known to consist of helium nuclei. The reaction released hydrogen nuclei, which Rutherford identified as components of all types of nuclei. He named them protons.

As early as 1920, Rutherford realized that a third type of subatomic particle must exist: one with no electrical charge but with a mass almost identical to that of the proton. Such a particle—the neutron—would account for the difference between the total mass of the electrons and protons in an atom and the actual atomic mass.

The neutron eluded detection for many years, however, since the particle detectors used at that time depended on the charge of a particle to produce a visible trace. Then, in 1932, the British physicist James Chadwick developed an ingenious

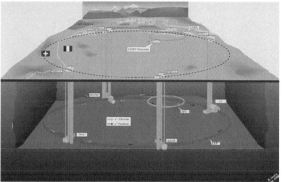

▲ Aerial view of the CERN installation, located on the French-Swiss border near Geneva. The larger circle marks the location of the LEP (Large Electron-Positron) collider. The LEP (right) occupies a circular tunnel 320 ft. (100 m) underground and 16.7 miles (27 km) in circumference. The same tunnel will house the LHC (Large Hadron Collider), in which physicists hope to find traces of one or more types of Higgs bosons.

technique for detecting neutrons. Chadwick bombarded a beryllium target with alpha particles to release neutrons. These neutrons then passed through paraffin (hydrocarbon) wax, where some of them knocked hydrogen nuclei out of the hydrocarbon molecules. The wax had the second function of blocking the passage of alpha particles, so the traces left by positively charged protons in a particle detector behind the paraffin could be indirectly attributed to free neutrons.

Quantum mechanics and structure

Chadwick's confirmation of the existence of the neutron completed a triad of particles—proton, neutron, and electron—that is sufficient to describe the chemical behavior and some of the physical properties of the elements. Theoretical physicists used these components to build an atomic model based on the wavelike motion of electrons around a nucleus of protons and neutrons. In that model, the electrons in an atom can exist only in certain states, called wave functions, that are defined by three quantum numbers.

The principal quantum number, n, is related to the total energy of an electron in a given state and has whole-number values greater than zero. A second quantum number, l, refers to the total angular momentum of an electron in a given state and may be zero or a positive whole number up to $n - 1$. The third quantum number, m, refers to the component of angular momentum along an arbitrary axis. The permitted values of m for a given state are whole numbers from $-l$ to l and zero.

Atomic spectra and spin

Experimental confirmation of the quantum model comes from atomic spectra, in which specific frequencies of light are absorbed or emitted as electrons pass from one state to another. Each frequency corresponds to a particular photon energy according to the equation $energy = h\nu$, in which h is a number called Planck's constant and ν is the frequency of light. In fact, the motions of electrons in all atoms other than those of hydrogen are so intertwined that it is more correct to refer to this energy as being the energy difference between two states of the atom as a whole.

Low-resolution atomic spectra are adequately explained by changes in the values of the three quantum numbers n, l, and m. Close inspection of certain high-resolution atomic spectra reveals details that call for a fourth quantum number, however. In 1925, the Dutch physicists Samuel

▼ Particles viewed in a bubble chamber (left), and an analysis of their movements (right). The tracks have been made by the interaction of neutrinos, kaons, protons, and pions.

Goudsmit and George Uhlenbeck realized that such details are consistent with the electron having a magnetic moment that can be aligned either with or against a magnetic field.

Goudsmit and Uhlenbeck attributed that magnetic moment to a spinning motion, reasoning that a spinning charged object should cause a magnetic field in the same way that a current circulating in the coils of an electromagnet produces a magnetic field. The fourth quantum number is s, and its permitted values are ½ and –½.

The proposal that an electron could have intrinsic angular momentum, or spin, met resistance from many scientists at first. Nevertheless, it was supported in 1927 by the British theoretical physicist Paul Dirac, who introduced the U.S. physicist Albert Einstein's concept of relativity into the quantum description of atoms. Since then, many other elementary particles have been confirmed to have intrinsic angular momentum.

Antiparticles

Apart from supporting the existence of spin, Dirac's relativistic description of the electron predicted a second fundamental aspect of elementary particles: the existence of antimatter. This predic-

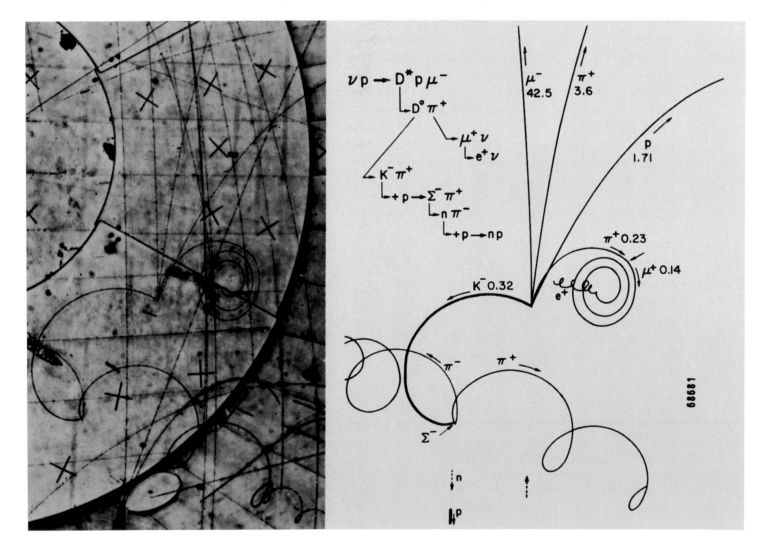

◀ The collider detector at the Fermi National Accelerator Laboratory near Chicago. Calorimeters containing photomultipliers surround the region where collisions between protons and antiprotons take place.

tion arose because the equation that describes the properties of an electron has two possible solution—one positive and one negative just as the square root of 100 can be 10 or −10.

In the case of the equation that describes an electron, the alternative solution is a particle identical to the electron in every respect but charge, which has the same magnitude but the opposite sign. In 1932, the U.S. physicist Carl Anderson found evidence for pairs of electrons and antielectrons, called positrons, in the debris of collisions between cosmic rays and atoms.

Whenever a positron meets an electron, the particle–antiparticle pair self destructs with the simultaneous release of energy, often in the form of a pair of gamma-ray photons. The amount of energy released (E) is related to the combined mass of the particle–antiparticle pair (m) by Einstein's famous $E = mc^2$ equation, where c is the speed of light in a vacuum. The combined kinetic energy of the particle–antiparticle pair is a second component in the total energy released.

Since the discovery of the positron, it has been shown that all particles have corresponding antimatter particles that differ by having the opposite value of some property and with which they can self annihilate to release energy. Some particles, such as the photon, are their own antiparticles.

Cosmic rays and colliders

Carl Anderson's observation of electron–positron pairs formed by cosmic-ray collisions was but one example of the interactions that are used to generate subatomic particles. Cosmic rays are fast-moving subatomic particles that rain down on Earth from outer space. Most react with molecules in the upper atmosphere to produce cascades of other particles.

When a cosmic ray collides with an atmospheric particle, the combined kinetic energy of the particles adds to the energy equivalent of their mass (by $E = mc^2$) to form pure energy. That energy then gives rise to various combinations of subatomic particles and antiparticles, as long as certain conservation laws are obeyed. One such law requires the total electrical charge to be unchanged by the interaction. The greater the energy of a collision, the more massive can be the particles it produces.

The artificial equivalents of cosmic-ray collisions are produced by creating beams of fast-moving particles in particle accelerators, then causing the particles in those beams to collide. Since the kinetic energies of the particles in the beams can be controlled, so can the total energy of the collisions between particles.

Since their first use in the late 1920s, particle accelerators have been used to produce evidence for hundreds of subatomic particles. Those particles have been characterized in terms of charge, mass, and spin by observing the geometries of their traces in particle detectors, particularly when subjected to electromagnetic fields. Some small chargeless particles are detected by the recoil effect, whereby their momentum as they depart from the scene of an interaction is matched and opposed by the combined momentum of larger or more easily detected particles.

Leptons

According to a theory called the standard model, six subatomic particles are fundamental elementary particles called leptons, which have no detectable structure. They form three pairs: the electron and electron neutrino (e and v_e), the muon and muon neutrino (μ and v_μ), and the tau lepton and tau neutrino (τ and v_τ). Each of the six leptons has a fundamental antiparticle.

The principal lepton of each pair is many orders of magnitude more massive than its neutrino partner. The principal leptons also have

▶ The L3 detector at CERN, where electrons moving one way around the ring collide with positrons moving the other way. A large magnetic field surrounds the detector, which is enclosed within enormous iron doors.

negative charges equal to that of the electron, while their neutrino partners are uncharged. All the leptons, including neutrinos, have spin = ½.

The electron and the neutrinos are the only stable leptons. The muon and tau lepton—respectively, around 200 and 3,500 times as heavy as an electron—decay rapidly and are not found in normal matter. The decay of a heavy lepton releases its corresponding neutrino together with a lighter lepton and its antineutrino or a lighter antilepton and its neutrino. The decay of a tau lepton always produces a tau neutrino and might produce a muon and a muon antineutrino or a positron and an electron neutrino, for example. Alternatively, the decay might produce a lepton neutrino with a quark and an antiquark (see below).

Hadrons and quarks

Apart from leptons, the other group of subatomic particles that constitute matter and antimatter are the hadrons. In the mid-1960s, the U.S. physicists Murray Gell-Mann and George Zweig developed a model that describes hadrons as consisting of quarks. In their model, quarks are subatomic species that cannot exist on their own but that can be characterized by their contributions to the properties of the hadrons they form.

Like leptons, quarks are grouped in three pairs. The lightest quarks, and the only ones to occur in stable matter, are the up and down quarks. They have respective masses 10 and 20 times that of an electron and respective charges of ⅔ and –⅓. The proton contains two up quarks and one down—denoted "uud"—resulting in a charge of (2 x ⅔) – ⅓ = +1. The neutron contains one up quark and two down ("udd"), which is consistent with its zero electrical charge.

The next heaviest quarks are the charm and strange quarks with respective masses 3,000 and 400 times that of an electron and respective charges of ⅔ and –⅓. The heaviest quarks are the top and bottom quark, with respective masses more than 330,000 and 9,200 times that of an electron and respective charges of ⅔ and –⅓. The top quark is so heavy that it was only in 1995 that it became possible to engineer collisions with enough energy to form particles that contain it.

Baryons and mesons

Quarks can combine in triplets or duets. Triplets, of which protons and neutrons are examples, are called baryons. Particles that contain more than one triplet of quarks are characterized by a baryon number that is the number of such triplets, so a helium nucleus has a baryon number of 4, for example. Duets of quarks, called mesons, consist of a quark and an antiparticle of a different quark.

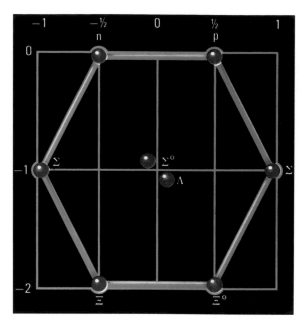

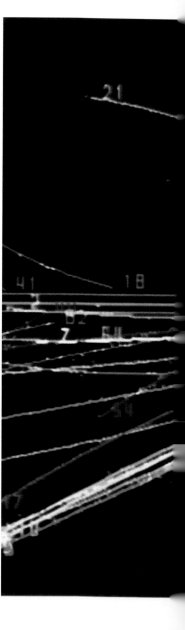

◀ A quark plot for Σ and Ξ particles helps predict the existence of new particles and explain the behavior of those already known.

Fermions and bosons

Leptons and hadrons can be classified as fermions or bosons according to their spin characteristics. Those that consist of an odd number of spin-½ particles have a half-integral total spin—½, 3⁄2, 5⁄2, and so on—and are called fermions. Particles that have zero or integral total spin are called bosons.

An important difference between fermions and bosons arises from quantum mechanics. No two fermions can share the same quantum numbers, effectively prohibiting two fermions from occupying the same space and so preventing all matter from collapsing into a single point. Bosons, on the other hand, are subject to no such constraint, and any number of bosons can occupy the same region of space.

Gauge bosons—the photon

The four forces that act between subatomic particles are, in order of increasing strength, gravity, the weak nuclear force, the electromagnetic force, and the strong nuclear force. The gauge bosons are particles with zero or integral spin that mediate these forces between other particles according to their characteristics.

The most familiar gauge boson is the photon, a massless spin-1 particle that mediates the electromagnetic force between electrically charged particles. Unlike the photons emitted by a glowing filament, for example, the photons that mediate the electromagnetic force switch in and out of existence as a consequence of transitory fluctuations in the mass–energy of interacting particles. These fluctuations are consistent with a tenet of quantum mechanics called the Heisenberg principle, whereby the position and momentum—and therefore the energy—of a particle cannot be defined beyond a certain degree of precision.

The consequence of this exchange of virtual protons is the existence of the familiar attraction between particles of opposite charges and repulsion between particles of like charges, which acts even at the subatomic level. The electromagnetic interaction also acts over great distances because its mediating gauge bosons have no mass.

Electroweak theory—W⁺, W⁻, and Z⁰

The weak force, which governs the radioactive decays of certain nuclei, for example, was first proposed to be mediated by gauge bosons W⁺, W⁻, and Z⁰ as early as 1967. At that time, a Pakistani theoretical physicist, Abdus Salam, and a U.S. physicist, Steven Weinberg, had no way of proving their theory, since the particles' masses of around 160,000 times the mass of an electron require collision energies around 100 GeV (giga electron volts) to produce them. In 1983, these massive relatives of the photon were produced in collisions at CERN (the European Center for Nuclear Research) near Geneva.

The charged W bosons take part in nuclear reactions where charge changes hands. In a beta decay, for example, a neutron (udd baryon) transmutes into a proton (uud baryon) with the emission of an electron. As one of the down quarks of the neutron (charge $-\frac{1}{3}$) becomes an up quark (charge $\frac{2}{3}$), a W⁻ particle momentarily comes into existence before decaying to form an electron and an electron antineutrino. The amount of energy borrowed to bring the W⁻ particle into fleeting existence is so great as to make its lifetime too short to be observed in the laboratory.

At the high interaction energies obtained in a collider, however, the lifetimes of the bosons W⁺, W⁻, and Z⁰ are sufficient for them to act over greater distances without decaying to form lighter particles. Under these conditions, the weak interactions become as prevalent as the electromagnetic interactions conveyed by photons. This similarity supports the electroweak theory, which asserts that electromagnetism and the weak nuclear force are different aspects of one force.

▼ This computer image has been processed to identify the types of particle present when accelerated subatomic particles hit their target to produce showers of short-lived particles. Analysis of the tracks reveals the nature of the interactions that take place at the heart of the subatomic particle collision. Free quarks have never been observed, but the tracks are consistent with quark theory, which predicts the formation of new particles under these conditions.

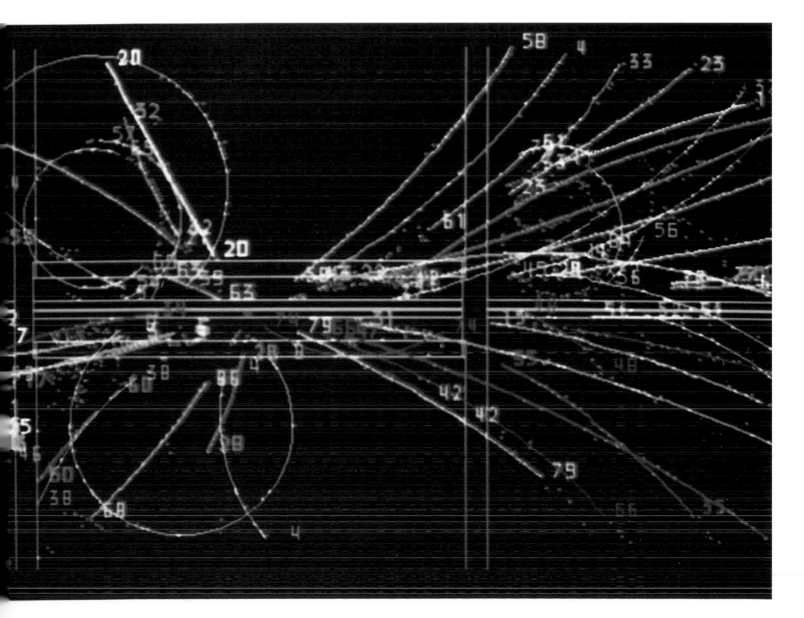

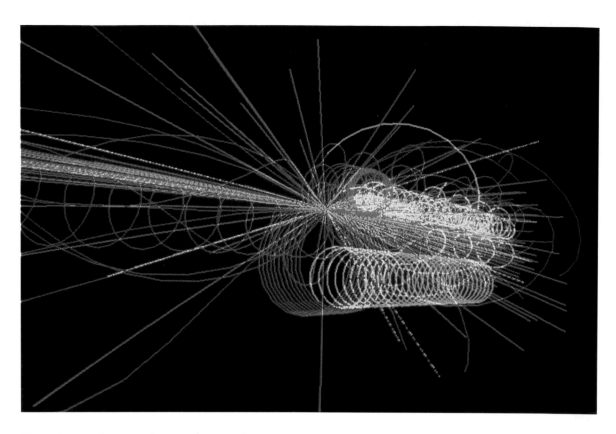

▶ A computer simulation of the type of display particle physicists expect to see from the detector of the Large Hadron Collider (LHC) at CERN. The LHC is due to start operating in 2005.

Quantum chromodynamics—gluons

Developed in the 1970s, quantum chromodynamics rationalizes the strong nuclear force that holds quarks together in terms of attractions between quarks that have different values of a property called color charge. Each type of quark can have a red, green, or blue color charge, and antiquarks have anticolors—antired, antigreen, or antiblue.

The color charges have no bearing on the color of matter, but they help visualize the ways in which quarks can come together to form baryons and mesons. The general rule is that stable quark combinations are colorless, so a baryon must have a quark of each color to be stable, just as red, green, and blue light mix to give white light. In a similar way, a stable meson must combine a quark of a given color with an antiquark of the matching anticolor—green and antigreen, for example. The requirement for quarks to form colorless groups prevents single quarks from existing in isolation, just as it prevents four quarks from grouping together, unless as a pair of mesons.

The origin of the strong internuclear force is the compulsion of quarks to form colorless groups; it is mediated by bosons called gluons, so called because they appear to glue together the quarks in subatomic particles. Like photons, gluons are massless particles that have a spin of 1. Unlike photons, which are electrically neutral, gluons carry charges pertaining to the force that they mediate: a color charge and an anticolor charge. There are eight gluons with different combinations of color and anticolor charges.

When a quark and a gluon interact, the anticolor of the gluon bleaches out the color charge of the quark and replaces it with its own color charge. Since there is a dense and constant flux of virtual gluons between quarks, it is impossible to determine the color of a given quark at any time. All that can be determined is that for any baryon there must be one quark of each color at any time and that any meson must be a quark-antiquark duet with matching color and anticolor charges.

A consequence of the color charge of gluons is that they, like quarks, only occur in colorless bundles of gluons. If a quark-bearing particle is given sufficient energy to emit a real (rather than virtual) gluon, that gluon has sufficient energy to spontaneously give rise to more quarks, antiquarks, and gluons. In doing so, the real gluon forms a new system of quarks and gluons that form into colorless groupings.

The residual strong force

Given that the quarks in protons and neutrons group together to form colorless baryons, it might seem that there would be no net color charge to generate a strong-force interaction between the baryons in a given nucleus. If this were strictly the case, the nuclei of atoms other than hydrogen would fly apart under the electrostatic repulsion between like charges. In fact, fluctuations in color charges give rise to a residual strong attraction between baryons, just as fluctuations in charge distribution causes an electrostatic attraction between neutral molecules.

Gravity and gravitons

While being the weakest of all forces, gravity acts over the greatest distances; furthermore, it is always attractive—there is no such thing as gravitational repulsion between masses.

Physicists assume that gravity is mediated by bosons, which they call gravitons. These bosons must be of negligible mass, otherwise they would decay before covering the distances over which gravity can act. Also, general relativity requires gravitons to be spin-2 bosons. Beyond these scant details, little is known of the nature of gravity.

Unified field theories

Many theoretical physicists believe that gravity, electromagnetism, and the strong and weak forces are different facets of a single force that are only discernable because of the low-energy environment that now exists in the Universe.

Experiments with W and Z gauge bosons produced in particle colliders since the mid-1980s confirmed that those bosons do indeed function in the same way as photons—confirming electroweak theory—at collision energies that correspond to ambient temperatures around $2 \times 10^{10}°F$ ($10^{10}°C$). (Collision energies are related to temperature because the hotter the temperature, the faster particles move.) According to the Big Bang theory, the temperatures at which the electrostatic and weak forces merge existed only until 10^{-10} seconds after the start of the Universe.

The electroweak and strong forces are thought likely to merge at temperatures above $2 \times 10^{29}°F$ ($10^{29}°C$)—the temperature 10^{-38} seconds after the birth of the Universe—and the gravitational force would join them at still higher temperatures. The collision energies corresponding to such temperatures are way beyond the scope of any conceivable particle accelerator, so the further investigation of the unification of forces might be by mathematical models alone.

The Higgs boson

While a practical investigation of the unification of the forces remains out of reach, particle physicists have a challenge that is only slightly more mundane. The standard model requires the existence of one or more particles, called Higgs bosons, that could interact with the W and Z gauge bosons to give them their masses.

While Higgs bosons have not yet been observed, some calculations predict their masses to be ten times greater than the W and Z bosons. Particle physicists hope to find such particles in the debris of proton–antiproton collisions in a device called a large-hadron collider.

FACT FILE

- *Some of the findings of particle physics have profound implications for cosmology. Neutrinos, which were once believed to be massless, are stable particles present in vast quantities in the Universe. If their mass can be confirmed to be greater than $\frac{1}{20,000}$ that of an electron, their presence may be sufficient to halt the expansion of the Universe and cause its eventual collapse under the force of gravity.*

- *The search for a Theory of Everything based on the unification of the electroweak force with the strong force and gravity may yet prove to be in vain. If so, a promising alternative candidate is superstring theory, which envisages subatomic particles as quantized vibrations of stringlike matter in up to 10 dimensions. This theory adds six "compactified" dimensions to the four familiar dimensions of space and time.*

- *The predominance of matter over antimatter is a puzzling feature of the known Universe, since high-energy collisions in colliders yield both antimatter and matter, leading to the question of what happened to all the antimatter formed in the early Universe. A possible explanation for this apparent imbalance might be found in a curious lack of symmetry in the weak nuclear force.*

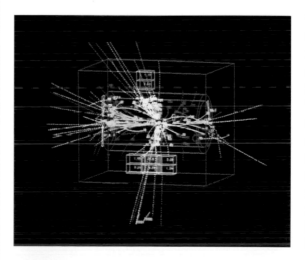

◄ This computer display shows the tracks of particles produced by a matter–antimatter annihilation at CERN. The purple and blue tracks show the paths of high-energy hadrons, while the yellow and green paths are of lower-energy particles. The UA1 detector—represented by the red outline—is the size of a three-story house.

SEE ALSO: Atomic structure • Binding energy • Bubble and cloud chamber • Electromagnetism • Energy, mass, and weight • Particle accelerator • Particle detector

Elevator

An elevator is basically a means of vertical transportation between the floors of a building, comprising an enclosed car balanced by a counterweight and moved by a wire rope.

The earliest elevators were man powered, using pulleys and a control rope passing through the car, a system still found occasionally in some small-goods elevators and builders' hoists. The first powered elevators were developed in the mid-19th century, using an extending hydraulic ram operated by water pressure to carry the car.

The first electric elevators were sturdy and simple and designed for use with direct current (DC) power. The introduction of alternating current (AC) supplies increased design problems, and until the mid-1920s, electric elevators used high-speed motors that turned the main drive wheel through a worm reduction gear.

The first practical variable voltage-control system was a DC hoist motor with power from a motor generator running off an AC supply. Today, geared motors provide the power for most elevators at up to 400 ft. (122 m) per minute. At higher speeds, the slow-speed gearless motor has advantages in speed of travel and in running costs.

Control mechanisms

Although the constant introduction of new materials, such as laminated plastics and stainless steel, has changed the appearance of elevator cars, the basic travel system has changed little during the last 50 years. By contrast, the control system has changed out of all recognition since the early days, when a pull on a rope actuated a pressure valve or moved a sliding bar across the control panel.

Push-button and touch-button controls in the car and at landing stations, automatic acceleration and deceleration, and the demand for greater speeds has led to unified control systems that provide the fastest service from the minimum of cars.

One of the objects today is to provide a minimum travel time. The simplest system provides service when any call button is depressed. The first call is the first answered; the passenger presses a button in the car to register a destination, and the car is dispatched to that floor. Other calls are registered in simple "first come, first served" sequence .

Automatic controls

The simplest automatic control system requires only one call button on each floor, no matter how many elevators there may be in the service bank. The approach of a car is signaled by an illuminated up or down arrow.

◀ A typical modern elevator system, with glass-sided cars moving up and down the center of the building. These elevators are designed to add to the architectural appeal of the building itself and are not hidden away as they used to be in the building's interior workings. Some modern glass elevators rise on the outside of the building, giving passengers views out over the surrounding area.

All landing calls are divided into sectors, each comprising a number of adjacent floors. The number of sectors equals the number of cars, and a car becomes available to answer a demand for sector service when the doors have closed and there are no assigned calls to be cleared.

As the car becomes available, it is allocated to the dispatching system, and the nearest car to a priority sector is allocated to it. The car is chosen by an electronic assembly that constantly compares the car's location with priority demand. In many systems, time is saved by initiating the dispatch sequence immediately after passengers have stopped entering or leaving the car, a situation detected by photoelectric cells in the door edge.

Most control systems are electromechanical, but an increasing number of installations use microprocessor systems with a complex arrangement of logic circuits to control car movements. In 1995, the Schindler Elevator Company developed a new elevator programming system to decrease travel time. The Miconic 10 replaces the up/down buttons with a keypad that eliminates the need for floor buttons inside the elevator. The user enters the desired floor number into the keypad, and the system computer chooses the most direct elevator.

As buildings have become taller, elevator speeds have increased to as much as 1,800 ft. (549 m) per minute, though a maximum is set for passenger comfort. Local lifts may be used to serve groups of floors rather than the entire building.

Counterweights

The cars of passenger elevators are usually counterbalanced by a heavy counterweight equal to the weight of the empty car plus about 45 percent of its maximum load. The effect is to reduce the amount of power needed to raise the car and to provide traction between the ropes and drive sheave.

Safety considerations

Passenger safety is an important feature of elevator design. Under normal circumstances, car speed is controlled by governor switches acting on the motor and brake circuits. If the speed of a descending car exceeds a preset limit, powerful braking arms (activated by a cable connected to a governor unit on the winding machine) contact the guide rails to stop the car smoothly and safely. Hydraulic or spring-operated buffers are situated at the bottom of all elevator shafts to safely stop loaded cars traveling at full speed.

In many modern installations, there are devices to sense the weight of the loaded car, and when the car is fully loaded, it will bypass all landing calls and service only calls registered within

the car. If the weighing mechanism detects an overload, the starting circuits will not function.

Door interlocks are fitted so that the car will not move until all the doors are fully closed, to prevent the landing doors from opening unless a car is present and to ensure that the car doors remain closed until the car has stopped at a landing. Additional devices reopen the doors if they begin to close as a passenger is entering or leaving.

Paternoster elevator

A type of elevator once fairly common but now less used is the paternoster, comprising a set of cars on a pair of endless drive chains. There are no doors on the cars or on the landing stations, and the cars do not stop but move slowly enough to allow passengers to step in and out. The cars travel up on one side of the chain loop, over the top, and down the other side. Each car is attached to the chains by pivots at its top so that it always hangs vertically as it passes over the top of the loop or under the bottom.

▲ The entrance hall of the Regency Hotel in Atlanta, Georgia. Panoramic cars glide up and down the central column, providing a view of the lobby.

SEE ALSO:

ELECTRIC MOTOR • ELECTRONICS • ELEVATOR, GRAIN • GOVERNOR • LOGIC • SKYSCRAPER

Elevator, Grain

Bulk materials, such as grain, often have to be raised from one level to another using the least possible floor space and in the shortest time possible; elevators are used for this type of handling.

There are various types of elevators in general use, but the principal types are the bucket, pneumatic, chain, and Archimedes' screw elevators. They are often used in handling materials other than grain.

Bucket elevator

Bucket elevators are widely used in a range of industries for handling materials as diverse as grain or limestone. Both the lift heights and the capacities of these machines vary greatly, for example, from 10 ft. (3 m) of lift height at 2 tons (1.8 tonnes) per hour to as much as 300 ft. (91 m) of lift height at a rate of 2,000 tons (1,800 tonnes) per hour in a large bulk-grain intake system. It is essential that the type of elevator used is matched to the material to be handled, and this important function is achieved by using either a centrifugal or a positive discharge unit.

In the centrifugal machines, the material leaves the bucket at a tangent to its path, impelled by natural forces; in the positive discharge machines, the buckets are completely inverted at the discharge point. The buckets are transported by either a belt or a chain. In the centrifugal discharge machines, the use of the belt is more usual; the positive discharge units have a chain or possibly twin chains on the larger units.

◀ The hose of a pneumatic elevator unloading grain from the hold of a ship. Static elevator installations may be part of a silo complex, discharging the grain into bins. Mobile units discharge into mills, silos, or vehicles.

Pneumatic elevator

The pneumatic elevator is extremely popular in docks for the unloading of ocean-going ships into lighters or shore installations at rates as high as 2,000 tons (1,800 tonnes) per hour. Such large capacities are needed to ensure rapid unloading of bulk-cargo ships with loads of up to 60,000 tons (54,000 tonnes). The grain is drawn up through hoses by suction created by a centrifugal fan or rotary blower operating at the discharge end. The operation of the flexible intake hoses on jibs allows this system to effectively solve the problems of trimming the hold and simultaneously accommodating variations in height owing to tidal changes. On a smaller scale, in the region of 70 to 80 tons (63–72 tonnes) per hour, similar systems are mounted on trailers and powered by an integral diesel engine. This small unit benefits from its mobility and operates just as flexibly as the static unit. Pneumatic elevators may be used with bucket elevators to clean out the bottom of a hold.

Chain elevator

A chain elevator consists of a steel tube enclosing a continuous chain that has extensions or paddles on the links to carry the grain along. Machines of this type operate on the en masse principle, which is that once the supply of material to the unit is started, it is allowed to fill the elevator from inlet to outlet; thus, the particles of the material being conveyed propel each other along in conjunction with the chain of the machine. This operation can be done effectively either horizontally or vertically or by using a combination.

Archimedes' screw elevator

An Archimedes' screw elevator, often referred to as an auger, operates on the en masse principle. It is generally inclined at an angle of 70 to 80 degrees to the horizontal, with a length of approximately 30 ft. (9 m). Mounted on a two-wheeled chassis and with capacities of 20 to 30 tons (18–27 tonnes) per hour, machines of this style are common in the agricultural industry.

Vertical screw elevators are an extension of the horizontal Archimedes' screw conveyor principle and also operate on an en masse basis, but by a series of variations of the pitch and diameter of the blades, they can carry material at a predetermined loading vertically up the machine.

SEE ALSO: ELEVATOR • FREIGHT HANDLING

Embryology

A new human life begins when a female ovum is fertilized by a male sperm. One day after fertilization has taken place, the ovum, which measures about 0.2 mm in diameter, begins to divide, doubling the number of cells with each division. At the same time as the cells are increasing in number, they are also being gently moved from the fallopian tube, where fertilization took place, down into the womb. This movement is achieved by tiny cilia lining the wall of the fallopian tube. By the fourth or fifth day, the processes of cell division have resulted in a hollow ball of about 140 cells called a blastocyst. This ball attaches itself to the wall of the womb where it begins to eat away at the mother's tissue until it has become embedded beneath the surface. While this is occurring, cells inside the blastocyst divide into two layers called the endoderm and ectoderm.

The endoderm spreads around the inner surface of one part of the ball to form a large cavity filled with yolk—the source of nutrients for the early development of the fetus. The ectoderm spreads over the other interior surface of the ball to form a fluid-filled membrane called the amniotic sac. This sac will help to protect the embryo as it grows. The outer cells of the blastocyst also begin to form long narrow projections called villi, which spread outward into the wall of the womb, where they connect with the mother's blood vessels and form the placenta. After two weeks, the developing cells are completely embedded in the womb and are now called an embryo. A stem between the amniotic sac and the womb eventually becomes the umbilical cord, which connects the baby to the mother across the placenta. By this point, all of the necessary structures are in place for the embryo to begin rapid development.

In the third week, another layer of cells develops between the endoderm and ectoderm. This layer, called the mesoderm, is the development of a thickening of the ectoderm called the "primitive streak." These three layers will eventually form all of the organs and tissues of the body. The endoderm will become the liver, pancreas, gallbladder, lungs, and lining of the digestive system. The ectoderm will develop into the teeth, nails, hair, and skin, as well as the nervous system and sense organs. The mesoderm will create the bone, cartilage, muscle, connective tissue, sex glands, and kidneys.

By the end of the third week, the embryo has grown to about ⅛ in. (2.5 mm) long and has begun to develop a heart, a spinal cord, a brain, a mouth, and an anus.

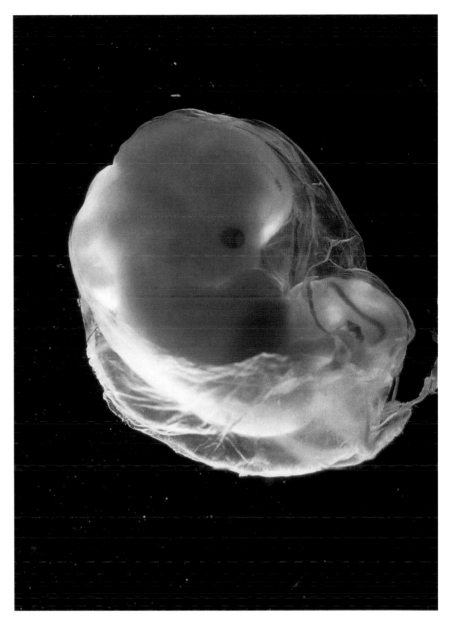

▲ Side view of an eight-week-old fetus surrounded by its amnion membrane. The fetus measures ¾ in. (20 mm) from the top of its head to its rump. The eye is visible as a dark spot on the head.

The next stage is complex in that the embryo must undergo a series of foldings in different directions that will redistribute its developing organs and ultimately give it the beginnings of a human form. During this process, the yolk sac diminishes in size, eventually disappearing altogether. The embryo now begins to grow rapidly. The heart and brain become much greater in size, and by the fifth week, the eyes, ears, and limbs have begun to appear. One week later, the embryo shows all the major structures of the body. The only exceptions are the sex organs, which, though present, do not begin to develop into either male or female until the 14th week after conception. By the 8th week, the 1 in. (24.5 mm) long embryo is called a fetus. Growth continues in the womb until, nine months after conception, the mother gives birth.

Genes in development

There have been many breakthroughs in recent years in our understanding of the development of the human embryo and why defects may occur. The breakthroughs started with research on the fruit fly, *Drosophila*. In the late 1970s, researchers realized that mutations of genes controlling early development would probably be lethal, and therefore, conventional research, which has always looked at adult animals, would have missed these gene mutations. They then screened fruit flies for the genes that, when they mutated, would give rise to dead larvae with recognizable abnormalities, such as missing segments, or conversion of one type of segment into another.

Most of these genes have now been cloned, and scientists know what part of the body they are expressed in—that is, the part they control the design of—and at what stage of development. The result of all this effort has been a virtual gene-by-gene account of how *Drosophila* develops from a single-celled egg to a complex larva with many differentiated tissues and body parts.

Surprisingly, higher animals, including vertebrates, mammals, and even humans, contain genes that have considerable parallels with the fruit fly. Thus, the *Drosophila* work has enabled scientists to identify many genes in vertebrates that would have been difficult or impossible to find directly.

Selector genes

Researchers have found that there is an important class of genes—homeotic, or selector, genes—that codes for parts of the body rather than for separate tissues or cells. Such a gene might be expressed in the front half of the body but not in the rear half. These homeotic genes code for transcription factors, whose function is to regulate the expression of other genes; they lie near the top of a hierarchy of gene regulation. Second, the body plan is specified by concentrations within each cell of chemicals that act as inducing factors, or morphogens. The crucial element is the concentration gradient—that is, the way the concentration increases over a short distance. Third, the stability of gene expression depends often and perhaps always on positive feedback, whereby a gene is kept active by the product it makes.

The fruit fly research has shown that the mechanisms of embryonic development are based on some simple rules. Every egg is slightly asymmetrical, regardless of species, so there is always a gradient that can trigger the formation of a gradient of morphogens.

The gradient leads to activation of one or several of the homeotic genes in different parts of the

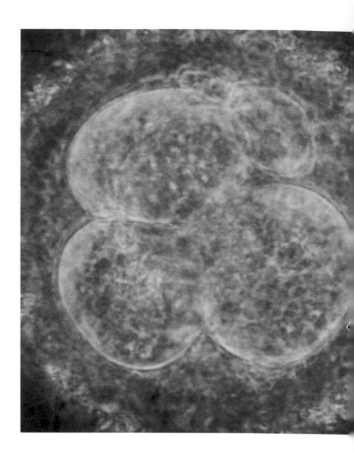

▶ Light micrograph of a primitive human embryo, composed of four cells following the initial mitotic divisions that ultimately transform a single-celled organism into one composed of millions of cells.

embryo; the exact concentration of the gradient determines which genes will be activated. These gene products turn on other genes that produce further sources and targets for further morphogen gradients, which activate other combinations of homeotic genes.

Each small, multicellular region of the embryo soon becomes uniquely specified by the activation of a combination of homeotic genes. Once established, these codings are maintained by positive feedback, and the gradients are no longer necessary. Later on in the embryo's development, each combination of morphogens will trigger the genes involved in the eventual differentiation of particular organs and tissues.

Growing organs

In 1998, scientists at the University of Wisconsin announced that they had successfully cultured stem cells from human blastocysts. This research may ultimately lead to the artificial creation of organs and tissues that could be used for transplants. It may also be possible to inject cultured cells directly into tissue—heart cells, for example could be grown and then injected into a diseased heart to support damaged tissue. Much work, however, still needs to be done before these ideas can become a reality.

SEE ALSO: BIOENGINEERING • CELL BIOLOGY • GENETIC ENGINEERING • GENETICS • MOLECULAR BIOLOGY • TRANSPLANT

Enamel, Vitreous

In enameling, a thin layer of glass is fused to the surface of a metal. Being a glass, enamel has a hard glossy surface that is resistant to corrosion, scratching, and staining. These properties led to its widespread use for household goods, such as bathtubs and cooking utensils, but today its major applications include finishes on kitchen equipment and buildings. The term enamel (more correctly, vitreous or porcelain enamel) should not be confused with the use of this word as applied to high-gloss paints.

The technique of enameling to create jewelry and pictures has its origins in antiquity and was known to the early Egyptians, the Celts, and the Romans and was developed even more by the Byzantines.

Industrial enameling was first developed commercially in the 1850s in Austria and Germany with the enameling of sheet steel. During the latter half of the 19th century, mass-produced enamel goods became available. Improvements to enameling technology continued throughout the 20th century and continue today.

Preparation of powdered glass

In large-scale industrial applications, a continuous smelter is used. The well-mixed raw materials are fed in at one end and the molten glass flows out at the other. It is then cooled by pouring into cold water or onto a cooled metal surface. This glass, called frit, is easily ground to small particles in a ball mill. For sheet steel enameling, the frit is milled with clay, certain electrolytes, and water to provide a stable suspension, or slurry. The particle size of a base coat enamel can be about 0.003 in. (0.08 mm), but cover coats are finer, usually less than 0.002 in. (0.05 mm) in diameter.

The chemical composition of the glass varies according to the job it must do, but it is important that the rates of expansion on heating and contraction on cooling are compatible with those of the metal to be enameled. A typical ground coat, which is the first coat to be applied in sheet-steel enameling, might contain 39 to 42 percent borax, 19 to 21 percent feldspar, 28 to 30 percent silica, 7 to 9 percent sodium carbonate, and small amounts of other chemicals, including cobalt or sometimes molybdenum oxides, to help the enamel to adhere well to the metal. The next layer of enamel is the cover coat (more than one may be applied), and it may contain 23 to 26 percent borax, 13 to 15 percent feldspar, 33 to 36 percent silica, 9 to 13 percent sodium carbonate, and various other chemicals, including 5 to 7 per-

◄ After being coated with enamel slurry, bath tubs travel on an overhead conveyor through a furnace at a temperature of 1560°F (850°C).

cent titanium oxide. Titanium oxide is added for opacity, and other opaque materials also used include zirconia, antimony oxide, and molybdenum oxide. Titanium enamels have excellent covering power—one thin coating about three thousandths of an inch thick will mask a dark colored ground coat. Colored enamels are produced by the addition of metal oxides.

The enameling process

It is most important that the metal surface is clean before the frit is applied, and the surface should be clean for all subsequent enamel coats. The most common industrial metals are steels, enameling iron, and sometimes cast iron. The sheet-metal articles are thoroughly cleaned in a series of baths including detergent, acid, alkali, and water for thorough rinsing. To enhance enamel bonding, sometimes a thin film of nickel is plated on.

Most enameling is done by the wet process: a thick slurry of the frit is applied by spraying or dipping followed by draining. The dry process is used for cast iron enameling. Here the first coat is applied wet, but the subsequent cover coats are applied by dusting the powdered glass onto the heated article; several dusting and heating cycles are needed for uniformity.

After drying, the enamel is fired either in intermittent box-type furnaces or in a continuous tunnel-type furnace. In the latter case, the articles travel slowly through the furnace on a conveyor, the journey taking about 20 minutes, but they remain in the hot part of the furnace only for

about four minutes. Ground coats are normally fired at about 1470 to 1560°F (800–850°C), while cover coats are fired for shorter times at a slightly lower temperature. Some enamels can also be fired at somewhat lower temperatures—typically about 1020°F (550°C)—and are suitable for enameling aluminum.

On heating, the glass melts and draws up with surface tension to the metal. It is not known exactly why it bonds so well, but probably it is a combination of physical gripping of the rough metal surface (no matter how smooth a metal may appear, it is actually full of minute hills and valleys) and the formation of chemical bonds between the glass and metal.

◀ An early example of ninth century Byzantine *cloisonné* work—the Hope Beresford Cross. The individual cells for the various colored enamels were made of thin gold strips.

▶ Like glass or pottery, the firing of enamel takes only a few minutes. Here a dish is carefully placed in the muffle furnace.

Jewelry and craft enameling

In many ways, the procedures are similar to industrial enameling, but often on an individual scale. The glass formulas differ—a typical craft enamel consisting of 33 percent silica, 33 percent red lead, 9 percent borax, 12 percent sodium carbonate, 7 percent potassium nitrate, and small percentages of other chemicals. Metallic oxides may be added to the frit as coloring agents, up to 15 percent. There are three basic types of enamel: transparent, translucent, and opaque.

The metals used most frequently are copper or copper alloys, but silver, gold, platinum, and stainless steel may also be enameled. The frit is usually applied by dusting it evenly onto the metal surface. If necessary, the surface can be coated with an adhesive, usually gum tragacanth, to make the powdered glass stick. Alternatively, the frit may be slurried.

There are various design effects in craft enameling: *cloisonné*, *champlevé*, and *basse taille*. In cloisonné, the metal surface is divided into individual cells by thin strips of metal, which have been soldered or fixed in a colorless flux (glass) to the surface. These cells can then be filled with different colored enamels without any fear of mixing. Champlevé was known to the Romans but was not widely used until the 12th century. In this technique, cavities are scooped out of the metal to hold the enamel. A thick metal base is needed in order to achieve this. For basse taille, the metal surface is designed in low relief and then covered all over with transparent enamel so that the design beneath shows through the enamel.

FACT FILE

- *Very few examples have survived of the fragile* plique-à-jour *enamels, which were produced mainly between the 14th and 16th centuries, and were intended to have the translucent appearance of stained glass. Originating in Byzantium (today's Istanbul), the process involved firing translucent enamels into wire patterns fixed to thin metal or metal backings and then removing the backing to enable a light source, such as a candle, to shine through.*

- *The Chinese emperor Kiang-hsi (1661–1722) founded enameling factories. Their main function was to produce incense vessels based on the forms of ancient bronzes. These vessels were then donated to the Buddhist temples he inaugurated around Peking.*

SEE ALSO: ALLOY • CERAMICS • CHINA AND PORCELAIN • FURNACE • GLASS • GOLD • IRON AND STEEL • METALWORKING • SURFACE TREATMENTS

Endocrinology

The endocrine system consist of groups of specialized cells called endocrine glands and is made up of the adrenal glands, the gonads, (ovaries and testes), the pancreas, the parathyroids, the pituitary, the thyroid, and the placenta in pregnant women. These glands produce chemicals that help to regulate and maintain various functions of the body, enabling it to respond to changing needs. The glands of the endocrine system are the most important in the body and the vital chemicals they produce are called hormones.

The endocrine glands

There are two adrenal glands, one on the upper part of each kidney. Each adrenal gland is divided into two parts called the adrenal cortex and the adrenal medulla. The adrenal cortex secretes steroids, such as aldosterone, which act upon the kidneys to maintain a fine balance within the blood of potassium, chloride, and sodium. The cortex also produces cortisol, which acts as an anti-inflammatory, helps to prevent allergic reactions, and breaks down protein into amino acids and then converts them to glucose.

The adrenal medulla produces epinephrine and norepinephrine (also known as adrenaline and noradrenaline) in response to stressful or dangerous situations that induce feelings such as fear or anger. These hormones have a number of different effects. They prepare the body to take action by diverting blood from nonessential parts of the body. They cause the pupils of the eyes to dilate, allowing them to take in more light, and the bronchiole muscles to relax, thus increasing the supply of oxygen to the blood.

The gonads are different in males and females—ovaries in females, testes in males. In both sexes, however, these glands are involved in sexual reproduction and sexual development.

The pancreas secretes the chemicals insulin and glucagon, which together maintain a correct balance of sugar levels in the blood. The pancreas also secretes digestive enzymes into the intestine to help break down food.

The parathyroid and thyroid glands are found together just below the Adam's apple in the neck. The thyroid produces hormones that adjust the metabolic rate—the speed the body uses food and oxygen to produce energy. This gland also produces the hormone thyroxine, which stimulates growth in children and speeds up the reactions of enzymes that help to produce energy. The parathyroids secrete parathormone, which keeps a correct balance of calcium in the blood.

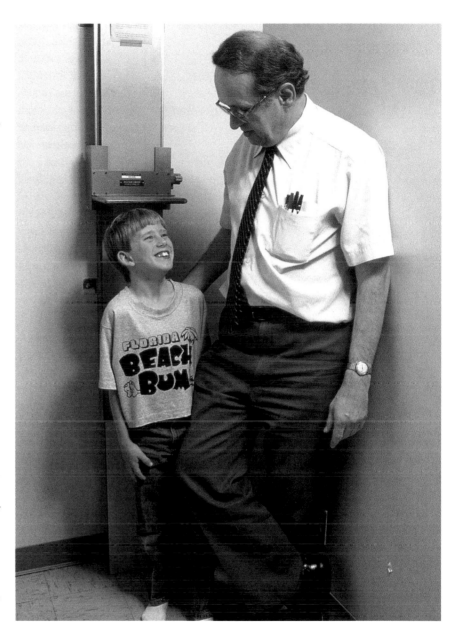

▲ An 11 year old boy undergoing treatment with a growth hormone is shown here being measured by his doctor. Growth hormone is synthesized and stored in the anterior pituitary gland and under normal conditions promotes growth of the long bones in the limbs and increases protein synthesis. Childhood deficiency of growth hormone results in dwarfism, whereas excess production causes gigantism.

The pituitary secretes more hormones than any other gland in the endocrine system. It is divided into two parts, called the anterior and posterior pituitary. Between them, they produce eight hormones that are involved in such areas as growth, reproduction, and the maintenance of plasma levels in the blood. The anterior pituitary produces six hormones, one of which is the human growth hormone, HGH. This is important in the normal development of children. If too little is produced, dwarfism results. Conversely, too much HGH causes gigantism. The posterior pituitary produces two hormones—oxytocin and an antidiuretic hormone called ADH. The antidiuretic hormone has the effect of increasing the rate at which the kidneys withdraw water from the urine. Oxytocin is responsible for the contractions that cause a pregnant mother to give

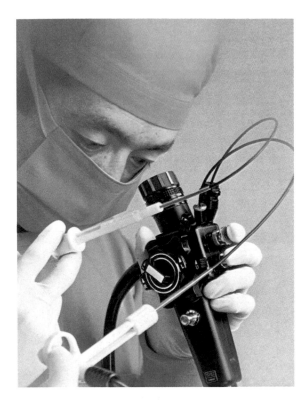

Endoscopes at work

A flexible fiber-optic endoscope can be used to look into many hollow parts of the body, including the abdominal cavity, esophagus, rectum, bladder, lungs, stomach, intestines, uterus, and knee joints—an endoscope is flexible enough to wriggle around any organ. Endoscopes cannot be used to view the interior of solid organs, such as the liver, but this situation may change with greater miniaturization.

Although all endoscopes operate on a similar principle, the instrument is given a number of different names according to where in the body it is used. Any particular endoscope may be used for diagnosis or surgery, as the need arises.

To provide mobility, a wide range of devices can be attached to endoscopes. A kind of pulley is used to thread an endoscope along curved parts of the body, such as the colon. Some endoscopes have steering mechanisms, and others clearing mechanisms. The larger endoscopes have airways incorporated into them. With an air compressor attached, a physician may distend an organ to improve access for operations or viewing. Other endoscopes have a vacuum channel for removing fluids. Despite the great complexity of the most advanced endoscopes, they are remarkably compact, usually being about the diameter of a pencil.

Diagnosis

Endoscopes are most often used as a diagnostic tool. More particularly, endoscopy is at its most valuable when it saves a patient from complicated or risky exploratory surgical operations.

◄ An endoscope being used to locate and remove a polyp from the patient's colon. This is a common disorder that can cause bleeding from the bowel. Using the white handles, the physician removes the polyp with tiny forceps and a snare.

▼ A cutaway diagram of an endoscope tube, showing bundles of fiber optics. The fibers do not transmit heat, which might damage body tissues.

In some cases, such as the treatment of peptic ulcers, endoscopy is the only way of certain diagnosis without surgery. Physical examination of the stomach may not help, and X-ray results may be misleading, but a physician can examine the stomach wall with an endoscope and actually see any signs of ulceration.

Endoscopy had been so successful in diagnosis of diseases of the upper gastrointestinal tract that many surgeons use it as first choice rather than X rays. Endoscopy is also preferred for regular monitoring to detect recurrence of symptoms in many conditions.

Jaundice

The diagnosis of jaundice has been one of endoscopy's successes. The condition is recognizable by a yellow tinge on the skin and the white of the eye. A tiny tube is passed from an endoscope into the patient's biliary and pancreatic systems. A dye is injected so that the biliary and pancreatic ducts show up clearly on X rays. Examining the X ray can show up a gallstone or cancer of the pancreas, either of which may be causing the jaundice.

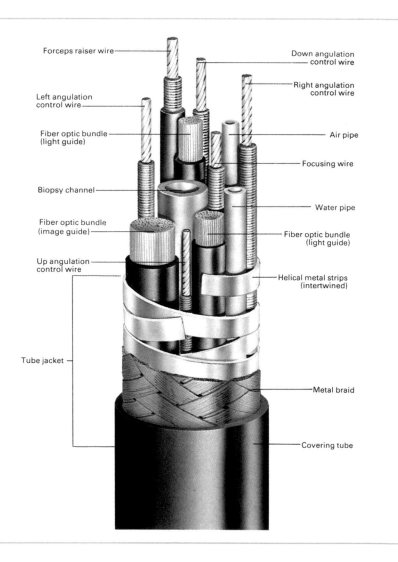

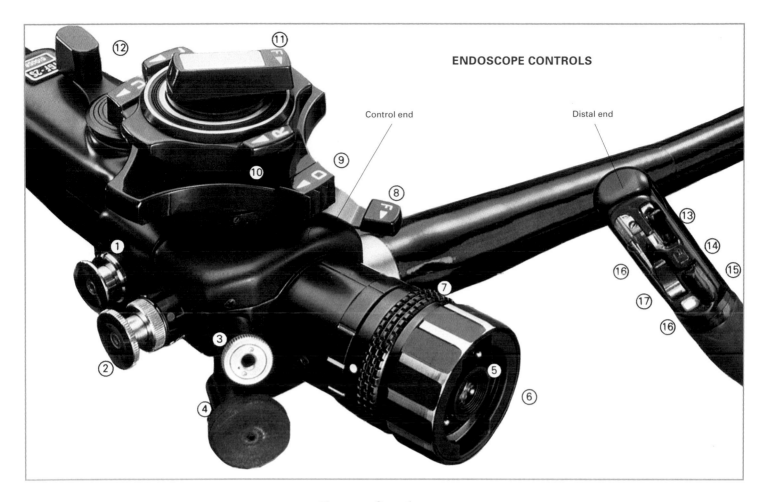

ENDOSCOPE CONTROLS

Control end

Distal end

Surgery

The most advanced kinds of endoscope can be used for surgery, with suitable attachments. Surgery may range from electric cauterization to removal of small pieces of tissue for biopsy. Attachments may range from clamps and forceps to cutting instruments and lasers.

Endoscopy can have major advantages over conventional surgical procedures. Removal of polyps in the colon traditionally demanded a complex surgical operation and a two-week stay in hospital. Now, using an endoscope, the operation is quick, and the patient can return home the next day. Gallstones may be removed with similar equipment. The bile duct is enlarged, and a special basket attached to the endoscope is used to remove the stones. This condition is common in elderly people, who would have difficulty in coping with full-scale surgery.

Endoscopy is well known for its use in laser surgery, particularly to treat major hemorrhaging of the gastrointestinal tract of the elderly. Glass fiber is unsuitable for transmitting laser light, so the endoscope is modified by using a quartz fiber instead. The hemorrhage is located by the surgeon looking through the endoscope. The tip of the quartz fiber is placed in position over the site, and the laser is triggered, causing the blood to coagulate and stop the bleeding.

Types of endoscope

Endoscopes are named according to the area of the body in which they are used. An endoscope used in the stomach is called a gastroscope, and it is as thin and flexible as possible so that it can pass easily down the patient's throat. Gastroscopes can also detect bleeding and tumors.

A bronchoscope is a flexible fiber-optic instrument used to explore the lungs. Rigid endoscopes have difficulty passing beyond the trachea, but with its controllable tip, the smaller bronchi can be explored to remove objects lodged in the lungs or even to remove cancers or cysts.

If a patient has severe pain or injury in the abdomen, a laparoscope may be passed through the wall of the abdomen to locate bleeding or damaged organs. A further use for a laparoscope is to confirm an ectopic pregnancy—a condition in which the fetus develops outside the womb.

There is a specific endoscope for use in many other parts of the body; they include an amnioscope, to check the development of a fetus inside the uterus; a colonoscope, to treat tumors and polyps in the colon; and a ventriculoscope, to explore the fluid-filled spaces around the brain.

▲ A typical endoscope has a number of control mechanisms located near the eyepiece of the instrument: (1) combined air and lens-washing control, (2) suction button, (3) small-channel nonreturn valve, (4) large-channel nonreturn valve, (5) viewing lens, (6) eyepiece, (7) focusing ring, (8) brake for up-down control, (9) up-down control for distal end, (10) left-right angulation for distal end, (11) brake for left-right control, (12) forceps raiser control, (13) forceps raiser for small channel, (14) objective lens, (15) air and water outlet, (16) viewing lights, (17) forceps raiser for large channel.

SEE ALSO: ELECTRONICS IN MEDICINE • FIBER OPTICS • INSTANT-PICTURE CAMERA • LASER AND MASER • LENS • MICROSURGERY • SURGERY

Energy, Mass, and Weight

Energy is the capacity of matter or radiation to do work; rest mass is a measure of the quantity of matter in an object. Energy and mass are different facets of a single entity called mass–energy. Weight is a force experienced by an object in a gravitational field by virtue of that object's mass.

The nature of energy

Energy is difficult to describe in absolute terms, since it is such a fundamental concept. It is also a recently developed concept: even the laws of motion—published in 1687 by the British physicist and mathematician Sir Isaac Newton—made no reference to energy, confining themselves instead to force, mass, momentum, and velocity.

The term *energy*—from the Greek *ergon*, meaning "work"—was first used in its current scientific sense in 1807 by Thomas Young, a British physician and physicist. Young described the energy that an object has by virtue of its motion, which is now called kinetic energy. Soon after, another form of mechanical energy was recognized: potential energy—the energy that arises from the position of an object at the top of a slope or at the end of a taut spring, for example. Potential energy is so called because it has the potential to be converted into kinetic energy by such an object accelerating under the pull of gravity or the tension in the spring, respectively.

In the early decades of the 19th century, many scientists believed that heat was a manifestation of an invisible fluid, called caloric, possessed by hot objects. Then in the 1840s, the British physicist James Joule performed a series of experiments to demonstrate that heat was a form of energy. In 1840, he showed that the rate at which heat is generated by an electrical current passing through a wire is proportional to the square of the current, and in 1847, he measured the amount of heat generated in water by the action of a paddle driven by a falling mass on a string.

The first law: conservation of energy

Joule's experiments helped establish the notion that energy exists in a variety of forms and that suitable devices can interconvert different forms of energy. Also in the 1840s, other experimenters showed the relationship between heat, chemical energy, and the motion of muscles. In 1850, the German physicist Rudolf Clausius and the British physicist William Thomson, who was later made Baron Kelvin, independently proposed what is now called the first law of thermodynamics: that energy can neither be created nor destroyed.

▲ Water loses potential energy as it falls from a higher level to a lower one. In the cascade of water in the foreground, some of this energy is converted into sound energy and some is converted into heat energy as the temperature of the water at the foot of the cascade rises. The hydroelectric plant in the background converts some of the potential energy of the falling water first into the kinetic energy of rotating turbines, then into electrical energy.

Mechanical energy

When a bullet is in motion, it possesses a form of energy that it does not have when it is at rest. This energy, called kinetic energy, is proportional to the mass of the bullet and the square of its speed. When the bullet hits a target, some of this energy is transformed into chemical energy as chemical bonds break in the deforming target and bullet itself, while some kinetic energy is transformed into heat and sound energies.

A mass raised against gravitational force possesses potential energy because it has a potential to move toward the ground or down a slope. If allowed to move under the gravitational pull, such a mass gains kinetic energy as it loses potential energy. That kinetic energy can, for example, hammer a foundation pile into the ground. In the case of a swinging pendulum, energy repeatedly exchanges between its kinetic and potential forms: the maximum of kinetic energy—the value at the bottom of the swing—is exactly the same as the difference in potential energy between the top and the bottom of the swing.

While a gravitational field is the most familiar cause of potential energy, other causes exist. A charged object has electrostatic potential energy by virtue of its position in an electric field, for example, and a magnetized object has magnetic potential energy in a magnetic field.

Equations of energy

The kinetic energy (K.E.) of an object in linear motion—motion along a line—is linked to the product of its mass (m) and the square of its velocity (v) by the equation K.E. = $\frac{1}{2}mv^2$. A similar equation links the kinetic energy of a rotating object to its moment of inertia (I) and its angular velocity (ω), namely, K.E. = $\frac{1}{2}I\omega^2$.

The change in gravitational potential energy (ΔP.E.) for an object that moves through a vertical distance in a gravitational field depends on its mass, the change in height (Δh), and the acceleration of an object in freefall in that field (g) according to the equation ΔP.E. = $mg\Delta h$. Note that the equation refers to *changes* in vertical position and potential energy rather than absolute values, because absolute potential energy is impossible to specify. An object on the ground does not have zero potential energy, since it would lose further potential energy if it fell down a well, for example.

Heat and sound energy

Heat and sound are manifestations of the movements of particles on an atomic scale. As such, they are directly related to the kinetic and potential energies of those particles.

The heat energy of an object is the sum of the kinetic energies of motion of all its particles. A major component of heat energy is the translational kinetic energy of particles, which is associated with the linear motion of gas molecules and the vibrations of particles within the lattice structure of a solid. In the case of vibrating particles, kinetic and potential energies are in constant interchange, just as they are in a pendulum. In this case, however, the potential energy changes arise from changes in the separations of molecules within each other's electrostatic fields.

Other components of heat energy include the kinetic energies of rotating molecules and the energies of vibrating molecules, whose bonds stretch and deform in a regularly repeating manner. Note that a single molecule may possess all three types of energy as it vibrates in a lattice, rotates, and undergoes internal vibrations. The kinetic energies associated with each type of motion obey the same equations as the equations that exist for macroscopic (large) objects.

Sound energy is carried through a medium as waves of compression, which generate fluctuations in the kinetic and potential energies of the particles of that medium. Just as for molecules in a lattice, the changes in potential energy arise from changes in the separations of molecules in the medium. This is why sound cannot pass through a vacuum: there are no particles to carry the fluctuations of kinetic and potential energy.

Chemical energy

Atoms consist of negatively charged electrons in motion around positively charged nuclei. Those electrons have kinetic energy because they have a mass and are in motion; they also have varying potential energies because they have charge and can change positions within an electric field.

When two atoms are in close proximity, the electric field of each is modified by the nucleus and electrons of the other. As a result, the electrostatic potential energy of each electron and nucleus in the atom pair depends on the distance between the two atoms, measured as the distance between their nuclei. A chemical bond forms when the minimum value of the total potential energy of the atom pair occurs at an internuclear distance similar to the radii of the atoms.

In methane (CH_4)—the main component of natural gas—each molecule has a geometry that is the best compromise of internuclear separations for one carbon atom and four hydrogens. Similarly, the internuclear distance in an oxygen (O_2) molecule corresponds to the lowest potential energy for two oxygen atoms. When a methane molecule and two oxygen molecules come together, however, their atoms can regroup in a way that reduces their chemical potential energy: they can form one molecule of carbon dioxide (CO_2) and two of water (H_2O). If this happens, the excess chemical energy is released as heat.

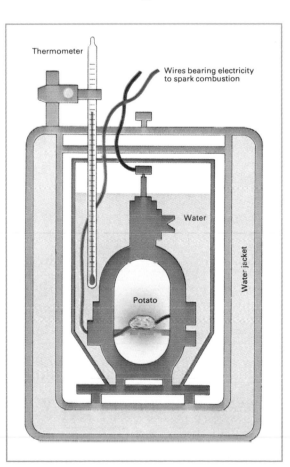

◀ A bomb calorimeter measures the amount of chemical energy released as heat when a substance is burned in oxygen in a sealed metal vessel. The combustion heats the water in the jacket around the bomb, and the heat change of the reaction can be calculated from the increase in temperature. This technique gives an indication of the chemical energy available from food.

Electrical energy

Electrical energy is the capacity to do work that arises from the increase in electrostatic potential energy that occurs when mutually repulsive charges concentrate in one place. When those charge concentrations are neutralized—by electrons flowing from negative to positive through the coils of a motor, for example—the drop in electrostatic potential energy can be transformed into mechanical energy and heat.

Electromagnetic energy

The energy in the magnetic field of a permanent magnet enables that field to move a piece of iron; similarly, the energy of the electric field of a charged object can move another charged object. Electromagnetic radiation—light, infrared, gamma rays, and other forms—conveys energy in the form of photons. It is in this form that Earth receives energy from the Sun, for example.

A photon is a massless "particle" of electromagnetic radiation whose energy oscillates between its electric field and its magnetic field. The frequency with which those interchanges occur determines the energy of the photon.

Efficiency and entropy

The efficiency of a process is the proportion of energy that it converts into useful energy. In a coal-fired power station, for example, efficiency is measured as the proportion of the chemical energy of coal, released as heat by burning, that is converted into useful electrical energy. The efficiency of a power station can never be greater than 40 percent, since the majority of heat flees through the chimney and through cooling water to be dispersed in the environment.

The inefficiency of power stations is but one example of a fundamental fact of nature: that high-grade energy, such as chemical energy, tends to be converted into low-grade energy from which little work can be obtained, such as dispersed heat. The "grade" of energy is expressed in terms of entropy— a measure of disorder.

The second law of thermodynamics, formulated in 1850 by Clausius and Thomson, observes that an energy-converting process will not occur if it requires a decrease in the disorder, or entropy, of the Universe. Even processes that appear to generate high-grade energy, such as the accumulation of chemical energy in growing plants, must be accompanied by a greater dispersal of low-grade energy. In the case of plants, the majority of the high-grade energy in photons of sunlight becomes low-grade heat energy; only a small proportion is finally converted into high-grade chemical energy in plant tissues.

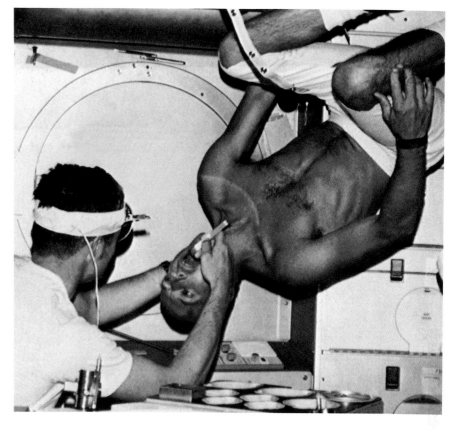

▲ An astronaut undergoes an oral examination while in orbit. The restraining strap visible at the top of the picture prevents him from floating away. Long-term weightlessness has numerous physiological effects. Joints settle in midway positions, for example, while blood collects in the head and drains from the feet in the absence of gravity, which would normally draw blood toward the feet.

The nature of mass

The mass of an object is simply defined as the quantity of matter in that object. In 1789, the French chemist Antoine Lavoisier proposed a law of conservation of matter, whereby matter can neither be created nor destroyed. Lavoisier used this law as a basis for the development of modern chemistry, observing that the initial and final masses in chemical reactions are always equal.

Classical physicists defined mass in terms of inertia—the resistance to acceleration by a force. A cannonball, for example, requires a much greater force to set it rolling at a particular speed than does a basketball. The greater inertia of the cannonball is due to its greater mass, and the observation is as true in space as it is on Earth.

Relativity and mass–energy

Until the 20th century, the conservation laws for energy and matter were held to be fundamental truths of the Universe, and no example was found to contradict them. This view changed in 1905, when the U.S. physicist Albert Einstein published his Special Theory of Relativity.

Einstein had been considering the results of an experiment, conducted in 1887, that showed the speed of sunlight to be identical whether the observer on Earth's surface is approaching or receding from the Sun. Einstein concluded that the speed of light is absolute—its measured value does not depend on the speed of the observer— and that it cannot be exceeded by any object.

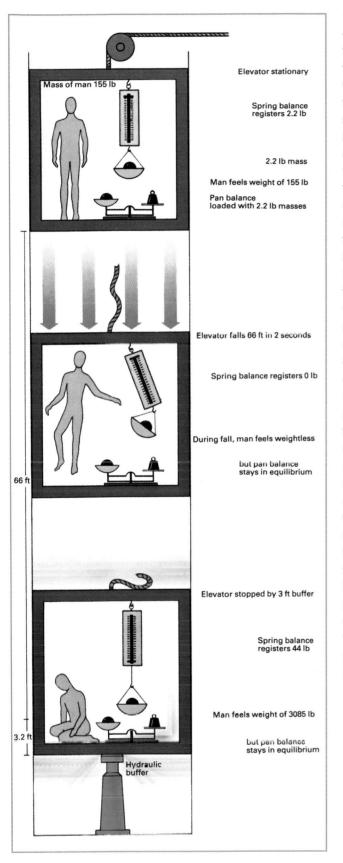

Elevator stationary

Mass of man 155 lb

Spring balance registers 2.2 lb

2.2 lb mass

Man feels weight of 155 lb

Pan balance loaded with 2.2 lb masses

Elevator falls 66 ft in 2 seconds

Spring balance registers 0 lb

During fall, man feels weightless

but pan balance stays in equilibrium

66 ft

Elevator stopped by 3 ft buffer

Spring balance registers 44 lb

3.2 ft

Man feels weight of 3085 lb

but pan balance stays in equilibrium

Hydraulic buffer

◀ In theory, the occupant of a frictionless elevator in falling freely without air resistance would have no sensation of weight, since both the elevator and its occupant would accelerate at the same rate and the occupant would feel no upward force from the floor. A mass on a spring balance would register no weight for the same reason, whereas masses on a balance would continue to be in equilibrium. At the end of the fall, the upward acceleration necessary to bring the elevator and its contents to a halt is much greater than the acceleration of gravity, causing the occupant to experience a sudden and drastic increase in weight and making the mass on the spring balance register an artificially increased value for its weight. The masses on the balance would still be in equilibrium.

object has when not in motion—its rest mass—is equivalent to an amount of energy (E) given by the equation E = mc^2, where m is rest mass and c is the speed of light in a vacuum.

The equivalence of energy and mass led Einstein to propose the existence of a more fundamental substance, of which mass and energy are different aspects. He called this mass–energy. The equivalence of mass and energy has been eloquently confirmed by the release of energy at the cost of mass in nuclear reactions.

Mass and weight

Weight is the force of gravity on an object that has mass in a gravitational field. The size of that force increases in direct proportion to mass, so an object with a mass of four units experiences twice the pull experienced by an object with a mass of two units. If no other force acts on those two objects, Newton's second law of motion (force = mass x acceleration) predicts that both objects will accelerate at the same rate, as will any other object with mass. For this reason, it is convenient to measure the strength of a gravitational field in terms of the acceleration owing to gravity.

On Earth, acceleration owing to gravity is approximately 32 ft. (9.75 m) per second per second—in one second, the speed of a falling body increases by 32 ft. per second (9.75 m/s). On the Moon, the acceleration owing to gravity is around one-sixth that on Earth. Consequently, objects on the Moon weigh one-sixth their weight on Earth.

Weightlessness

A person experiences weightlessness when he or she is accelerating toward the source of the gravitational pull at the acceleration owing to gravity. This phenomenon happens in an orbiting spacecraft because the orbital motion is equivalent to a constant acceleration towards the center of the orbit. Put differently, the force of gravity is the centripetal force that sustains the orbital motion.

Weightlessness can be reproduced in Earth's atmosphere by flying an airplane on a parabolic trajectory—the path followed by a stone when thrown at an upward angle. The pilot ensures that the airplane maintains a downward acceleration of 32 ft. per second squared (9.75 m/s²)—even when flying upward—so that the occupants of the airplane are in constant freefall. In this manner, conditions of zero gravity can be simulated for several minutes in a single session, providing valuable training for potential astronauts.

Einstein postulated that the speed of an object is limited by its mass increasing as its speed approaches that of light. As the mass increases, so does the rate at which it must acquire energy in order to accelerate. At the speed of light, the mass becomes infinite and it cannot accelerate further. The same theory proposed that the mass that an

SEE ALSO: ANTIMATTER • ENERGY RESOURCES • ENERGY STORAGE • NUCLEAR REACTOR • RELATIVITY • THERMODYNAMICS

Energy Resources

▲ Geothermal power plants are an economical source of energy in countries like Iceland, which sits on a volcanic ridge in the Atlantic Ocean. Because Earth's crust is very thin at this point, water can be evaporated into steam just a few feet below the surface. This type of energy is clean and sustainable, as well as cheap to run.

Our use of energy has steadily grown during our existence on Earth, from the fires of primitive ancestors to the modern very intensive use in the developed world. Only recently has there been any suggestion that the amount of energy available may not be enough to meet all the requirements. Energy planners are faced with two problems of growing urgency: how to ensure an adequate supply of energy for the foreseeable future and how to curb the damage to the environment from burning fossil fuels. Fossil fuels are by far the most important source of energy. About 40 percent of the world's primary energy needs are met by oil, 27 percent by coal, 21 percent by natural gas, 6 percent by hydroelectricity, and 6 percent by nuclear electricity. However, Earth's supplies of fossil fuels are being consumed 100,000 times faster than they are being formed. With new concerns about atmospheric pollution and global warming, the search is on to find alternative, sustainable, and clean sources of energy.

Predictions by the International Energy Agency expect world energy demand to increase by 65 percent by 2020, two-thirds of which will come from China and other developing nations. While fossil fuels are expected to provide 95 percent of this increased demand, carbon dioxide emissions would increase by 70 percent as a consequence. Although renewable energy sources are expected to provide 8 percent of the energy market, the continuing low cost of fossil fuels over this period is likely to prevent any significant expansion of the sector.

Part of the increasing demand for energy is the industrial nations' various huge needs, which have not been preplanned but have rather arisen independently of each other. A change in social attitudes, maybe forced by lack of energy, could alter these requirements, just as the discovery of new oil reserves can change the picture as well. One school of opinion believes that it would be preferable to make better use of energy by, for example, insulating homes, using solar energy to run them, and growing food at home.

Energy requirements

Units of energy are measured in joules or in a more familiar unit, calories. The energy in food is usually quoted in calories or kilocalories. Power stations, however, are usually rated in power units, watts, which do not take into account the time over which the power is used. Energy sources can therefore be quoted in a variety of units, but here the basic power unit of watts (and the multiples kilowatts, kW, and megawatts, MW) will be used.

Considerable care is needed when comparing estimates of available energy and energy usage from different sources. The use of different conversion factors and alternative approaches to the estimation of reserves can give significantly different figures. In addition, energy sources such as the use of animal dung or wood in underdeveloped countries are almost impossible to quantify. Often energy usage is expressed in units that relate more directly to the production of primary fuels, such as the tons of coal equivalent (approximately 8 MWh) and barrels of oil (approximately 10.5 MWh).

Humans need only 0.15 kW per person as food for light effort (1 kW = 239 calories/sec.), but Europeans used a total of 5 kW per person in 1970, both for food and for other uses. In the underdeveloped countries, the figure was about 0.5 kW, while in the United States it was 10 kW.

So far, most of the energy used around the world has been obtained from the combustion of fossil fuel—coal, oil, and natural gas. Demand for oil is increasing as more people drive cars and travel on airplanes, and it could reach 113 million barrels per day by 2020.

The biggest rise, however, is expected in the consumption of natural gas, mainly for use in generating electricity. Gas turbine plants are more energy efficient than oil or coal-fired plants and emit less sulfur dioxide, carbon dioxide, and particulates. The demand for coal is expected to be maintained, chiefly to provide electricity in the industrialized world, though it will still be used as a primary energy source for industry in China. Overall, electricity consumption worldwide is predicted to rise by 76 percent by 2020 to 22×10^{12} kWh per year.

Fossil fuels represent the accumulation of 400 million years of solar energy transformed by photosynthesis in plants. Although technology is developing to extract even the poorest reserves, on any reasonable timescale they must be regarded as nonrenewable resources, and the end of humanity's brief fossil fuel period of 2,000 years is in sight. What are the alternatives?

Renewable energy sources

Renewable energy sources are, as the name suggests, resources that are constantly being replaced and are generally less polluting. Typical examples include heat from the Sun, wind energy, water power, and geothermal energy. Other potential sources are biomass (trees and plants), municipal solid waste, and the more controversial nuclear forms of power.

Power from the Sun

Of all the alternative sources of energy, solar power is among the most attractive. It is clean, plentiful, and free for the taking. About 30 percent of the Sun's radiation is reflected by Earth's atmosphere, 20 percent is absorbed by it, and 50 percent reaches Earth's surface. In favorable regions, the average intensity at the surface is 600 MW per km^2 over a nine-hour day. This is certainly a valuable and underused resource—an area of around 25,000 acres (100 km^2) receives an energy input that is equivalent to the total present world usage—but is not easy to exploit. With

▼ Solar panels, like this array near Barstow in California, are an ideal way to harness the energy from the Sun. The panels can be tilted to follow the path of the Sun during the day. This array focuses the sunlight on a tower that uses the heat to drive a steam turbine producing electricity.

present technology, only around 15 percent of the solar power in an area can be converted to electricity, so large collector areas are required.

There are several ways to use solar energy. The simplest and oldest is conversion to heat, as in the rooftop solar panels sometimes used to supplement domestic water-heating systems. Solar water-heating systems use a collector, a rectangular box with a transparent cover containing tubes carrying water, and mounted on a black absorber plate. The heated water runs or is pumped to a storage tank, which is usually well insulated. Some houses are designed to trap heat within their structure by using large south-facing windows known as sunspaces. The floors of such buildings are covered with bricks or tiles that absorb heat during the day and release it back into the house when the temperature falls at night.

The most promising lines of research are in photovoltaic devices (PVs), the "solar cells" that are used to power space satellites and pocket calculators. Based on silicon wafers, PV cells convert radiant energy directly to electrical energy with efficiencies of 12 to 16 percent. New types of cell, which reach efficiencies of more than 30 percent, are under development. PV cells are used as roof and wall cladding to heat buildings in the winter and run air conditioning in the summer. PV systems can be expensive to run, consequently they tend to be used in places where there is no electricity supply. One problem in using such systems is their "intermittency"—when the sun is not shining they cannot make electricity, and therefore, they need a battery device to store surplus energy. Germany is the leader in applying PV technology and has unveiled plans for the world's biggest PV solar power plant. It will be built in the state of Thuringia and will generate 4 MW.

Approximately 50 MW of PV solar plant is installed around the world every year to the value of $700 million, and the market is rising rapidly. The bulk of American-made solar energy equipment is sold to the developing world, where the absence of electricity distribution grids makes solar energy particularly attractive. Small installations can drive telecommunications equipment, water pumps, and refrigerators.

A more sophisticated approach is to collect solar energy over a wide area and concentrate it onto a boiler to raise steam that can then drive a conventional turbine and generate electricity. As with PV systems, this method works only intermittently and relies on a natural gas backup system to heat the water on sunless days. Thermal solar plants in Daggett, California, together produce about 400 MW—equivalent to a full-size nuclear installation.

Storage, always a problem with electricity generation, is particularly acute for solar electricity, since production is determined by the weather rather than by demand. A radical solution is to use solar electricity to electrolyze water into its constituent gases of hydrogen and oxygen. The hydrogen could then be stored, transported, and used as a clean-burning fuel, the only emission being water vapor. Some planners foresee a full-scale "hydrogen economy," where new and safe methods of storing hydrogen will allow it to be used as the prime fuel for industry and transportation. Experimental cars that burn hydrogen are already running, though many practical concerns over their safety remain to be solved.

Water power

Evaporation by the Sun and rainfall on high ground represents one of the largest renewable concentrations of solar energy. The power of water is harnessed by allowing it to fall under gravity through turbines that drive electric generators, and consequently, this source of energy is referred to as hydroelectric power. About 10 percent of the United States' electricity is currently generated by hydroelectric power. The potential world capacity of hydroelectric power is about 2.9×10^6 MW, but only 7 percent is being used. Unfortunately, many of the unused sources are far from centers of population and industry, and transmission costs, which are very high, cannot be ignored. Furthermore, such schemes may affect the environment, for example, by altering the flow of rivers and changing the ecology of a region.

Tidal power

The total worldwide potential power of the tide is 3×10^6 MW, the energy coming from the rotation of the Earth. However, the power available from usable shallow seas and estuaries having tidal ranges of more than 10 ft. (3 m) is merely 64,000 MW, and the actual electrical output that could be generated is put at 13,000 MW. One tidal barrage in operation is a small plant on the River Rance in France, producing electricity at an average power of 100 MW—compared with a large power plant's 1,000 MW. Tidal power can make only a minor contribution to world requirements,

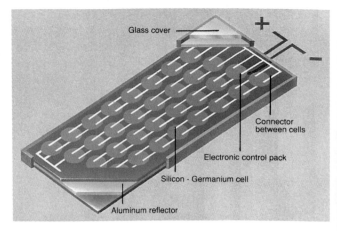

▲ Solar panels consist of a number of individual photovoltaic cells joined together. Each cell produces only a low voltage, but by making suitable connections, the output can be chosen for each application. The low efficiency of solar cells means that large numbers, covering a huge area, are needed to produce a significant amount of power.

mainly by improving the overall efficiency of a regional electricity supply in conjunction with pumped storage systems.

Geothermal power

Heat sources deep beneath Earth's crust can also be tapped to provide energy. Hot molten rock warms water trapped in nearby strata forming geothermal reservoirs that either come to the surface naturally, as with geysers, or can be extracted by sinking wells. This hot water can be used in its natural form to heat houses and factories or converted into steam to make electricity. The total installed generating capacity is about 1,200 MW. Assuming that about 1 percent of the potential energy available can be tapped and converted to electricity with an efficiency of 25 percent, the potential yield is estimated to be 3×10^6 MW per year. This source of energy is highly significant to a country like Iceland that has no fossil fuel. The Geysers geothermal field in northern California is the largest source of this type of energy in the world, producing an equivalent amount of power to that of two large coal or nuclear power plants.

Another possible source of thermal energy is the temperature gradient of the sea. In some areas, the surface temperature heated by the Sun is at around 77°F (25°C) while the temperature 3,300 ft. (1,000 m) down is 41°F (5°C) with the difference being sufficient to drive a heat engine.

Wind power

Man has been using the power of the wind as an energy source for thousands of years. Simple windmills were first built to pump water in China in 200 B.C.E. and to grind grain in the Middle East and Persia. By the 11th century, windmills were being used extensively for producing food, but it was the Dutch who refined the design and used it for draining lakes and marshes. Then, in the 19th century, windmills were set up in the New World to provide electricity and pump water for farms and industries.

The first heavy-duty wind turbines for commercial production of electricity appeared in Denmark in 1890, but their popularity as an energy source has fluctuated with the scarcity and price of oil. The 1970s oil crisis prompted further research into the design of wind turbines and has resulted in the modern "wind farms" capable of inputting significant amounts of energy into the utility grid at comparable costs to conventional power plants.

Wind turbines look very different from old-fashioned windmills, usually having two or three blades, called rotors, that can be vertically or horizontally mounted. Standing 100 ft. (30 m) off the ground, they take advantage of faster and less turbulent winds at that level. As the wind blows, it causes a pocket of air to form on the downwind side of the blade, which pulls the blade toward it, turning the rotor. This lift, together with the drag of the wind's force against the front side of the blade, spins the rotor like a propeller and turns the shaft to generate electricity.

Wind energy is the fastest growing energy technology in the world. Much research is being put into the development of low-cost turbines capable of generating up to 1 MW of power per turbine. Wind turbines can be used as stand-alone systems to provide electricity and communications for farms and homes, often in combination with a photovoltaic cell. More often they are used in large numbers to input power to a utility grid. Of necessity, this system requires turbines to be placed in exposed and windy areas, but the need to cover large tracts of the countryside has led to some opposition to their installation.

▼ Over the centuries, windmills have been used to power water pumps and provide electricity to homes and farms. With modern turbine designs, wind power can now provide a substantial amount of electricity to the utility grid without producing any pollution.

Vegetation as a power source

Biomass energy, derived from plants and trees, is a form of stored solar energy. Biomass can be turned into energy by burning it directly or by converting it into a gaseous or liquid fuel. Its use as a liquid fuel is of particular importance, as one-third of the world's energy is used in transport. The two most commonly produced biofuels, as they are called, are methanol and ethanol. Ethanol is increasingly being used as an automobile fuel throughout the Americas, usually blended with gasoline. In the United States, it is made from corn and other grains, but it is an expensive fuel compared with gasoline on a gallon-for-gallon basis. Efforts are being made to find other biomass crops that would produce enough ethanol to power the nation's cars on an economic basis. Biodiesel made from various kinds of vegetable oils is also under investigation, and researchers are trying to develop a strain of oil-producing algae. Research is also proceeding on the use of photosynthesis processes to directly split water into hydrogen and oxygen gases that can be used as fuels.

Energy on the road

Of the world's production of oil, about half is burned up in road vehicles. With about 500 million vehicles on the roads and the number rising rapidly, we cannot expect an early move away from fossil fuels for road transportation. In some areas, especially the large urban areas, emissions of carbon monoxide, nitrogen oxides, and hydrocarbons are reaching worrying proportions. The average tankful of gasoline releases up to 400 lbs. (180 kg) of carbon dioxide to play its part in the global greenhouse effect.

Automobile manufacturers are researching methods of making cleaner and fuel-efficient engines, but in the longer term, more drastic solutions will be required. California has taken a lead by legislating that one in 50 of all new cars sold in the state from 1998 will be required not to produce any air pollution at all. This is a severe condition and only one technology could feasibly meet the deadline—the electric car.

So far, electric traction has found application in only a few low-powered and specialized vehicles, such as golf carts and delivery vehicles. Although the attractions are obvious—no immediate pollution, low noise, efficient use of energy—the chief obstacle to the widespread use of electric vehicles is the cumbersome lead–acid battery. A practical electric car would need lead–acid batteries weighing up to 1,000 lbs. (450 kg) to give a range of a mere 100 miles (160 km).

Fortunately, the Californian deadline has spurred manufacturers to research new types of battery. Of the two systems under development, the sodium-sulfur battery is the more promising. It contains electrodes of sulfur and molten sodium enclosed in a ceramic casing. With a weight-for-weight capacity three times that of a lead–acid battery, it could run a car for an accept-

◀ The blue glow of Cerenkov radiation, produced when fast electrons travel through water, is a sign of the vast rate of energy production in a nuclear reactor.

ENERGY FROM THE OCEANS

A great deal of heat is stored in the world's oceans, equivalent to 250 billion barrels of oil per day. The surface waters become warmer than the deeper layers, and this temperature difference creates a thermal gradient that can be exploited to drive a turbine and produce electricity in a process known as ocean thermal energy conversion (OTEC).

The idea was pioneered by a French engineer, Jacques d'Arsonval, in 1881. Three types of system have been designed. The closed-cycle system circulates a working fluid such as ammonia, which has a low boiling point, through the plant, heating it with warm seawater. The fluid vaporizes and drives a turbine to generate electricity before being condensed with cold seawater and recycled.

Open-cycle systems actually boil pumped seawater by operating at low pressures. The water is flashed to steam and used to drive a turbine. Hybrid systems use the steam to vaporize a working fluid in a closed system. In 1998, an experimental OTEC plant produced a 255 kW output of electricity.

able 150 to 200 miles (240–320 km) between recharges. However, with an operating temperature of around 660°F (350°C), it poses problems of corrosion and safety. The other possibility is a nickel–metal hydride battery, but this is not yet sufficiently developed. Despite these developments, these new technologies cannot compete with gasoline for energy storage per pound, and it requires several hours to charge a battery.

Engineers are also looking at ways to make electric cars more efficient so that they waste less energy. New lightweight electric motors with electronic controls can deliver 100 horsepower (75 kW) and weigh only 100 lbs. (45 kg).

Of course, the electricity has to come from somewhere, and for the near future, power stations will continue to depend heavily on fossil fuels. However, economies of scale ensure that the pollution emitted by the central generation of electricity to run cars would be considerably less than that emitted from the gasoline-powered vehicles they replace. The immediate benefit is that the emissions are removed from the places where they do the most harm—the congested centers of our ever growing cities.

Hydrogen

Hydrogen is the most plentiful element in the Universe. As a fuel, it offers unlimited potential for clean energy, but it has a number of drawbacks that make it difficult to use and store. Hydrogen does not occur naturally as a gas on Earth but is usually combined with another element, particularly oxygen (as water) or carbon (in hydrocarbons). Water can be split into its components using electricity, though some bacteria can do this naturally using sunlight. Heating the hydrocarbons in natural gas, a process known as reforming, is currently the main source of hydrogen as a fuel. Liquid hydrogen is used to power rockets, as it is high in energy and produces little pollution. Hydrogen fuel cells are used on board the space shuttle to power its systems, with the added benefit of pure water as a waste product from the reaction, which can then be drunk by the crew. There is a lot of research into fuel cells being carried out, as a source of electricity and heat for buildings and to power electric vehicles. Initially, these fuel cells will run off intermediate sources, such as natural gas, gasoline, or methanol, but it is envisaged that pure hydrogen will eventually be used once a method has been found to store this highly inflammable gas safely.

At Los Alamos National Laboratory, researchers are investigating a process that will turn coal and water slurry into hydrogen and then electricity using a high-temperature solid-oxide fuel cell. Conversion energy efficiencies of around 50 percent can be obtained with solid-oxide fuel cells, which can reuse the waste heat generated by the process. Because the process is anaerobic, it needs no oxygen input for combustion, and it also pro-

◀ Nuclear fusion is considered to be the most likely source of energy for centuries to come. This view is of the inside of the tokamak in an experimental fusion system, the Joint European Torus, at Culham, Oxfordshire in the United Kingdom.

duces less nitrogen oxide compounds than would result from burning coal in a normal power plant. At least twice as much energy per unit of fuel used can be produced by the process, which has the added benefit that it can be adapted for use with other fossil fuels and even biomass. Carbon dioxide formed during the process is reacted with magnesium or calcium silicates to lock it into stable mineral carbonates.

Nuclear energy

Nuclear reactors use radioactive fuel to produce heat by fission, which is then used to make electricity in a more or less conventional way. The initial fuel, uranium-235, is in short supply, but breeder reactors produce more fissile material than they use.

It may thus appear that nuclear fission is the answer to the world's energy needs, but a major drawback is the amount of radioactive waste produced. This waste takes several hundred years to decay to a safe level and is being produced in increasing amounts. At present, it can only be stored. The safe transport of fuel elements is another serious problem.

Fusion, the other means of producing nuclear energy, would be much safer, using deuterium (from sea water) and tritium (from lithium, which is plentiful). So far, however, no practical methods of controlling fusion reactions have been developed. The problems involved in meeting the world's energy requirements are not all technical—just as complex are the social and political

aspects. There are, however, many known ways of increasing the efficiency with which we use our energy resources. Some experts believe a reasonable annual increase in demand could be met without a large expansion of fission power, with its attendant radioactive waste problems, and without depleting our resources of fossil hydrocarbons. However, with the introduction of the Kyoto Protocol on reducing carbon dioxide emissions, some countries are prepared to keep their nuclear power capabilities to help them meet their commitments on gas emissions while ensuring a regular power supply.

The promise of fusion

In the longer term, far into the next century, problems of energy supply and pollution may be eased by nuclear fusion. There are two ways to release the energy of the atomic nucleus: fission and fusion. In fission, energy is released by breaking up large nuclei, such as uranium or plutonium. This is the principle underlying the nuclear power industry, but it has its attendant problem of nuclear waste transportation and storage.

Fusion energy is released by forcing small nuclei together rather than by splitting large nuclei apart. It is the source that powers the Sun and the hydrogen bomb. In both cases, hydrogen nuclei are fused to create helium. Fusion can release much more energy than fission and is cleaner and with less danger of pollution.

Physicists and engineers around the world are working together to find ways of controlling

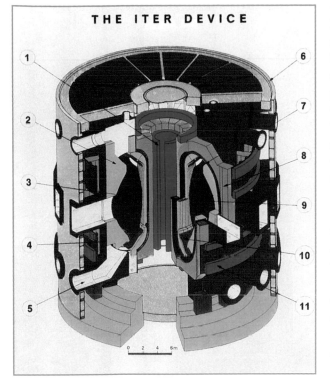

◄ A cutaway view of the ITER device. The central solenoid (1) generates a large current—25 million amps—that heats the gas inside the tokamak to some 200 million K. The shield/blanket (2) converts the fast neutrons produced by fusion reactions with the plasma (3) into heat at a few hundred degrees, which can then be used to drive a generator. The plasma is contained within a vacuum vessel (4), and exhaust products are extracted through the plasma exhaust (5). A cryostat (6) uses liquid helium to keep the vessel at just a few degrees above absolute zero, enabling superconducting coils (7, 8, and 11) to produce the magnetic field needed to contain the plasma. The first wall (9) has to contain the immense heat within the plasma, while the diverter plates (10) direct the spent helium away through the plasma exhaust.

confine and control the reacting plasma and induce an electrical current through it.

ITER will be intrinsically safe. Unlike fission reactors, the amount of fuel inside ITER at any one time is so tiny that there is no danger of a runaway reaction. The waste products will not be radioactive, but neutrons produced in the reaction will induce radioactivity in the structure of the machine. This is one problem engineers will need to address before fusion becomes a practical proposition.

ITER will operate for at least 15 years. It will not generate electricity but will give physicists and engineers the know-how they need to build a fusion power station. It could be the middle of the 21st century before fusion energy plays a part in our everyday lives.

FACT FILE

■ The ancient Chinese used natural gas as a fuel before 1000 B.C.E., drilling deep through rock to release the gas, which they then transported through pipelines constructed from bamboo. The gas was used for lighting as well as heating and cooking. The coal mined during the same period was used as a supplement to the gas.

■ Asphalt, one of the earliest energy sources, was being burned as a fuel in the Middle East as early as 6000 B.C.E. In Mesopotamia, asphalt was used to fuel furnaces for bricks and pottery up to the sixth century B.C.E., after which, despite the existence of huge surface deposits, its use almost disappeared.

■ Liquid wastes from industrial processes have become an important addition to the catalog of energy sources. Wastes, such as petroleum and solvent derivatives, and even heavy sludges, can be treated so that they can be atomized into small droplets that can then be injected into a combustion chamber in the presence of oxygen. A Philadelphia plant imports 3 million gallons (10 million liters) of waste per annum to burn for steam production.

nuclear fusion. A number of small projects have been set up around the world, but three teams from the European Union, Japan, and Russia have been collaborating on a reactor that could produce power at a commercial level—the International Thermonuclear Experimental Reactor, or ITER.

Devising and building a 1,000 megawatt reactor like ITER is a formidable task. A draft design, expected to be ready by the end of 2000, will allow the costs of the project to be estimated. If ITER goes ahead on schedule, it should be completed by 2005 at a cost of at least $7.5 billion. The reactor is likely to be built at Cadarache in France.

The fuel used will be deuterium and tritium, heavy forms of hydrogen. Ample deuterium is found in water, and tritium can be made from naturally occurring deposits of lithium metal. Extremely high temperatures are required first to ionize the gases and then to impart sufficient kinetic energy to the nuclei to overcome their electrostatic repulsion and collide, allowing the strong nuclear forces to take over and fuse them. In the Sun, the reactions proceed at a stately 15 million K, but ITER will maintain temperatures of approximately 200 million K.

No material container can possibly withstand such temperatures. The ionized gas (or plasma) will be confined in a vacuum in a doughnut-shaped magnetic field in a device called a tokamak. The vessel will be about 52 ft. (16 m) in diameter and contain a magnetic field 200,000 times as strong as that of Earth, generated by 16 giant superconducting magnets, each cooled to 4.5 degrees above absolute zero. The magnets

SEE ALSO: Biofuel • Energy, mass, and weight • Energy storage • Fission • Fuel cell • Fusion • Gasoline, synthetic • Hydroelectric power • Hydrogen • Solar energy • Tidal power • Wave power • Wind power

Energy Storage

Energy cannot be created or destroyed, but it can be converted from one form to another. Apart from solar and nuclear energy, the original source of energy is invariably some natural form in which energy was stored, and storage of the original resource, such as carrying fuel in the tank of a vehicle, is one form of storage very widely used. There are, however, a number of cases where, having released the energy from its natural storage, it is advantageous to store it again for later recovery, even if storing involves a further conversion process and loss of some of the potential of the energy for doing useful work.

The reasons for such storage are to even out fluctuations in demand, to store energy that might otherwise be wasted so that it can be used later, to accumulate energy over a long period for release very rapidly, and to convey energy to where it is required when continuous transmission systems are not practical.

Pumped storage systems

The only large-scale method of storing energy that has been developed to operate with the main electric supply system is known as pumped storage. A large electric machine that can be used either as a motor or a generator is connected to a water turbine and a water pump. This combination of machines is positioned close to a large water reservoir and connected by a series of pipes to a second reservoir placed at a much higher level. The head (difference in level) may vary from 100 to 2,300 ft. (30–700 m) or occasionally even more. Such arrangements are normally found in mountainous country. During off-peak times (usually nights) when there is plenty of electrical generating capacity available elsewhere that would be uneconomical to shut down, power is supplied to the pumped storage station and used to pump water from the lower reservoir to the high reservoir. At times of high demand (the daytime peak-load periods), the pump is disconnected and water is allowed to flow back downhill through the turbine, driving the electrical machine as a generator. The flow of water can be very quickly regulated so that the machine will meet almost instantaneously any demand placed on it, up to its maximum capacity.

It is normal for this type of system to generate power for a total of four or five hours each day and to pump up the corresponding amount of water during a period of about six hours during the night. There are inevitable losses in all the machines concerned and friction losses in the

A pumped storage project at Ffestiniog, Wales. The upper reservoir is 1,000 ft. (300 m) above the lower plant.

pipes, so the total amount of energy recovered is approximately 70 percent of that absorbed during the pumping operation.

Compressed-air and -gas systems

Compressors are frequently used to compress air into large pressure vessels from which energy can be drawn as demand arises. Such systems are very commonly used to operate large numbers of small pneumatic tools and other equipment in factories. To provide individual electricity-driven tools would be very expensive and inefficient in terms of energy consumption. The compressed-air system allows high-efficiency motor-driven compressor systems to be used and also gives a steady electric power supply even if the individual tools present a fluctuating demand. The overall efficiencies for this sort of system are around 50 percent, but the other advantages outweigh the losses.

Compression of gas is also a method of storing up energy in both pneumatic and hydraulic control and power systems. In these systems, the pneumatic or hydraulic power may be used to operate parts of machines, for example, to open and close doors on trains and buses. Pneumatic systems use essentially the same pressure vessel previously described; in hydraulic systems where oil is the working fluid, a receiver is provided with a flexible diaphragm separating the oil from a trapped volume of air or gas. As oil is forced into the receiver, the diaphragm is pressed back and the air on the other side becomes compressed; when the oil flows out again, the energy stored in the air is recovered.

Compressed air can also be used for the storage of electrical energy. In one system at Huntorf, Germany, off-peak electric power is used to pump air into an underground storage cavern. It is then stored under pressure until required to drive two 290 MW (megawatt) turbogenerators, which run for two hours a day to meet peak power requirements. As well as using natural or artificially created underground caverns, investigations are being made into the possibilities of using the natural storage left when a gas well has been exhausted. Alternatively, reinforced concrete storage vessels could also be constructed to contain the pressurized air.

A relatively recent development is the use of very-high-pressure pneumatic storage batteries. These use containers machined from solid metal to hold gas at very high pressures. Air is used for pressures of up to 600 million lbs. per sq. in. (415 x 10⁵ bar), a helium and air mix for pressures up to

▼ The operating principles of a gyrobus. Power from the pickup arm drives the motor generator to spin the flywheel.

10 billion lbs. per sq. in. (6,896 x 10⁵ bar), and pure helium up to 17 billion lbs. per sq. in. (11,725 x 10⁵ bar). The stored power can be released immediately or over a period of time and is safe for use where electric sparks would be dangerous. At present, these pneumatic batteries are mainly used for military applications, such as driving gyroscopes in guidance systems.

Electric storage batteries

The most common type of storage battery is the lead-acid accumulator, which has to be charged up over a period of about 10 hours; when discharged, about 90 percent of the actual current-storing capacity (amps x time) is recovered, but as the discharge voltage is lower than the charging voltage, the actual energy recovered is only about 75 percent of that used to charge the battery.

For vehicle uses, the weight of the battery is particularly important, and great efforts have been made to reduce the weight for a given output. This aim has partly been met by the development of alkali batteries, which have nickel and cadmium or nickel and iron plates in a potassium hydroxide solution. These batteries are very rugged both mechanically and electrically and have found considerable application to electric vehicle drives, though they are still heavier than the equivalent lead–acid batteries. The current energy recovery is about 75 to 80 percent, but the energy return is only 60 to 65 percent.

High power densities and cycle efficiencies are offered by high-temperature batteries such as the lithium alloy–iron sulfide and sodium–sulfur batteries. The sodium–sulfur design has a working temperature of over 572°F (300°C) and has sodium and sulfur electrodes, which are in a liquid state at the working temperature, and an alumina electrolyte, which is solid. The output per unit weight (around 140 watt hours/kg) is more than five times that of the established lead–acid battery.

Another form of electrical energy storage involves the electrolysis of water to form hydrogen and oxygen gases, which are stored and then allowed to recombine in a fuel cell to generate electricity. Such fuel cells are used to supply power on the space shuttle.

The increasing use of portable electronic devices, such as radios and calculators, has led to a requirement for small rechargeable batteries. Sealed nickel–cadmium cells are often used, but higher energy densities are offered by zinc–silver oxide cells. An alternative approach to meeting small power requirements in portable equipment is to use large capacitors rated at several Farads. These have particular advantages when repeated charge–discharge cycles are involved.

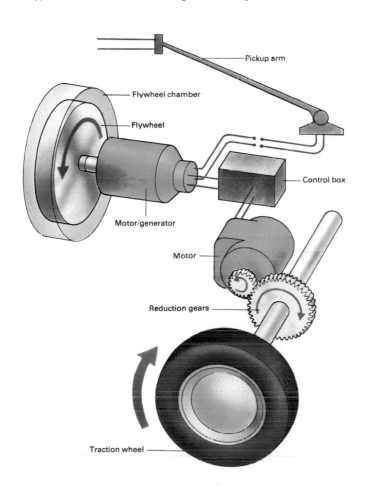

Pickup arm

Flywheel chamber

Flywheel

Motor/generator

Control box

Motor

Reduction gears

Traction wheel

GEOTHERMAL ENERGY

Groundwater can be used as a low-grade heat storage reservoir (far right). Waste heat, pumped underground, is recovered when needed by a heat pump. Geothermal heat pumps that extract naturally occurring low-grade heat from groundwater or earth and upgrade it to heat a house (right) can be profitably installed in the backyard. Though often expensive to install, these systems are highly cost efficient, using 25 to 50 percent less electricity than conventional heating systems. The heat is carried in a solution of water and antifreeze through a series of high-density polyethylene pipes that may run horizontally underground to a depth of 4 to 6 ft. (1.2–1.8 m) or vertically into the ground to a depth of 100 to 400 ft. (30–120 m). During the summer, the heat pump may be used in reverse to carry heat away from the building and into the soil or groundwater. These systems can also produce free hot water in the summer and reduced-cost hot water in the winter. Heat pumps are often low in maintenance and reduce the need for fossil fuels, making them an environmentally friendly source of energy.

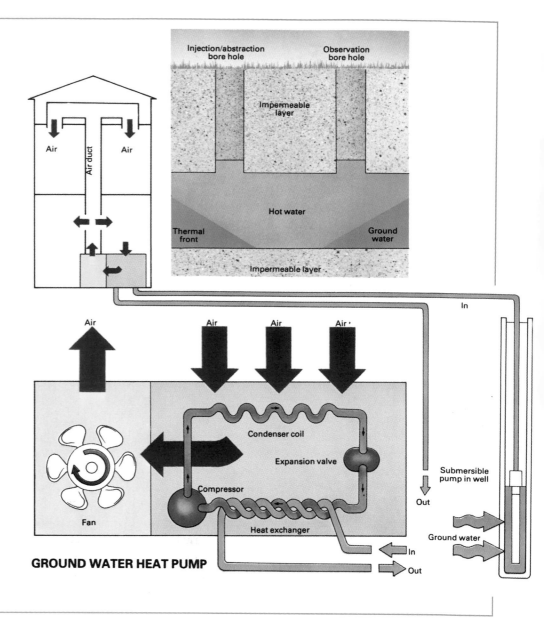

GROUND WATER HEAT PUMP

Thermal storage

Electric heating is an inefficient process because the original generation of electricity involves conversion from fuel to heat to mechanical power and then to electric power with efficiencies of 40 percent or lower. Conversion of the electric energy back to heat is clearly wasteful, but the overall inefficiency can sometimes be justified on account of cleanliness and convenience, particularly if the efficiency of the overall system can be increased by using power at the low-demand periods. Such systems can be used for heating by means of storage heater systems.

Electric resistance wires (similar to those found in an ordinary electric heater) are arranged to pass through a large mass of refractory (heat resisting) material, which has a high heat capacity (it absorbs a large amount of heat for a comparatively small temperature change). Air passages are provided through the refractory material, and the whole assembly is contained in a casing that is thermally insulated so that heat will not be lost to the surroundings. Arrangements are made to allow air to flow through the whole assembly as required, and the air then carries away heat to the surrounding space. The flow of air can be controlled by vanes, which are generally operated automatically according to the outside temperature. A fan may also be used to assist the movement of the heated air.

Such systems are normally operated with a time-controlled switch so that heating not only takes place during the night but also so that heat may be released at any time. The efficiency of all electric space-heating systems is in fact 100 percent, as there is no loss of heat except to the surrounding space where the heat is required.

SEE ALSO:

BATTERY • ENERGY, MASS, AND WEIGHT • ENERGY RESOURCES • FLYWHEEL • FUEL CELL • HEAT PUMP • HYDRAULICS • HYDROELECTRIC POWER • PNEUMATIC TOOL

Engine Cooling Systems

Because of very high operating temperatures within an internal combustion engine, the system must be cooled in order to prevent seizing of moving parts, that is, jamming of the pistons in the cylinders. There are two main types of cooling system: water cooled and air cooled.

Water-cooled systems

Water-cooled systems employ a radiator, which is traditionally made of copper and brass, though some modern designs have plastic tanks. Radiators made of these materials will not rust. A tank at the top of the radiator is connected to a brass tank at the bottom via a mesh of copper tubing. Radiators also have metal fins that increase the surface over which the heat dissipates. The other major component is the water pump, which is usually mounted on the front of the engine and driven by the fan belt from the crankshaft.

The engine cylinder block and the cylinder head are castings that have waterways cast into them. The block and head are connected to the radiator at the top and bottom by rubber hoses. When the engine is running, the water is pumped out of the bottom of the radiator into the block, where it circulates around the cylinders and through the head gasket into the head past the combustion chambers (the hottest part of the engine, where the fuel mixture is ignited). While circulating around these engine parts, the water absorbs heat and removes it. The water then reaches the thermostat, which is a valve operated by heat. The thermostat stays closed if the engine is cold until the water is heated to the correct operating temperature. Then it opens and the water flows through the top hose back into the radiator, where it is cooled as it passes down through the copper tubing.

After the water has been cooled it re-enters the engine block, and the process continues. By varying the amount of water passing through the radiator, the thermostat maintains a constant engine temperature.

The fan is mounted on the front of the engine just behind the radiator. When the vehicle is moving, the air rushing through the radiator may be sufficient to cool the water, but the fan is necessary to cool the system when the engine is idling. The fan is normally operated by the fan belt from the crankshaft, but there are some types of fans with blades whose pitch is variable. The blade-pitch variation is controlled by another thermostat or by the speed of the fan by means of centrifugal force. Other types of fan are driven by electric motors, turned on and off as necessary by a thermostatic switch.

COOLING SYSTEM

This cutaway of an automobile water-cooling system shows how the fan draws in air, which cools the water as it passes down through the radiator. The water is then pumped under pressure through the water passages of the cylinder head and engine block. It is then circulated to the radiator for cooling again. A thermostat controls the cooling capacity by regulating the circulation. In this way, a constant temperature is maintained.

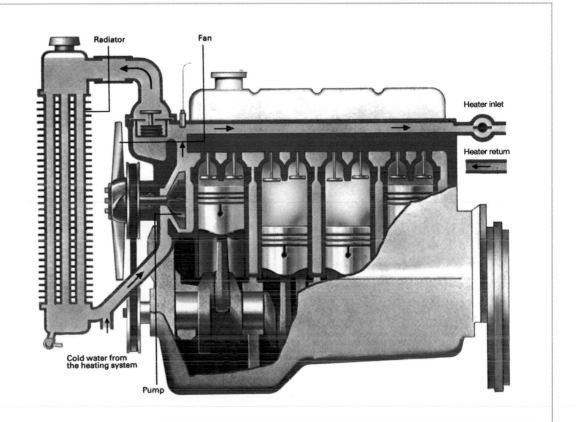

Radiator

Fan

Heater inlet

Heater return

Cold water from the heating system

Pump

Antifreeze

Water expands when frozen and if allowed to freeze in the engine block will crack it, so in cold weather, antifreeze must be added to the system. Antifreeze is essentially alcohol, which has a much lower freezing temperature than water. The most commonly used form of antifreeze is ethylene glycol. Today many cars are equipped with permanent antifreeze at the factory and are designed to operate on it all year round.

Water-cooled systems are usually pressurized—up to 14 lbs. per sq. in. (9.7 kN/m²)—to raise the boiling point of the system, thus improving the efficiency of the engine and the thermal coefficient of the radiator. The radiator cap on such a system will be designed to withstand the pressure. If the system overheats, great care must be taken if the cap is removed while the fluid is still hot. A sudden release will cause boiling.

Although the radiator will not rust, it may become clogged up with particles from dirty water or rust from the inside of the engine. When this happens, the best treatment is to flush the radiator with chemicals in a reverse direction from the usual water flow, that is, from bottom to top, and under pressure from a hose. Antifreeze, however, contains corrosion inhibitors that reduce the need for flushing to only once a year.

The most common failure of water-cooled systems is failure of the rubber hoses, causing leakage of the coolant. A temperature gauge used to be provided on the dashboard of the car, but for reasons of economy, many manufacturers have replaced it with a warning light that shines if overheating occurs.

Air-cooled systems

Air-cooled engines—such as in the Volkswagen Beetle—have fins on the cylinder bores to give the largest surface area for dispersal of heat. The air is drawn in by a large fan. A thermostat, which is operated by the heat of the engine, directs the air toward or away from the fins. The main advantages with this system are that the engine casting is simpler and the radiator, water pump, hoses, and antifreeze are all unnecessary.

The larger the engine, however, the less efficient the air-cooling system becomes, because much larger fans would be needed. Water is a far more efficient coolant than air. Air-cooled engines also tend to be more noisy in operation, because fans are more noisy than pumps and because the water jacket in a water-cooled engine block deadens much of the mechanical noise produced by the engine. Aero-engines are usually air cooled because the propeller acts as an efficient cooling fan.

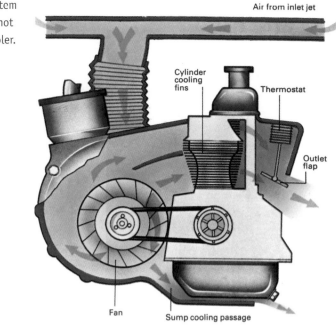

▶ The air-cooling system on the Fiat 126 does not incorporate an oil cooler. Instead, the air is channeled down to the sump.

▼ The high-performance Porsche 2.7 liter motor is air cooled. The belt-driven fan and its ducting are in the foreground. The exhaust valves are sodium filled to aid cooling of the valve head; the sodium melts and circulates. The lubrication system is designed for maximum cooling—the engine is fitted with an oil filter that does not restrict flow and an oil cooler with a thermostat.

SEE ALSO: AUTOMOBILE • INTERNAL COMBUSTION ENGINE • THERMOSTAT

Engraving and Etching

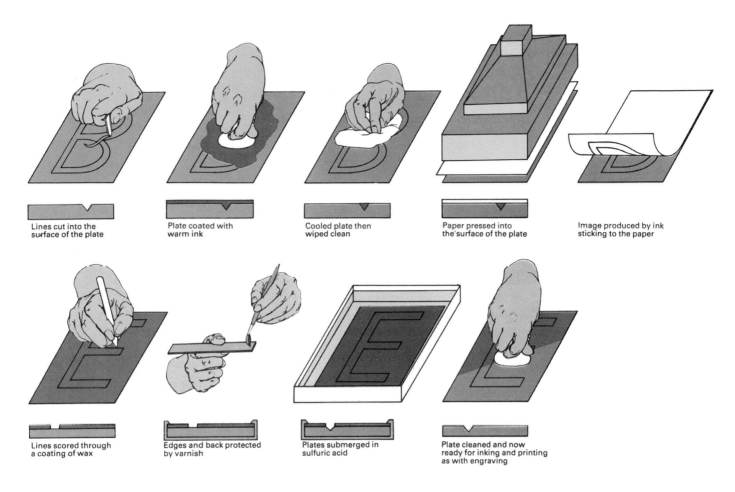

Lines cut into the
surface of the plate

Plate coated with
warm ink

Cooled plate then
wiped clean

Paper pressed into
the surface of the plate

Image produced by ink
sticking to the paper

Lines scored through
a coating of wax

Edges and back protected
by varnish

Plates submerged in
sulfuric acid

Plate cleaned and now
ready for inking and printing
as with engraving

Engraving and etching on metal are old crafts. Although their use as printmaking processes dates only from the 15th century, they were in use long before that by metalworkers as a means of decorating arms, armor, and jewelry by incising a design into the surface of the metal.

In the middle of the 15th century, the idea of printing from engraved or etched plates occurred at almost the same time in the Rhine valley in Germany and in northern Italy. In order to keep a record of their original designs, goldsmiths filled the engraved or etched lines in a metal plate with a black greasy mixture and pressed a piece of paper against the plate to pick up the ink from the grooves.

With the invention of photography, the crafts of engraving and etching as a means of reproduction of pictures died out, but these processes are widely used by artists as media in their own right. The techniques are defined under the general heading of intaglio processes. Plates of steel, copper, or zinc less than ⅛ in. (3 mm) thick are used. Grooves, pitted areas, and textures are bitten into the plate with acid (etching, aquatint, soft ground) or directly cut or scratched by the artist using sharp tools (engraving, drypoint, mezzo-

tint). To obtain a print from such a plate, ink is pushed into the grooves and the surface of the plate is wiped clean with muslin. The plate is placed on the bed of a copperplate printing press; a sheet of dampened paper is laid on the plate and backed by several layers of fine felt blankets. When taken through the press under pressure, the blankets force the paper into the grooves, where it picks up the ink. Despite all the progress in commercial printing presses, no one has managed to invent a satisfactory automatic process.

Engraving

The engraver's tool is called a burin or graver, and its action is limited to lines and dots. The art of the engraver has been to manipulate this tool to advantage, building up a variety of tones and textures by varying the width, depth, and size of the lines and dots. An engraving is differentiated from other types of prints by its sharpness and clarity.

The tool is a short, highly tempered steel bar about ¼ in. (6 mm) thick, square or lozenge-shaped in section. One end is bent up into a mushroom-shaped handle so that when the tool lies flat on the plate the handle comes up comfortably into the palm of the hand. A facet is cut at

▲ In line engraving (top), a design is made by cutting directly into the surface of a copper plate. In etching (bottom), the design is scored through a wax coat and treated with sulfuric acid, which eats away at any exposed copper to leave the required pattern. In both cases, the patterns are printed in a similar manner.

a 45 to 60 degree angle on the other end, and the engraving is done with the sharpened tip of the tool by holding it at a shallow angle to the plate and pushing it slowly forward. As the tool cuts grooves in the metal, it generates a chip that is removed at the end of the line with the side of the tool. The bigger the angle of the tool to the plate, the wider and deeper the incision. The greater the amount of ink that the line can hold, the darker it will print. Curved lines are executed by turning the plate rather than the tool. Shaded areas may be indicated by the use of parallel lines and crosshatching. Round dots are executed by placing the tip of the tool on the plate and turning the plate in a circle; it is also possible to execute triangular dots by pushing the tip of the tool into the plate and pulling it out.

Mezzotint

Mezzotint is a tonal technique, invented in the middle of the 17th century and used to copy paintings. It is a time-consuming process, requiring elaborate preparation of the plate. The plate is prepared with a chisel-shaped tool made of hard steel called a rocker. The end of the tool is rounded, and has grooves in it numbering from 45 to 120 per inch; one side of it is sharpened so

that the sharp edge is serrated by the grooves. This tool is then rocked across the surface of the plate in as many as 80 different directions until the entire area of the plate is covered with inumerable tiny holes, and so shiny dots of polished surface remain. When the plate is ready, other sharp tools, called burnishers and scrapers, are used to scrape away the texture to varying depths. The ink held by the plate determines how dark it will print: the more the texture is scraped away, the lighter that area will print. This technique produces large areas of tone, but the designs are often indistinct. For this reason, etched or engraved lines are sometimes used in combination with mezzotint.

Etching

The principle of etching is to protect the surface of the plate with a thin layer of acid-resistant substance called an etching ground. The plate is heated and this ground, made of asphaltum, beeswax, and resin, is melted onto the surface of the plate and evened out with a roller. When the plate is cooled, it is smoked with tapers to harden the ground and to make it evenly black to facilitate seeing the drawing. The drawing is scratched through the ground, and the plate is bathed in an

▲ Top left: a burin is used to engrave a plate. A burin produces a long thin chip, which is removed with the side of the tool.

Top right: a demonstration of the mezzotint technique using a rocker.

Bottom left: the artist has inked the copper plate and is now wiping off the excess ink.

Bottom right: the press forces the paper into the inked lines.

acid solution. The longer the plate is left in the solution, the deeper the lines and the darker they will appear in the final print.

Aquatint

Aquatint is a tonal etching method invented in France in the 18th century. The surface of the plate is covered with a thin, even layer of fine powdered resin. The plate is heated from beneath, and as the powder melts, it forms a uniform surface of acid-resistant granules that firmly adhere to it. The acid will bite into the plate around each granule; the deeper the bite the darker the tone will be. For different tones, the plate is removed from the acid and the lightest tones stopped out with liquid varnish on a brush. This process is repeated until the varying tones are achieved. The resin is washed off the finished etching with methylated spirits.

Sugar aquatint

In a sugar aquatint, the drawing is made with a brush using a solution of sugar and India ink. The plate is then coated with diluted acid-resistant varnish, which, because it is diluted with turpentine, does not disturb the sugar in the drawing. The plate is then immersed in water; the sugar swells and dissolves, lifting off the varnish in the drawn lines and leaving the image exposed. An aquatint ground is laid, and the plate is bitten in the acid. Both aquatint and sugar aquatint are often used in combinations with engraved or etched lines in order to give more precise definition to the final image.

Glass etching

There are several methods for creating etched designs on glass. In one of the most common, the surface of the glass is coated with a layer of paraffin or beeswax onto which an image is drawn using a sharp metal needle. The glass is then placed in a bath of hydrofluoric acid, which cuts into the areas of glass exposed by the metal needle. This technique may be used to create smooth or rough and frosted surface effects, depending on the type of glass and the amount of time the glass is allowed to remain in the acid bath.

Other applications

The principles of engraving and etching are used in many applications by science and industry. Currency is usually printed by engraved plates to make it hard to counterfeit. Toolmakers use etching and engraving methods to incise trademarks, measurements, and other vital data on their products. Metallurgists etch metal samples directly without using a resist (ground) before examining

► Engraving a traditional design on a silver plate in Indonesia. Metal engraving originated long before this technique was used to create printed images.

► The etching process. This copper plate has been coated with an acid-resistant substance called a ground. This is then smoked, using tapers, to create a uniform black work surface.

► Using precision tools and a magnifying glass, the artist scratches the design into the black ground, revealing the copper beneath.

► In this instance, acid is pushed carefully into the lines with a feather. The acid bites into the areas of exposed metal.

them under microscopes. This technique has the effect of making metal grain characteristics stand out more clearly. Photo engraving (or gravure) processes are used for the reproduction of photographs by a printing press.

SEE ALSO: ARMOR • COUNTERFEITING AND FORGERY • GLASS • INK • NEWSPAPER PRODUCTION • PRINTING

Environmental Science

Environmental scientists may be experts in physics, biology, geology, climatology, or even mathematics, and their job is to investigate how human beings interact with the environment and how we affect it. By bringing together the threads of many different investigations, they give a global picture of what is happening to Earth as a result not just of technological activity but also of natural activity.

Disaster predictions

The work of environmental scientists covers the air we breathe, the flow of water, and the soil we depend on for our crops. At the beginning of 1991, pundits were fearing a major environmental disaster—and they were proved correct, but not in the way they expected. The cause for their worries was the impending Gulf War. Their worst fears were realized when Iraqi action set hundreds of oil wells ablaze, their smoke turning day into night in Kuwait. The news media predicted that the fires would take years to extinguish and that the resulting pall of smoke would affect huge areas of the globe.

In fact, the fires were put out within eight months. The smoke stayed close to the ground, and crops beyond the Gulf region were not unduly affected. There were, however, serious side effects from the vast lakes of up to 150 million barrels of unburned oil that gushed from the uncapped wells. Efforts were then diverted into bulldozing dikes to prevent the oil from spilling into the Gulf. Pumps were used to suck the oil up from the lakes, but this in turn led to problems of storage. Over a period of years, underground water supplies to the region could be irreversibly polluted by oil seepage. It takes only 2 pints (approximately one liter) of oil to pollute 250,000 gallons (a million liters) of drinking water.

Even the air was at risk of pollution from the lakes of standing oil. Experts from the World Conservation Monitoring Centre feared that hydrocarbons evaporating from the oil could affect the health of people living in the area. Wildlife, too, suffered: birds trying to land on what appeared to be a lake of water became instantly coated with sludge.

Ozone depletion

For a number of years, environmental scientists warned of damage to the layer of ozone (a form of oxygen molecule) that lies some 15 miles (25 km) above Earth's surface. This layer is vital to life on Earth, as it screens the Sun's most harmful ultra-

▶ Oil fires raged in Kuwait after the Gulf War. The fires were extinguished within eight months using a Hungarian machine known as Big Wind that literally blew out the flames. There was serious damage to the local environment, but the effects did not spread far beyond the Gulf, as had initially been feared.

violet rays. Yet in the early 1980s, scientists in the Antarctic found that the ozone layer there was severely depleted—there was a hole in the ozone layer over the Antarctic. Looking for the cause, they pinpointed a reaction between the ozone and gases called CFCs—chlorofluorocarbons, used widely in such household items as refrigerators, fire extinguishers, and aerosol sprays. At low temperatures and under the influence of ultraviolet light, CFCs broke down the ozone molecules.

The scientists reported their findings amid much skepticism. However, when Australian doctors began reporting an increased incidence of melanoma, a form of skin cancer, which is the result of excessive skin exposure to ultraviolet light, public concern was aroused. In Chile, also affected by the ozone hole, sheep that spent their lives in the open began to go blind from cataracts. While there is no proof that either of these occurred as result of the ozone hole, the link was made in many people's minds.

In the spring of 1992, there was international alarm as measurements made over northern Europe showed that an ozone hole was also opening up over the Arctic. The eruption of Mount Pinatubo the year before had increased the number of particles in the upper atmosphere, speeding up the ozone-depleting reactions. It was feared that up to 1 percent of the ozone layer could be depleted each day—leading to a 25 percent drop by the end of the Northern Hemisphere's spring. Regrettably, the ozone actually produced by industrial pollution occurs at the wrong level in the atmosphere and at the wrong time to have any effect on the ozone hole.

Governments finally began to take action to force industry to replace CFCs with other materials that would not have the same effects. In February 1992, President George Bush committed the United States to cease production of CFCs by the end of 1995, and shortly afterwards, the European Union agreed likewise. As CFCs take five years to reach the ozone layer and persist for up to a century, environmental scientists were concerned that the extra effects of manufactured CFCs in addition to volcanic eruptions could have a major effect on world agriculture. Ultraviolet light can damage young crops, particularly in the spring when the ozone hole is at its worst. CFCs are now banned from use in all developed countries, and under the terms of the Montreal Protocol, developing countries must find safer alternatives by 2010.

Global warming

Environmental scientists have long been aware that the composition of the atmosphere is changing. The proportion of carbon dioxide in particular, but also of other gases that are lumped together as greenhouse gases, is increasing.

The name of this phenomenon comes from the tendency of these gases to block the flow of heat away from Earth's surface. As long as the flow outwards is in equilibrium with the inflow of solar warmth, the globe remains at an equitable temperature. If the greenhouse gases interfere with this flow, the world will heat up, with drastic changes in the world's agriculture as some areas dry up, others become wetter, and the viability of staple crops such as rice and wheat changes in their traditional growing areas. An increase in global temperature could also affect the sea level, as snow and ice currently on land masses melt, with clear consequences for the large populations that live close to sea level.

While many experts are convinced that global warming should be taken seriously, it is not so easy to persuade governments to take drastic steps to curb industrial output of greenhouse gases, which are produced both naturally and by human activities. Carbon dioxide is released into the atmosphere by using natural gas, coal, and oil—fossil fuels—to generate electricity and fuel for road transportation. A further contribution

▼ A symbol of global warming—crops will suffer dramatically as huge areas turn into desert. Loss of productive land to drought could cause migration of large numbers of people to regions where food is plentiful, and put new stresses on the area they move to. Careful management of water supplies and development of drought-tolerant crops could do a great deal to relieve such pressures.

comes from the burning of forests in the developing countries of the world as people clear land to grow crops. At the Earth Summit in June 1992 many developing nations were hoping to force the United States—the world's biggest producer of greenhouse gases—to join them in agreeing to curb its own activities and maintain output of carbon dioxide at no more than 1990 levels by the year 2000.

In December 1997, 160 countries that are party to the United Nations Framework Convention on Climate Change agreed to cut collective emissions of greenhouse gases by 5.2 percent in a legal document called the Kyoto Protocol. Central to the plan is a set of binding emissions targets to be met by the developed nations. These limits vary between countries—the United States has committed itself to reducing its emissions by 7 percent of its 1990 levels, the European Union by 8 percent, and Japan by 6 percent over a period of five years up to 2012.

Six major greenhouse gases are covered by the targets—carbon dioxide, methane, nitrous oxide, hydrofluorocarbons, perfluorocarbons, and sulfur hexafluoride. These last three are industrial gases that are particularly long-lived in the atmosphere. They were brought in to replace CFCs, but are believed to be just as damaging to the upper atmosphere.

These emission targets will be offset by the development of carbon "sinks." Sinks are systems

that absorb large amounts of carbon dioxide and include the oceans and large forests. Under the Kyoto Protocol, countries will be encouraged to plant new areas of trees and reforest areas that have been destroyed by logging or clearance. Other measures encourage improvements in energy efficiency, reformation of the energy and transportation sectors—particularly the use of motor transport—and promotion of renewable energy sources.

Developing countries are in a slightly different position over greenhouse gas emissions, as their economic growth is dependent on cheap fuel sources and old-fashioned technology. Under the Kyoto Protocol, these countries will be encouraged to adopt cleaner manufacturing techniques and given help to construct environmentally sound power plants.

The Earth Summit and Agenda 21

The Earth Summit, which took place in Rio de Janeiro, Brazil, was convened to address urgent problems in environmental protection and socioeconomic development. It was a defining moment in the recognition of environmental matters, as it acknowledged that global cooperation was needed to address problems such as climate change and greenhouse gases, where pollution could not be confined within national boundaries. Over 100 heads of state attended the meeting, which gave the resulting policy document, Agenda 21, credibility and made environmental concerns a top priority. Fundamental to the plan was the concept of "sustainable development" first put forward by the Norwegian prime minister Gro Harlem Bruntland in the late 1980s. Under this concept, nations could continue to grow economically without causing further damage to the environment. Managing ecosystems would lead to better living standards for all by reducing poverty, ill-health, and hunger.

Agenda 21 was a holistic view of sustainable development, covering poverty, population growth, water resources, climate change, desertification, toxic chemicals, energy resources, forestry, agriculture, biodiversity, and technology transfer. Its key aim was that it should be a dynamic program, responsive to the different needs, capabilities, and priorities of individual countries and regions.

▲ Air pollution knows no boundaries, as this smoggy view of Hong Kong shows. Forest fires burning out of control on islands in Indonesia in the late 1990s created enormous palls of smoke that traveled hundreds of miles and blotted out the Sun in nearby Singapore and Malaysia for several weeks. Particulates in the smoke also caused a huge rise in respiratory illnesses, such as asthma.

At the first review of progress in 1997, it was noted that some of the targets proposed in Rio were being met, but the failure of others was preventing the concept of sustainable development from being reached. Population growth appeared to be slowing, food production was rising, and the environmental quality in some regions was improving. However, fresh water is becoming scarce in some parts of the world, productive land and forests continue to be lost at an unacceptable rate, and 60 percent of global fish stocks are said to be overfished or fully depleted.

◄ Scientists at a conference in Zimbabwe gathered on the dried-up bed of Darwendale reservoir in 1992, in an area that should have been submerged. Water shortages have hit many countries, including even some with normally wet climates, such as Britain and New Zealand.

FACT FILE

■ In the summer of 1992, work was completed in an effort to discover how Earth's atmosphere has changed over a vast time span. In Greenland, an international team of scientists drilled their way through a mile and a half (2.5 km) of ice, down to solid bedrock, through layers deposited as snow up to half a million years ago.

■ By extracting a core of ice as the hole was drilled, the scientists obtained a unique record of environmental conditions on Earth long before Homo sapiens appeared. The acidity of the sample indicated the presence of particles from ancient volcanic eruptions.

■ In the new core, scientists found evidence for the first time of "biomass burning"— that is, forest fires. These may have been caused by major volcanic eruptions or other natural events in the past. Like volcanic particles, the clouds of smoke from big fires could have a major effect on the global climate, reducing temperatures over a large part of Earth's surface.

■ Other measurements of isotopes in the ice core have revealed the varying temperatures of the polar regions over many thousands of years. For example, after the last ice age ended 10,700 years ago, the average temperature rose 13°F (7°C) within just 50 years, showing that rapid natural temperature changes can occur. Current global warming trends are about 1°F (0.5°C) per century. Such studies can help shed light on the complex links between atmospheric dust, carbon dioxide, and temperature.

Fresh water constitutes only 3 percent of the water found on Earth, and less than 1 percent of it is available for drinking, the rest being locked up at the poles and in glaciers. It is estimated that if current trends continue, two-thirds of the world's population will suffer moderate to severe water stress by 2030 as a result of overdemand and pollution of supplies. Scarcity of water would also have repercussions for the expansion of agriculture to meet growing populations' food needs. Despite a United Nations program in the 1980s that aimed to give everybody access to a safe supply of drinking water, some 20 percent of the global population still lack this vital resource, and nearly half have no adequate sanitation.

Other resources are under considerable threat. Reports presented to the 1997 review of the Earth Summit estimated that nearly 34 million acres (14 million ha) of forest are being cut down or burned every year. It is believed that animals and plants are being wiped out at a rate of 50,000 species per year through loss of habitat, development, and pollution. Some species are even being lost before they have been officially classified. Marine pollution, mainly as a result of land-based activities, is threatening the livelihood of people living along the coasts.

Toxic wastes continue to pose a danger both to human health and to ecosystems. About 3 million tons (2.7 million tonnes) are thought to cross national borders every year. In an effort to stop the practice of toxic waste being dumped in poorer countries, a ban on exportation was introduced in 1995, but it is not yet legally binding. Under Agenda 21, governments are committed to developing safer alternatives to toxic chemicals, transferring clean-up technologies to poorer countries, and helping to dispose of old nuclear plants and other contaminated sites.

SEE ALSO: CLIMATOLOGY • EARTH • ENERGY RESOURCES • FORESTRY • LIFE • POLLUTION MONITORING AND CONTROL • WATER SUPPLY

Enzyme

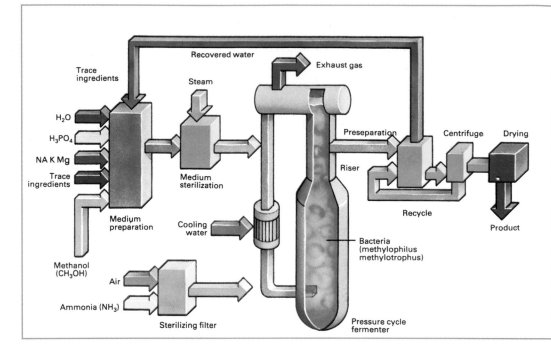

PROTEIN PRODUCTION

Yeast enzymes, when fermented, can produce bacterial protein as an end result. Here, yeasts are grown in a preparation containing methanol (produced from natural gas), water, phosphoric acid, sodium, potassium, magnesium, and various trace ingredients. After sterilization, the yeasts pass through an oxygen-rich fermenter vessel containing air and ammonia. Fermentation produces the bacterium *Methylophilus methylotrophus*, which is then dried, resulting in a protein-rich animal food.

Enzymes are biological catalysts that are vital to living organisms. Without enzymes, the process of turning the food an organism eats into energy that can be used to keep its cell functioning, for example, would be impossibly slow. It is not known how many enzymes exist; more than 1,000 have been listed and many more doubtless await discovery.

Those enzymes that have been isolated and identified in a pure state have proved to be proteins, and although most enzymes have not been positively identified as proteins, those conditions and substances that denature, or precipitate, proteins also inactivate enzymes. Some of these conditions and substances are extremes of acidity or alkalinity, the salts of heavy metals, ultraviolet light, and high temperatures. Most catalytic reactions speed up when heat is applied, and enzyme-assisted reactions are no exception. If the cell is heated, the reaction speeds up until the optimum temperature is reached. If the cell gets any hotter, the enzymes become progressively inactive and the reaction slows until eventually, at about 120°F (50°C), enzymes are completely denatured. The optimum temperature in the human body is between 86 and 104°F (30–40°C). Within this range, there is a maximum reaction speed at which no damage to the enzymes occurs. The destruction of enzymes at high temperatures is probably one reason that a prolonged raised body temperature, as in a fever, can prove fatal.

Enzymes promote the chemical processes collectively called metabolism. There are two aspects to metabolism: anabolism, which is the synthesis of complex molecules from simple ones, and catabolism, which is the degradation, or breaking down, of large molecules into simpler ones. The enzymes concerned in these processes may be classified in the following way: transferases transfer a substance from one molecule to another; isomerases rearrange molecules; lyases split complex substances into simpler ones; hydrolases act like lyases but use water in the reaction; ligases or synthetases are concerned with the synthesis of substances; and oxidoreductases are concerned with oxidizing and reducing substances.

Enzymes, unlike other catalysts, are specific—each is concerned with only one reaction and acts only upon a particular substrate. For example, the enzyme maltase is involved only in converting its substrate maltose into glucose. There are a few that act on more than one substrate, but even these take part in a limited range of reactions. The actions and interactions of enzymes are complex, and the absence of just one enzyme in the body can have catastrophic results for health.

There are many instances in which a large number of enzymes are required to maintain health. Any imbalance in these enzyme combinations, either because of over-production or deficiency, will upset the metabolism and can cause a chain of disorders.

 SEE ALSO: BEER AND BREWING • CATALYST • CELL BIOLOGY • DIGESTIVE SYSTEM • FERMENTATION • METABOLISM • WINEMAKING • YEAST

Epidemiology

The science of epidemiology is not only the study of epidemics: it is the study of who gets diseases and why. In its broad sense, it covers the whole of mathematical medicine. It also studies the efficacy of treatment, compares one treatment with another, allows health care providers to project future needs of populations, and measures the effectiveness of beneficial treatments and health workers.

Epidemics are no longer confined to just one country or continent. The growth of air travel and international trade has helped spread diseases around the globe more rapidly than ever before. Coupled with this is the ability of microorganisms to mutate and change into new strains, leading to the emergence of new diseases and the return of old ones, such as tuberculosis, which is again becoming a problem in countries where it was previously thought to have been brought under control. Other factors, such as poverty, civil strife, urbanization, and environmental change, all contribute to the spread of disease and make efforts to confine it difficult.

Recognizing that disease no longer has national boundaries, the World Health Organization in 1995 established a global surveillance network among its member countries to improve monitoring and reporting of communicable diseases. This network links national institutions such as the U.S. Centers for Disease Control and Prevention, the French Pasteur Institutes, and the U.K. Public Health Laboratory Service. Under current international health regulations, WHO member states are legally obliged to report diseases of international importance, particularly plague (*Yersinia pestis*), cholera, and yellow fever.

Influenza monitoring

One of the most monitored diseases in the world is the influenza virus. Since 1948, collaborating laboratories have sent details on local outbreaks and the strain of virus involved to one of four coordinating centers. The data is then assessed by experts, who make recommendations on the three strains to be included in the next season's influenza vaccine. The surveillance system is backed up by plans to combat pandemic outbreaks, as was brought into force in 1997, when an avian influenza virus that broke out in commercial chicken farms in Hong Kong crossed over into humans. Prompt dissemination of information to the public on the outbreak was followed up by the production of a suitable vaccine and diagnostic kits and elimination of all infected flocks.

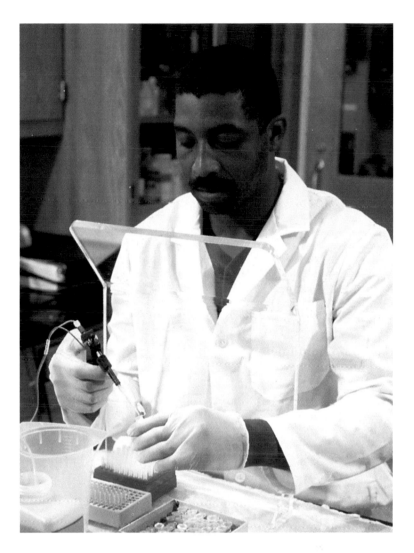

▲ A technician at the Center for Disease Control in Atlanta, Georgia, carries out an enzyme-linked immunosorbent assay on blood samples. In a double-blind trial of a new drug, samples are identified only by a random number, so no one carrying out the test can influence the results either consciously or unwittingly.

Tracking the AIDS virus

AIDS (acquired immune deficiency syndrome), which was first recognized in 1981, has been a challenge for epidemiologists, both for mapping where the disease started and how it spread and for projecting its future incidence and the resources needed to tackle it.

AIDS is caused by a virus, HIV (human immunodeficiency virus), which was first isolated in 1983. The origins of AIDS remains obscure, but HIV was first found in isolated individuals in the 1950s. HIV belongs to a group known as retroviruses, one group of which can cause leukemia in humans and animals. A related strain that occurs in monkeys and other ape species, simian immunodeficiency virus, is thought to be a likely contender as the origin of HIV, as it causes similar symptoms to AIDS among primates.

Although HIV was identified in the 1950s, the slow incubation time for its development into AIDS meant that the scale of its spread did not become apparent until the 1980s. By the end of 1999, it was estimated that 34.3 million people

◄ Speed is vital in spotting and checking the spread of diseases. At this center in the United Kingdom computers are used to log the results from over 25,000 clinical samples taken daily across the country and sent by phone. This network quickly reveals outbreaks of both infectious diseases and food poisoning, which can often be traced to individual batches of food.

The reemergence of tuberculosis

Tuberculosis, or TB, a disease that had been in decline for over 40 years, is once again causing concern around the world. Nearly two million people a year are dying from the disease and the epidemic is growing. Contributing to the rise in cases has been the spread of HIV, which weakens the immune system, and the emergence of drug-resistant strains of the bacteria that cause TB. In response to the rising number of cases of TB, WHO declared a global emergency in 1993, estimating that one billion people would become infected between 2000 and 2020, and 35 million would die if steps were not taken to control the disease.

TB is highly contagious and is spread through the air by droplet infection. Drugs to control it were not available until the 1950s, but already strains that are resistant to a single drug have been documented in every country surveyed. More worrying is the emergence of multidrug-resistant TB, which can withstand treatment using the two most powerful anti-TB drugs available, rifampicin and isoniazid. Drug resistance has arisen through incomplete treatment regimes and unreliable drug supplies. Even while they are being treated, the bacillus may become resistant, and this resistance can be passed on to a new host. Although drug-resistant TB can be cured, it often requires extensive chemotherapy, which is usually prohibitively expensive in poorer countries where the disease is rife.

To try to combat the increase in TB cases, a working group has been set up to recommend a strategy for the detection and cure of the disease. The plan has five elements—political commitment, microscopy services, drug supplies, surveillance and monitoring system, and efficacious treatment regimes backed up by reporting of results. Patients are diagnosed, using microscopy, and put under a strict treatment regime that is checked regularly by health workers to ensure that they complete the course of medicine. Sputum tests are carried out after two months and again at the end of the treatment. The patient's progress is documented throughout, and the outcome noted.

Since this system was introduced on a global scale, cure rates have been reported of up to 95 percent, even in the poorest countries. Following the full course of treatment is also slowing the development of multidrug-resistant TB, as infections are cleared up before they can be passed on.

around the world were infected with HIV, 24.5 million of them in sub-Saharan Africa, the worst affected region. The virus has been detected in over 200 countries and is spreading rapidly, especially in developing countries.

Regular reports on cases of AIDs have been collected by WHO since 1981. Because HIV cannot survive outside the body, transmission of the disease can pass from person to person only by exchange of blood and body fluids (chiefly through sexual contact) or from mother to child. The level of risk behavior, such as engaging in unprotected sex, is therefore key in the global spread of HIV, and prevalence of the disease varies from country to country, owing to many factors.

Epidemiological monitoring of HIV in particular population groups is called sentinel surveillance. Selected groups, particularly those at high risk of contracting the virus, are screened at regular intervals to indicate how levels of infection are changing over time in specific areas. Pregnant women, who routinely have blood taken for other purposes during their pregnancy, are often used as an indication of the prevalence of the virus among the sexually active adult population. As a tool, sentinel surveillance is a cheap and flexible method that can be sustained even in countries that have poor medical resources.

Analyzing the data from epidemiological monitoring of AIDS requires careful interpretation. Survey methods may vary and different case definitions apply between countries. There may also be a reluctance to diagnose AIDS cases because of the stigma associated with the disease. The long lead time between contracting HIV and the onset of AIDS can also give a misleading picture of the spread of the disease.

 SEE ALSO: Immunology • Medicine • Microbiology • Pathology • Vaccine

Ergonomics

◀ A designer's sketch, showing one idea for a solid-state instrument panel. The real ergonomic breakthrough in automobile design is in devices such as global positioning systems and head-up displays that project information onto the windshield so that the driver's line of vision need not be shifted.

Any realistic design requires that the designer makes trade-off decisions. People who buy goods expect them to be reliable, efficient, safe, easy to use, and appropriately priced. The manufacturer would probably add that they should be eye-catching, easy and cheap to manufacture, and appeal to a large section of the population. The difference between a good design and a poor one is the nature of the trade-off decisions, and these in turn depend on the criteria the designer sets before starting to work. For example, a designer may decide that low-cost manufacture is the most important thing and may sacrifice some aspects of safety and reliability or other factors to achieve this aim.

Ergonomics—the principle that underlines ergonomic design—is concerned with the interaction between humans and the environment in which they live and work. It is concerned with the home, offices, factories, hospitals, and schools and the vehicles that transport people between them. Its goals are to ensure that these interactions occur with ease, in safety, and without error, to the benefit of the individual and society. If they can be made pleasurable, so much the better.

The interactions ergonomics considers are those directly between a user and an object, bearing in mind the range of shapes, sizes, knowledge, and intentions of the user population, and also whether the interaction is intentional or accidental. It also considers the effect of this interaction on the society in which it is embedded.

Ergonomic design is the process by which the designed environment is matched to the characteristics of people and draws upon a wide body of knowledge and methods to achieve this aim.

Ergonomics ensures, for example, that automobile seats can be adjusted so they are comfortable for people of all sizes and shapes and that an ergonomically designed can opener will not injure the user's fingers. Ergonomic design goes even further; it includes not only everyday consumer goods but also complex systems, such as the cockpit and life-support systems of the space shuttle and the design of control rooms for nuclear plants. The philosophy behind ergonomic design is that things should be safe, easy, and comfortable to use; a person should not have to battle with the tools to do a task. Its importance lies in the fact that all technological developments are intended to benefit people.

Design through the ages

Ergonomics is not a new practice. When the early cave dwellers took to chipping flints to make hand tools, they were practicing ergonomics. Ergonomics embraces knowledge from a number of sources. The word itself was derived from the Greek and means "combining work with natural laws." It is also known as "human factors" and, occasionally, "engineering psychology," and it draws upon physics, physiology and anatomy, psychology of design, statistics, computer science, and engineering as its main sources.

Erosion

◄ Landslides can happen very suddenly, often changing the landscape beyond recognition. This hotel on the coast near Scarborough in northern England was originally some distance from the edge of the cliff. In a matter of weeks, the entire hotel had disappeared down the cliff face. A large crack can clearly be seen opening up behind the main building.

Erosion is the process of displacement of soil materials from the surface of Earth. It results principally from the passage of wind, water, or ice over or against the land surface. Erosion by ice occurs in sparsely populated areas and is of little economic or social consequence.

Erosion by wind and water is widespread and, in fact, is exacerbated by modification of the natural environment for economic exploitation. An indication of the scale of the problem is given by figures from the U.S. Soil Conservation Service, which estimated in 1987 that some 3 billion tons (2.7 billion tonnes) of soil were lost from United States farmland. It is estimated that over 40 percent of American farmland is losing soil faster than it is replaced by normal organic processes. To a large extent, this problem has been hidden by the fact that the considerable increases in crop yields, owing to the use of fertilizers, far outweigh the loss in production resulting from erosion.

Land surfaces are subject to erosion by wind and rainfall, depending on factors such as climate and vegetation. Water erosion is usually restricted to river channels or coastlines where water and land abut. Freeze-thaw cycles can also cause erosion, since repeated expansion and contraction of water within a solid matrix such as rock can cause it to split.

Control of soil erosion

Erosion by wind, known as deflation, is confined to areas of relatively flat land where rainfall is sparse or to flat areas that are heavily cultivated. In such areas, winds are strong and frequent, and there is not enough water in the soil to cause a cohesive effect. The speed of the wind can be reduced by windbreaks. A windbreak will reduce the speed of the wind at ground level for a distance of about 5 times its height on the windward side and 20 to 30 times on the leeward. The windbreak must, however, have a certain permeability to the wind, or serious turbulence (eddy currents) may result around the ends of the windbreak, resulting in local erosion.

Windbreaks usually consist of rows of trees planted at right angles to the prevailing winds. For maximum effectiveness, the rows should be no more than about 1,650 ft. (500 m) apart. Natural windbreaks have certain drawbacks: they compete with crops for moisture, nutrients, and space; they may harbor pests; and at the time of the year when crops are not growing, the foliage on the trees may not be dense enough to protect the soil from the wind. Sometimes scientifically designed artificial windbreaks of wood or other materials are used instead.

The surface of the ground is best protected from erosion by vegetation. This reduces wind speed at ground level, and the roots help to bind together the particles of soil; the absence of vegetation is the reason cultivated soil is particularly subject to erosion during the soil preparation and sowing season. Modern methods of sowing crops allow sowing to be done directly into the stubble and waste plant matter left from the last growing season, a technique known as stubble mulching.

Strip farming, a method of cultivating alternate strips 300 to 600 ft. (90–180 m) wide, not only prevents the soil's nutrients from being used up owing to overfarming but also helps prevent erosion because the planted strips act as windbreaks. It is also possible to protect the soil by spraying it with bitumen emulsion; this is an especially useful technique in areas where a very low annual rainfall may restrict the growth of a continuous vegetation cover.

▶ Erosion on beaches can be combatted by a system of groynes that stop the sand shifting up the beach and by building up defense structures like these interlocking spoked cement shapes that absorb and break the energy of the waves.

◀ Wind erosion constantly shifts the sands of the desert to form the familiar dunes landscape.

Shifting cultivation, where the land is left fallow for several years to allow poor soils to recover, also helps to minimize erosion. However, population pressures are reducing the amount of time for which the land can be left fallow, with a consequent increase in erosion. The widespread felling of trees, for commercial use of the wood or for use as fuel, is another serious cause of erosion.

The intensity of soil erosion by water depends on the velocity as well as the volume of water flow over the ground and therefore is worst in areas of steep slopes and heavy rainfall. Here again, stubble mulching is useful because it reduces rainsplash erosion, which results from the impact of raindrops on the ground, and also retards surface water flow. The use of cover crops is also helpful and widespread. In the tropics, a cover crop may be a perennial tree beneath which other crops are grown; in more temperate climates, it will be a winter annual that protects the bare ground when crops are not growing.

On slopes, contour plowing is practiced. Plowing along the contour rather than up and down the slope reduces the total runoff because water is stored in the furrow rather than channeled by it. (Channeling of runoff down a furrow results in a rapid erosion, causing gullies). Soil erosion can be reduced more than 50 percent by contour plowing.

Terracing of hillsides is another contour technique. A system of ditches and embankments is

Escalator and Moving Walkway

The modern escalator provides the most efficient method of moving large numbers of people from one level to another at a controlled and even rate. In its simplest form, it consists of a series of individual steps mounted between two endless chains that move upward or downward within a steel frame.

The pioneers of the escalator were Jesse Reno and Charles Seeberger, whose designs were produced independently in the early 1890s. In 1900 escalators were installed in Paris and New York. The first modern type of escalator, which did not appear until 1921, incorporated the best features of both the Reno and Seeberger designs. Today escalators are commonplace in railway stations, airports, and department stores.

▲ The escalator at Centre Georges Pompidou in Paris, France, is not only functional but also integral to the aesthetics of the building.

Top section
The top section houses the electrically powered driving machine and most of the controlling switch gear. The driving machine consists of an AC induction motor running at around 1,000 rpm and driving the escalator through a worm-type reduction gear. The main brake is spring-loaded into its on position, being held off by a DC electromagnet to enable the escalator to run. This arrangement is thus fail-safe; in the event of a power supply failure, the electromagnet will be de-energized, and the brake will be applied by the springs. A hand-winding wheel and a manual brake-release lever allow the escalator to be moved by hand if necessary.

The controlling unit includes rectifiers to provide the DC supply to the brake, a contactor to start the motor, and control relays linked to safety switches that will stop the machine in the event of an overload, drive chain breakage, or obstruction to the steps or handrail. The controller is also linked to the key-operated starting switches and the emergency stop buttons, and contains a device to prevent an up-traveling escalator from reversing its direction of travel in the event of drive mechanism failure. To reduce wear and running costs, some escalators are fitted with speed-control devices that run the machine at half speed when no passengers are using it. Photo-electric sensors, fitted at each end, switch the escalator to full speed when a passenger steps on and return it to half speed when all the passengers are cleared.

Center and bottom sections
The bottom section contains the step-return idler sprockets (toothed wheels around which the chain turns), step-chain safety switches, and curved track

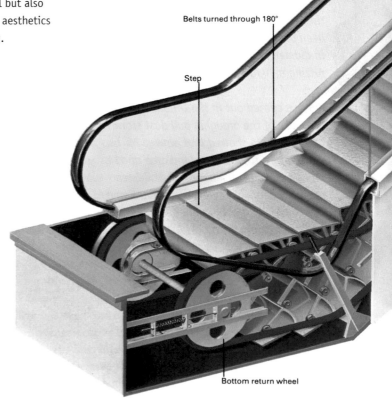

Belts turned through 180°

Step

Bottom return wheel

of the escalator from the horizontal plane into the angle of climb, which is usually 30 to 35 degrees. Between the top and bottom sections runs a welded box-type structure that carries the straight track sections.

The steps on which the passengers stand are normally assembled from aluminum pressure-die castings and steel pressings mounted on a frame, usually of cast aluminum, which runs on rollers on the main track sections and is driven by the two main chains, one on each side. Foothold on the step surface is provided by a

▼ A cutaway view of an escalator, which consists of a continuously moving series of individual steps mounted between two endless chains. The chains are driven around four toothed wheels by an induction motor. Each step moves on smaller wheels along rails, which are positioned so that the steps fold to give a horizontal surface at the top and bottom. The handrail is a moving belt of rubber and canvas.

Drive shaft and wheels

Endless chain

Handrail drive   Ratchet wheel

Inner rail

Returning steps

Top pair of wheels

Bottom pair of wheels

Outer rail

cleated board faced with aluminum or rubber. The moving handrails are made from layers of canvas covered with a rubber or plastic molding. They run in continuous loops in T shape guides along the tops of the balustrades at a speed closely linked with that of the steps. The balustrades and their skirtings allow a smooth passage for the steps, and all joints are securely masked. The running clearance of the steps has to comply with strict safety standards and the comb plates (the

metal teeth that project at the top and bottom of the fixed escalator base and provide the link between the moving treads and floor level) incorporate safety switches that will stop the escalator if any object is caught between the steps and the comb plate.

The tread width can vary between 2 and 4 ft. (0.6–1.2 m), and the speed of the escalator can range from 90 to 180 ft. per min. (27–54 m/min). When running at 145 ft. per min. (44 m/min), a single escalator powered by a 100 horsepower motor can carry up to 10,000 passengers an hour.

Moving walkways

A variation of the escalator is the moving walkway, which may run horizontally or on an incline of up to 15 degrees. The flat moving surface may consist of a continuous rubber belt or a series of jointed treads. These systems are often used for moving passengers around such places as airports and train stations.

SEE ALSO: ELECTRIC MOTOR • ELEVATOR • PHOTOELECTRIC CELL AND PHOTOMETRY

Evolution

Most scientists believe that all life on Earth is the product of, and participator in, a gradual and never-ending process of change they term evolution. The theory of evolution, although closely associated with the name of Charles Darwin, has itself evolved over the years, with many scientists contributing their ideas.

In the late 1790s, an English geologist, William Smith, while supervising the excavation of a canal, noticed the fossilized remains of long-dead creatures. He also noticed that fossils occurred in layers, or strata. After studying a fossil, Smith claimed that he could identify it by looking at the stratum from which it came.

Someone else with interest in fossils was the Scottish geologist Charles Lyell, who studied rock formations, particularly in relation to volcanoes. He came to the conclusion that Earth was many millions of years old, much older than had previously been thought. Lyell's findings were published in 1830, about the time Darwin, an English scientist, was undertaking his famous voyage on the *Beagle*. Darwin realized that the changes in species he observed would take many millennia, and Lyell's estimate of the antiquity of Earth worked in well with his theories.

In 1809, Jean Baptiste de Lamark, the French naturalist, had propounded his theory of evolution. His ideas concerned the inheritance of acquired characteristics, and he suggested that if a creature had a *besoin*, or need and desire for change, that desire caused the change, and the

▼ The tree of life. All life derives from single-celled prokaryotes. In the Precambrian era, plants and animals began developing along separate paths. Marine animals developed first; then bony fish evolved into amphibians, which in turn developed into mammals, including humans. The gaps in this record, however, make it open to dispute.

change could, moreover, be passed on to its progeny. Darwin himself toyed with a similar idea, "use and disuse heredity," which suggested that the organs of a creature gave off particles that collected in the sex organs and then passed on to the next generation, affecting their organs' structure.

The survival theory

Apart from Lyell, one of the scientists who had most influence on Darwin was the 19th-century political economist Thomas Malthus, who said in his book *An Essay on the Principles of Population* that nature produced far more offspring than would live to become adult and eventually reproduce. He noticed that there were thousands of seeds produced by, say, just one plant or eggs by just two frogs, yet over a period of time, the number of mature plants and frogs remained about the same. This idea formed the basis of Darwin's theories on natural selection. It was obvious that within a species individuals differ, and Darwin said that those individuals who were better at getting food and avoiding predators were more likely to survive and reproduce—this is the principle of the survival of the fittest.

At the same time Darwin was formulating his theory of natural selection, the naturalist Alfred Wallace had, as a result of his study of insects, reached much the same conclusion. He noted that although basically the same in structure, each variety of beetle differed in detail from the next according to its lifestyle.

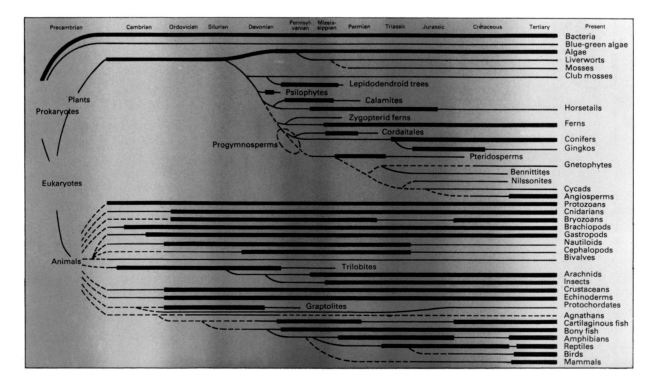

In 1859, Darwin published his book *On the Origin of Species* in which he put forward his theory that all life on Earth had a common ancestry and that different species had evolved from that common ancestry to fill different ecological niches. Darwin suggested that one of the mechanisms involved in producing changes in individuals and eventually in species was sexual reproduction. This theory became established only in the light of the work of the Austrian Gregor Mendel, who worked out the Mendelian Laws of Inheritance, which defined the likelihood of a particular parental characteristic being transmitted to the offspring.

Inherited characteristics

Scientists have discovered that living cells contain paired structures called chromosomes, each containing many genes made up of deoxyribonucleic acid (DNA). These genes are inherited from the parents and are the blueprints of the organism.

Each parent contributes one chromosome to each pair. The genes along the chromosomes are matched to each other. The gene for eye color from one parent, for example, might be for blue eyes, and the equivalent gene from the other parent might be for brown eyes. The brown-eye gene would dominate the recessive blue-eye gene, so the organism would have brown eyes.

When the organism with these two genes mates, only half the genetic material is passed on. This may be the half with the blue-eye gene or the half with the brown-eye gene. Depending on which genes come from the mate, the offspring could have either blue or brown eyes.

Occasionally, the genetic material undergoes a mutation—a radical change that produces a characteristic not present in either parent's genetic makeup. Often, the organism does not survive, or, if it does, it is handicapped and does not live long. Another change, however, might be wholly advantageous, enabling the organism to compete more successfully for food and mates. One such mutation occurred in the European peppered moth, *Biston betularia*. This species lives on and around trees. It is thought that many centuries ago, the trees that were its habitat were dark-barked pines and the moth itself was dark and well-camouflaged. Over the years, deciduous trees with lighter colored bark and a tendency to play host to lichens took over. The dark moth, now at a disadvantage, was easy prey, but a mutant with peppered wings that blended better into the new habitat became the dominant species until the Industrial Revolution. In areas that became heavily industrialized, soot and fumes darkened the tree bark, killed the lichen, and provided

▲ A 150 million year old fossil of an *Archaeopteryx*. The first discovered fossil of this species was found in south Germany in 1861, only two years after Darwin proposed his theory of evolution. It was crucial evidence in his support because it was a clear example of an intermediate between one type of creature and another. Its reptilian tail, claws, and teeth coexisted with birdlike feathers, a wishbone (which is a structure found only in birds), and chickenlike wings.

again a habitat in which those moths that were darker could survive. In these areas, the peppered species is virtually extinct, the peppering being not only disadvantageous but also recessive.

Life on Earth

Many scientists believe that life arose on Earth from a primeval "soup" made up of such substances as water, hydrogen, methane, and ammonia. In a famous experiment, researchers passed electric discharges (to simulate lightning) through a similar mixture in the absence of oxygen—thousands of millions of years ago Earth's atmosphere contained no oxygen. They found that much more complex organic compounds were synthesized, including amino acids—the basic protein building blocks.

It is suggested that from such beginnings arose the most primitive forms of life—blue-green algae and bacteria. These unicellular creatures are alone in being prokaryotes—cells with no nucleus. The cells of all other organisms (eukaryotes) have a nucleus, which contains the genetic material. Eukaryotes have one other important difference from prokaryotes—sexual reproduction, giving the possibility of faster rates of change and increasing diversification. Blue-green algae, probably the first life on Earth, paved the way for other organisms by producing oxygen as a by-product of photosynthesis.

Explosive

◀ High-explosive charges in a line of boreholes explode simultaneously to bring down a wall of rock in a limestone quarry.

▶ High-explosive slurry is poured into boreholes to surround electrical fuses. A single electrical impulse from a detonator will cause a simultaneous detonation along the line of boreholes.

An explosive is a substance or mixture that burns rapidly, releasing large quantities of gas and heat in a short period. The gases generated by explosives can be used to propel rockets, shells, and bullets or to form shock waves that shatter rocks or buildings in the vicinity of the explosion.

History

The first explosive was gunpowder—a mixture of saltpeter (potassium nitrate, KNO_3), sulfur, and carbon. The origins of gunpowder, also called black powder, are obscure. The Chinese were probably aware of the properties of saltpeter as early as the Chin dynasty (221–207 B.C.E.), although it was used only in fireworks and flares at first. Then in the mid-13th century, records show that the Chinese used black powder as a propellant for crude bamboo guns.

Also in the mid-13th century, Roger Bacon, an English monk, discovered the formulation of black powder. He recorded instructions for its preparation in the form of a Latin anagram in his *De Secretis Operibus Artis et Naturae* (Of the Secret Works of Art and Nature) of 1245. In the West, black powder was first used as a gun propellant in the 1320s, and in 1346, English troops used black powder as the propellant in cannons trained against the French at Crécy.

The modern formulation of gunpowder has remained unchanged for at least three centuries: 75 percent saltpeter, 15 percent charcoal (carbon), and 10 percent sulfur. A cheaper but less effective version, called B powder, has sodium nitrate instead of potassium nitrate. Although slower-burning explosives have replaced gunpowder as a gun propellant, it is still widely used in fireworks and blank cartridges and has even been used in the retrorockets of a space probe.

Explosion and detonation

The two modes of explosive combustion are explosion—sometimes called deflagration—and detonation. The principal difference between explosion and detonation is the rate at which the combustion front travels through the explosive.

Explosion is fast combustion, the burning front spreading layer by layer through the material at a velocity of up to around 1,300 ft. (400 m) per second, which is slow when compared with detonation. The relatively slow evolution of gases is suitable for use as propellants. Substances that deflagrate are called low explosives.

Detonation is characterized by a supersonic shock wave, or detonating wave, that travels through the explosive substance at typical speeds of 6,500 to 29,500 ft. (2,000–9,000 m) per second. The exact speed of the detonation wave depends on the composition of the explosive, and its pressure can reach 700 tons per sq. in. (100,000 bar). The gases formed in a detonation travel in the same direction as the detonation wave, which shatters objects in its path and leaves a region of low pressure behind it. Explosives that react by detonation are called high explosives; they are used in bombs and artillery shells and for blasting operations in mines and quarries.

Other characteristics

Apart from the velocity of explosion or detonation, the essential properties of chemical explosives are explosion temperature, sensitivity, and power. It is possible to measure absolute values of power and sensitivity for some explosives, such as gunpowder, nitrate mixtures, and nitro compounds; for other explosives, it is more usual to compare their power and sensitivity with picric acid (trinitrophenol, $C_6H_2(NO_3)_3OH$). Picric acid is assigned stability and power values of 100; more sensitive explosives have stability values less than 100, and more powerful explosives have power values greater than 100.

Sensitive detonating explosives, with stability values around 20, are used to initiate explosions. The shock waves can set off intermediary charges with stability values around 60, which in turn initiate the reactions in stable main charges.

Modern explosives

Modern explosives are of three main types: those based on unstable molecules, such as mercury fulminate and lead azide; those based on ammonium nitrate and the organic nitrate esters, such as nitrocellulose, nitroglycerine, and pentaerythritol tetranitrate (PETN); and those based on organic nitro compounds, such as picric acid, trinitrotoluene (TNT), tetryl, and RDX.

Unstable molecules

The molecules of certain solid substances can undergo rearrangement reactions to form gases. Such reactions release heat and large volumes of gas—the basic constituents of an explosion—and are readily triggered by mechanical shock or heat.

Mercury fulminate ($Hg(OCN)_2$) is used to make detonating caps. As can be seen from its formula, the gaseous products of the explosion include nitrogen and oxides of carbon. Lead azide ($Pb(N_3)_2$) is another detonating material; it produces nitrogen gas when it explodes.

Nitrate explosives

Ammonium nitrate (NH_3NO_3) and organic compounds that contain the nitrate group ($-ONO_2$) are capable of exploding because their molecules are self-sufficient in oxygen for the burning process. This means they do not require air to penetrate the explosive mass in order to burn. Nitrate mixtures are widely used for blasting pur-

poses, where their low cost and ease of handling are advantageous. In many cases, these mixtures are used as gels or slurries with water; TNT, which improves detonating properties; and gelling agent. The mix is poured into boreholes and ignited by a fuse.

The earliest nitrate explosive was guncotton, made by a German chemist, Christian Schönbein, in 1845 by nitrating cotton using a mixture of nitric and sulfuric acids. It consists mainly of nitrocellulose, $(C_6H_7O_2(NO_3)_3)_n$, but the fibrous nature of cotton hinders complete nitration, and a substantial quantity of the dinitrate is also present. The exact properties of the explosive depend on the amounts of dinitrate and trinitrate in the mix.

The manufacture of guncotton was blighted by frequent accidental explosions until 1875, when Sir Frederick Abel devised a method of pulping cotton to give a more stable product. Guncotton is easily gelled by solvents, when it can be pressed into shapes such as cords, flakes, or tubes. It is sensitive when dry—its stability rating is around 23—but less so when wet, when its stability value increases to around 120 relative to picric acid. The detonation velocity is around 24,000 ft. per sec. (7,300 m/s) for dry guncotton, falling to around 18,000 ft. per sec. (5,500 m/s) when wet.

In 1846, one year after the invention of guncotton, an Italian chemist, Ascanio Sobrero, prepared nitroglycerine by treating glycerol ($C_3H_5(OH)_3$) with a mixture of nitric and sulfuric acids. Nitroglycerine ($CH_2(NO_3)CH(NO_3)CH_2(NO_3)$) was a powerful liquid explosive, but its usefulness was limited by its great instability. Then in 1865, the Swedish chemist Alfred Nobel found that the liquid could be used safely if it was first absorbed into kieselguhr, a diatomaceous earth that consists of the fossilized remains of single-celled algae. Nobel named this product dynamite. By mixing 8 percent nitrocellulose with 92 percent nitroglycerine, he produced a stable semisolid gel, which he called blasting gelatin.

Nitroglycerine has a detonation velocity of 25,400 ft. per sec. (7,750 m/s), a power rating of 160, and an explosion temperature of around 8000°F (4400°C).

▼ Two methods for igniting an explosive charge. The electric detonator in the upper picture is connected to a distant explosive charge by twin cables. When the plunger drops, a current causes a spark at the far ends of the cables that ignites the charge. The lower picture shows a fuse that burns at a controlled rate, allowing time to take cover before the blast.

Pentaerythritol tetranitrate, or PETN, $C(CH_2NO_3)_4$, is a sensitive explosive (40) with a high power rating (166) and a detonation velocity of 26,500 ft. per sec. (8,100 m/s). It has a small critical diameter, and thus can sustain a detonation over great distances when packed at low filling densities in a detonating cord. PETN is also widely used as an intermediary charge.

One of the cheapest and most widely used high-explosive nitrate mixtures is ANFO (ammonium nitrate fuel-oil mixture) and a water-based ammonium-nitrate gel. These two types of explosives were developed in the 1950s and now supply more than 70 percent of the total demand for high explosives in the United States.

Nitro explosives

Nitro explosives are organic compounds that contain the nitro group ($-NO_2$). The first nitro explosive, picric acid, was prepared in 1771 by nitrating phenol (C_6H_5OH). It was not used as an explosive until around a century later, when it was found that a mercury fulminate cap could initiate its explosion. Picric acid is more stable than nitrocellulose or nitroglycerine but just as powerful. It withstands the shock of discharge from a gun, and in 1888, it replaced gunpowder as a shell filling.

TNT, $C_6H_2CH_3(NO_2)_3$, is made by reacting toluene with a nitrating mixture of nitric and sulfuric acids. Its sensitivity is 110, its power rating 95, and its detonation velocity 23,000 ft. per sec. (7,000 m/s). It is cheap and easy to make. Mixtures of TNT with ammonium nitrate—the amatols—are widely used to fill shells and bombs, as are mixtures with tetryl.

Tetryl (N-methyl-2,4,6,N-tetranitroaniline, $C_6H_2(NCH_3NO_2)(NO_3)_3$) is related to TNT. It requires careful extraction and preparation for use as an explosive, as it is powdery and toxic. It has a detonation velocity of 24,000 ft. per sec. (7,300 m/s), a power value of 120, and a sensitivity of 70. These characteristics make it useful as an intermediary for transferring a detonating shock wave from a detonator to a less sensitive main charge.

RDX, $(CH_2N \cdot NO_2)_3$, also called Hexogen or Cyclonite, was discovered in 1899 by Henning, a German chemist. Produced by nitrating hexamethylenetetramine, RDX is a very powerful explosive (167) with a high velocity of detonation, 27,500 ft. per sec. (8,400 m/s) and a moderate sensitivity of 55. Mixtures of RDX with TNT and aluminum are among the most powerful chemical explosives, and mixtures of RDX with various oils and plasticizers are useful plastic explosives.

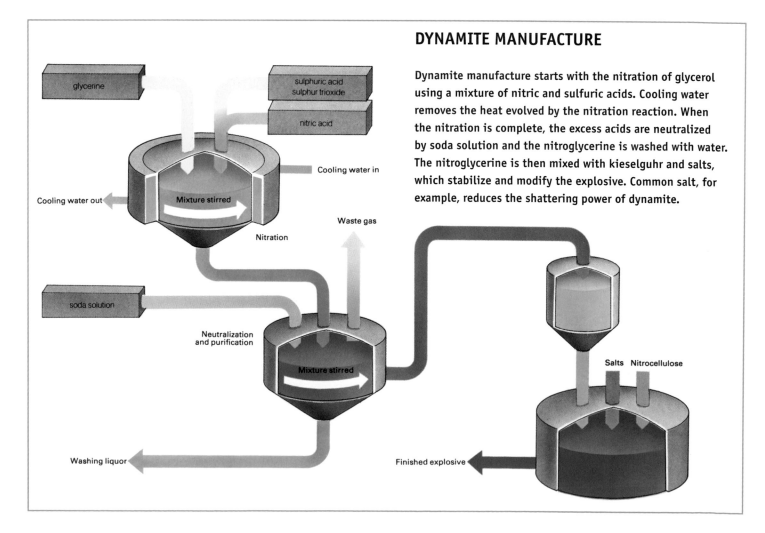

DYNAMITE MANUFACTURE

Dynamite manufacture starts with the nitration of glycerol using a mixture of nitric and sulfuric acids. Cooling water removes the heat evolved by the nitration reaction. When the nitration is complete, the excess acids are neutralized by soda solution and the nitroglycerine is washed with water. The nitroglycerine is then mixed with kieselguhr and salts, which stabilize and modify the explosive. Common salt, for example, reduces the shattering power of dynamite.

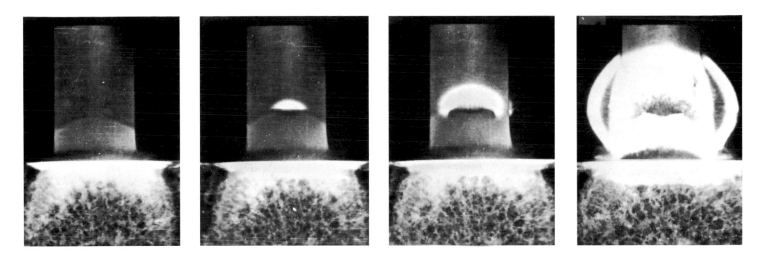

Nonchemical explosives

The two types of devices that do not use explosive chemical reactions are mechanical and nuclear explosives. Mechanical explosives are useful in coal mines, where the heat of a chemical explosion would be likely to ignite a methane explosion

▲ These frames of high-speed film show the progress of a detonation wave through a mixture of RDX and TNT. From left to right, there is an interval of two microseconds between the first three frames and then six microseconds between the third and fourth frames.

or fire. One such system consists of liquid carbon dioxide (CO_2) under pressure in a shell. The device is exploded by energizing a heating filament within the shell. The carbon dioxide vaporizes and develops a pressure that eventually ruptures the shell, releasing rapidly expanding gas without flames. Other systems use compressed air to rupture a shell.

Nuclear explosions are much more powerful than chemical or mechanical explosions, since they convert tiny amounts of mass into enormous amounts of energy. Underground nuclear explosions have been considered as a means of boosting petroleum extraction rates by fracturing rocks.

▶ This sheet-metal component consists of carbon steel with an aluminum bronze cladding. The layers were bonded together by placing them at a small separation, smearing explosive on the outer face of the bronze, then detonating the explosive to slam the bronze onto the steel. The energy of the impact forms a permanent bond between the two metal layers.

SEE ALSO: AMMUNITION • BOMB • GUN • MINE, EXPLOSIVE • MINING TECHNIQUES • QUARRYING • ROCKET AND SPACE PROPULSION

Eye

The eyes receive visual information about an organism's surroundings and pass it to the visual cortex in the brain for analysis and interpretation. Only a small area of the eyes is visible—the bulk is deeply set into the skull in hollows called orbits. For added protection, the eyelids can be closed voluntarily, to protect them against strong light, for example, or involuntarily, such as when there is sudden movement near the eye.

Blinking cleans and lubricates the eyeball by distributing fluid from the tear glands and sebaceous (fat-secreting) glands at the edges of the eyelids. The eyelids are lined with a thin layer of epithelial (membranous) tissue, which is contiguous with the front of the eye and prevents objects, such as dust and contact lenses, from slipping behind the eye. The eye will blink automatically and quickly when danger, such as a bug, approaches.

The tear glands are not strictly part of the eye. They are located in the upper part of the orbit and secrete a solution of sodium hydrogen carbonate and sodium chloride that moistens, lubricates, and cleanses the exposed area of the eye. The tear solution also contains lysozyme, an enzyme that helps to prevent infection.

The eyeball

The eyeball is completely enclosed by the sclera, or white of the eye—a tough, opaque outer layer made up of inelastic tissue that keeps the eye in shape. The front of the sclera is the cornea, a transparent disk that lets in and refracts (bends) light. Stimulation of nerve endings in the cornea causes tear production and reflex blinking and also makes the cornea sensitive to pain.

The inside of the sclera, but not the cornea, is lined by the choroid, a pigmented layer with many blood vessels. The black pigment reduces reflection of light inside the eye. At the front, the choroid is modified to form the iris, which is opaque and pigmented. The pigmentation ranges from none, as in pink-eyed albinos, to dark brown.

The iris opens and closes to vary the size of the pupil, which lets light through into the eye. The movement is controlled by involuntary muscles in the iris that respond to light levels; a high level of light causes the pupil to contract and restrict the amount of light passing through, and a low-intensity light causes the pupil to dilate to maximize the amount of light gathered.

The eyeball is divided into two parts—the anterior (front) and the posterior (rear), which is three times larger. The anterior eyeball contains

◄ Owls have tubular eyes that are deeper than they are wide. The cornea is huge, and the iris is capable of immense expansion and contraction, enabling owls to hunt at night.

the aqueous humor, a thin, liquid blood plasma that carries the supply of oxygen and nutrients to the lens and cornea. The aqueous humor is produced by the ciliary body, a thickened part of the choroid containing muscles, large blood vessels, and glands. The aqueous humor exerts a pressure of about 0.5 psi (25 mm of mercury) to keep the cornea and lens in shape.

The lens itself divides the anterior and posterior parts of the eye. It is a biconvex, transparent body attached by the suspensory ligament to the ciliary body. The lens further refracts the light and focuses it on the retina. The muscles in the ciliary body alter the shape of the lens, enabling it to focus on near or distant objects. The lens is made up of thin fibers and epithelial cells in concentric layers like an onion. The refractive power of the lens increases toward the center.

The space behind the lens is filled with the jellylike vitreous humor, which maintains the shape of the eye and helps to further refract light. Running through the vitreous humor from the back of the eye to the lens is the hyaloid canal that, in the embryo, contained a blood vessel supplying the lens. This blood vessel disappears after birth, leaving behind the canal.

The eye and vision

If the eye is thought of as a camera, then the retina would serve as the film. The retina is a layer of light-sensitive cells on the inside of the eye. In effect, it is a continuation of the optic nerve, which enters the eyeball at the back through the sclera and choroid. There are two types of cells—rods, which are sensitive to black, white, and shades of gray, and cones, which react to color. There are about twelve million rods and seven million cones.

Rods contain a pigment (rhodopsin or visual purple) made up of retinene (obtained from vitamin A) and opsin. Light causes the rhodopsin to decompose into its constituent parts and stimulates the nerve leading from the rod into the optic nerve and then to the visual cortex, where rhodopsin re-forms. Very little light is needed to stimulate the rods, so they are particularly important for night vision. The cones, however, need high levels of light to work, so, at night, colors appear muted or absent.

There are three types of cones—the first is sensitive to red, the second to green, and the third to blue. Colors are perceived according to which cones are stimulated by the wavelength of the light entering the eye. Cones are concentrated in one particular part of the eye—the macula—a small hollow in the middle of the retina and the point at which most light falls when the eye is at rest.

The center of the macula, the fovea, is packed with cone cells and is the area of sharpest vision. Cones diminish in concentration toward the edges of the retina. There are no light-sensitive

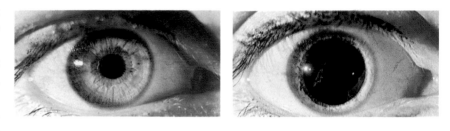

cells at the point where the optic nerve leaves the eye; this point is termed the blind spot. It does not appear as a blank in the image, because one eye compensates for the other and the image is projected onto the fovea.

Light is focused on the retina by accommodation, which varies the shape of the lens. To view a distant object, muscles in the ciliary body relax, tightening the suspensory ligament and stretching the lens to make it thinner. When viewing a close object, the ciliary muscles contract, the suspensory ligament relaxes and the lens thickens and shrinks.

Light from an object falls on the retina as a focused image, which stimulates the rod and cone nerve cells. This image is smaller than life size and upside down. The stimulation travels to the brain, which perceives the image the right way up and the correct size. Together, the two eyes send the brain a stereoscopic view, which gives the image depth and helps the brain to judge distance.

▲ In bright light (left) the muscles of the iris contract, causing the pupil to shrink. In dim light (right), the iris relaxes and so allows the pupil to expand.

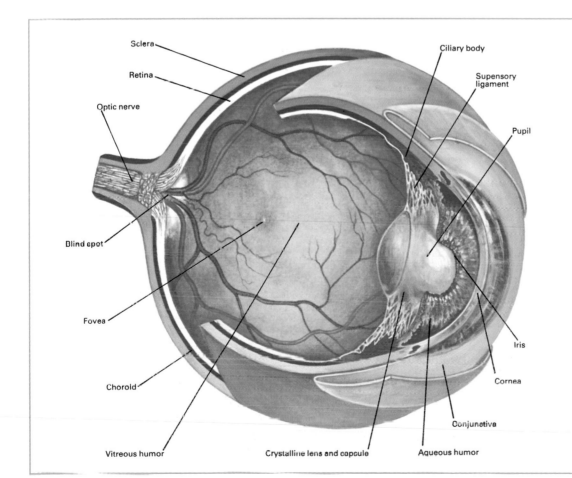

Sclera

Retina

Optic nerve

Blind spot

Fovea

Choroid

Vitreous humor

Crystalline lens and capsule

Aqueous humor

Conjunctiva

Cornea

Iris

Pupil

Supensory ligament

Ciliary body

EYEBALL

The eyeball, together with the muscles that control eye movement, blood vessels, nerves, and the lacrimal gland are lodged in a bony socket in the skull. The pupil determines the amount of light let into the eye by the contraction of the iris. Behind the iris, the aqueous humor nourishes the cornea and has little effect on light rays; it is renewed every four hours. The light rays pass through the lens, which refracts them to focus on the retina.

Quantifying vision

Vision is measured against a theoretical "normal" eye rated as 20/20 (or 6/6, the same formula expressed in meters). An eye with 20/20 vision can see at 20 ft. (6 m) what the normal eye can see at 20 ft. Two 20/20 eyes, and the ability to see a three-dimensional image, is normal. In practice, eyes can be above average. For example, a 20/13 (6/4) eye can see at 20 ft. (6m) what a normal eye can see only if it is within 13 ft. (4 m). Usually, adults' eyes are below average. A 20/30 (6/10) eye, for example, has to be at 20 ft. (6m) before it can see what a normal eye can see from 30 ft. (10 m).

Common eye defects

The most obvious eye defect to the onlooker is strabismus, or a squint. Each eyeball has six muscles between the sclera and the back of the orbit. These muscles are arranged in opposing pairs—the superior and inferior rectus, which allow the eye to look up and down, the superior and interior oblique, which rotate the eye, and the medial and lateral rectus, which turn the eye from side to side.

The brain coordinates these muscles so that they move together. In some individuals they are not properly coordinated, and one eye may "point" in an entirely different direction from the other. If uncorrected, this condition is serious, especially in the very young.

Myopia (nearsightedness) and hyperopia (farsightedness) are caused by a slight defect in the shape of the eyeball. In myopia, the light is focused at a point in front of, or short of, the retina, blurring the image on the retina. In hyperopia, the image reaches the retina before it is focused. Effectively, the image is focused behind the retina—the focus is too long and consequently the image is blurred.

Astigmatism is a defect in the cornea. If the cornea is not perfectly hemispherical, light rays do not come together at a single point on the retina, as they should, and there are two points of focus, causing blurred vision.

Presbyopia is the farsightedness associated with aging. It is caused by a loss of elasticity by the lens of the eye. As the muscles age, they become less efficient at accommodating the eye, so objects have to be held farther away from the eye to bring them into focus. All these defects are correctable, usually with prescription glasses or contact lenses.

Another common eye defect is the progressive visual impairment caused by cataracts—a whitish clouding of the crystalline lens. Usually, however, vision may be improved by surgical removal of the cataract.

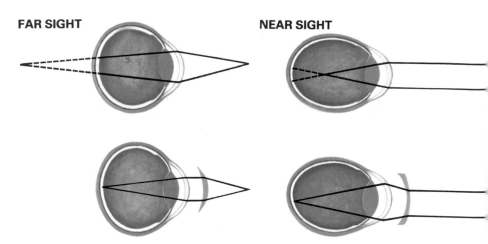

FAR SIGHT   **NEAR SIGHT**

Nonhuman eyes

The eyes of vertebrates are similar, differing only in small details, such as the shape of the lens. Within vertebrates, the main difference is between primates, who can see color, and the rest, who are thought not to be able to see color.

Some creatures, such as birds, cats, rabbits, and alligators, have a third eyelid, the nictitating membrane. It is transparent and can close over the whole of the exposed part of the eye, cleaning and protecting with little or no loss of vision. When closed, the membrane is situated in the bottom corner of the eye nearest the nose.

Compound eyes

Many kinds of arthropod (including shrimp, spiders, and insects) have compound eyes made up of hundreds of individual ommatidia, or optical units, which refract light and pass information to the optic nerve. The eye is roughly hemispherical. On the surface is the cornea equivalent—the cuticular lens. Below this lens are the vitrellae—four cells with transparent, refractive inner edges that form a crystalline cone. The cells below them are the retinulae. These, too, have refractive inner edges and contain the visual purple pigment.

The retinulae are the receptor cells and project down into an optic ganglion, which is connected to the large optic nerve that goes to the brain. A large number of facets in a compound eye give it a large field of vision. The extent to which creatures with compound eyes see is uncertain, but probably some can differentiate shapes and color. The main function of this type of eye seems to be to distinguish between intensities of light. Many arthropods have ocelli, or simple eyes, which are little more than light-sensitive spots.

▲ Farsightedness (top left) is the inability to focus close objects on the retina, owing to the eyeball being too short. The focal point occurs behind the retina, resulting in a blurred image. Farsightedness can be corrected by using glasses that bring the focus of the image forward onto the retina (bottom left). Nearsightedness (top right) occurs when the eyeball is too long and light rays from a distant object are focused in front of the retina. Glasses may also correct nearsightedness, by moving the focus of the image back onto the retina (bottom right).

 SEE ALSO: Brain • Contact lens • Enzyme • Light and optics • Ophthalmology • Optometry • Spectacles

Fabric Printing

Fabric printing probably originated in India between 2,000 and 2,500 years ago: the Greek geographer and writer Strabo reported the printing of cotton cloth in India around the start of the first millennium. The traditional Indian technique uses cut wooden blocks to transfer dye to fabric in regularly repeating patterns. Stencils are known to have been used for printing designs in China as long ago as the eighth century B.C.E. Most modern printing techniques are automated developments of block or stencil printing. Some printing is still done by hand using blocks; this technique can offer high-quality results for small print runs, but it is laborious and expensive.

Roller printing

The most widely applied printing technique is intaglio, or gravure, roller printing. This method uses a metal roller, often called a gravure roller, engraved with pits in the form of the design that is to be applied. The gravure roller is supplied by a furnishing roller, which dips into a trough that contains the dye mixture. An accurately ground and finely adjusted metal strip, called a doctor blade, scrapes the surface of the gravure roller before it comes into contact with the fabric. This blade has the dual function of ensuring that each pit receives dye and that the unetched parts of the roller's surface are free of dye.

As the roller rotates further, its surface comes into contact with the fabric, backed by a pressure cylinder. The pressure between the gravure roller and the fabric helps ensure an even transfer of dye to the fabric. A second doctor blade then removes any lint or fibers that the gravure roller might have picked up from the fabric before its surface comes into contact with the furnishing roller to receive more dye for another print.

While gravure printing can offer excellent results, the engraved metal gravure rollers are expensive. This fact and the fact that a separate roller is necessary for each color of a design make the process economically viable only when large quantities of fabric are to be printed.

Furthermore, a number of careful adjustments have to be made before each run: the doctor blades must be perfectly flush against the roller, the viscosity of the dye must be low enough to allow good transfer but not so low as to let the dye bleed from the printed areas, and the pressure of the pressure cylinder must be adequate for effective dye transfer. If more than one color is to be printed, the movement of the fabric through the printing machine must be adjusted such that

the position of each color component coincides with the others. Considerable lengths of fabric can be wasted during initial adjustments, so many thousands of yards (meters) of fabric must be printed in order to compensate for initial losses.

In relief roller printing, the surface of the printing roller is engraved such that raised parts of the design transfer dye to the fabric. In the relief-roller process, the amount of dye transferred depends on the thickness of the dye layer on the roller that furnishes the printing roller.

Screen printing

In screen printing, the pattern to be printed is produced on a fine mesh of a strong material, such as nylon, polyester, or metal, stretched tightly over a rectangular frame. The mesh is prepared by coating it with a photosensitive resin, then exposing to light those parts of the mesh where dye is not intended to transfer to the fabric. Subsequent washing leaves the exposed parts of the screen sealed and clears resin from the unexposed parts. The original process used a solid stencil or wax coating to form a similarly masked mesh—hence the term *silk-screen printing*.

▲ Traditional Indian printing using a carved wooden block. Each color of the pattern must be applied separately, taking great care to apply each block in the correct place.

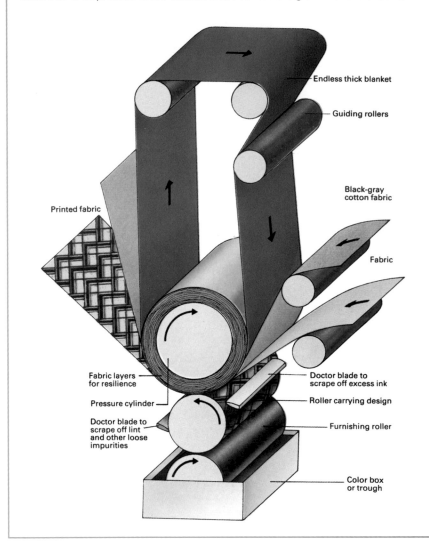

▼ An intaglio, or gravure, roller-printing machine uses an engraved roller to transfer dye to a fabric in the pattern of the engraved design. The dye is supplied from a trough at the bottom of the machine. A furnishing roller rotates in the trough and transfers dye to the engraved gravure roller. A doctor blade scrapes the surface of the gravure roller, leaving dye in its pits. Transfer occurs in the gap between the upper pressure roller and the gravure roller. A looped blanket and a strip of backing fabric assist the passage of the fabric through the machine and ensure an even pressure at the contact area between the gravure and the fabric.

Endless thick blanket

Guiding rollers

Black-gray cotton fabric

Printed fabric

Fabric

Fabric layers for resilience

Doctor blade to scrape off excess ink

Pressure cylinder

Roller carrying design

Doctor blade to scrape off lint and other loose impurities

Furnishing roller

Color box or trough

To print, the framed screen is placed on the cloth to be printed and a band of dye mixture is poured along one inner edge of the frame. A tough rubber blade, called a squeegee, then traverses the frame, forcing dye mixture through the open parts of the screen onto the fabric below. The frame is then lifted and the fabric removed.

In the manual process, now rarely used, cloth is fastened to a long table and operators move the screens along one frame's length at a time using a different screen for each color component. In mechanical systems, an endless belt carries the cloth through static frames; the screens are lowered, the printing stroke made by mechanical squeegee, and the screens lifted to permit the cloth to advance by one pattern repeat.

Screen preparation is cheap, and initial adjustments are rapid compared with roller printing, but screen printing is much slower than roller printing for long production runs. Screen printing is also limited to open designs, since unbroken patterns would reveal the overlaps between frames.

Transfer printing

Transfer printing is the most appropriate method for high-quality printing in small batches. The process uses waxy inks that sublime, or vaporize, from solid at around 390°F (200°C). The design is first printed on paper using a device that sublimes the dye into place as it crosses the paper. Once printed, the paper with the design is placed face down on the fabric to be printed and clamped in a hot press. The heat of the press causes the design to transfer from paper to fabric.

The advantage of dye sublimation and transfer is that it is an extremely flexible process, capable of producing one-off prints by using a computer-driven dye-sublimation printer to produce the design for transfer. The disadvantages of the process are the high cost of its raw materials and its slowness for high-volume printing.

Additional treatments

The dye mixtures used for most printing jobs consist of the dye itself, water or some other solvent, and a thickening agent, such as a gum or starch. The thickening agent prevents the dye mixture from spreading during printing so that the sharp edges of a design are maintained. After printing, the fabric is dried and the color fixed, usually by passing through a large steam chamber. Some combinations of dye and fiber require high-pressure steam to fix them. Some dyes must be oxidized to obtain the correct shade, and the fabric must be thoroughly washed to remove the thickener together with surplus dye. These postprint treatments are of vital importance for the development of dye color and fastness.

In some cases, a pigment-and-resin blend, rather like paint, is used as the coloring paste. The resin holds the pigment to the fabric, and its tenacity is developed by a short heat treatment—typically four minutes at 266°F (130°C).

In resist printing, where a dye-repellent substance is "printed" onto a fabric to produce a reverse design, the fabric must be dyed after the resist coating has been printed. Then, after the dye has been fixed, the resist coating, which is often a form of wax, is washed out using solvent.

SEE ALSO: CLOTHING MANUFACTURE • DYEING PROCESS • FIBER, NATURAL • FIBER, SYNTHETIC • INK • PRINTING

Fastener, Clothes

The fashion for buttoned boots in the 19th century prompted the U.S. engineer and part-time inventor Whitcomb Judson to invent an alternative type of fastener, based on the hook-and-eye principle that could be fastened by hand or with a movable guide. It was patented in 1893, and over the next 12 years, Judson took out several patents for improved designs.

It was a brilliant idea, but in practice the fastener had an annoying tendency to spring open. Also, fasteners had to be hand manufactured because the development of suitable machines proved too difficult.

In 1905, Judson invented another type of fastener that had the individual elements attached to a tape instead of each other as in a chain. In spite of this improvement, the design was still not satisfactory. Gideon Sundback, a Swedish electrical engineer who had been employed by Judson's company, set about improving the design. In 1913 he invented the hookless fastener, in which the individual elements, or teeth, were identical and interchangeable. He also invented machines to stamp out those parts and attach them to the tape.

Hookless fasteners were first used on garments in 1918, when a clothing manufacturer with a contract to supply flying suits ordered several thousand. The usefulness of fasteners began to catch on, and in 1923, B. F. Goodrich put fasteners on their galoshes. The name itself did not appear until 1926, when an enthusiastic marketing man demonstrating the fastener's advantages declared, "zip it's open, zip it's closed."

Modern designs

Modern zippers consist of a series of teeth clamped along the edge of a strong textile tape, which are interlocked with another series of teeth on a tape opposite by means of a slider. A stop is fitted at the bottom of each tape to prevent the slider from slipping off.

Each tooth has a small protrusion on its upper face and a hollow on its lower face. Teeth on opposite tapes are staggered so that the protrusion of one fits into the hollow of the opposite tooth on the adjoining tape. The teeth are interlocked by the slider, which consists of two channels that diverge at the top and converge at the bottom. It works by splaying the teeth out as it runs, allowing the head of a tooth to pass throught the gap between a pair of teeth opposite, and vice versa. They are interlocked by the narrow part of the slide, drawing them together in precise contact. The working components of

the zipper may be made of either metal or nylon, and some zippers are designed so that the slide may be disengaged from one side at the bottom to allow the article to be opened out flat. Some types of zipper do not have individual teeth but instead consist of a fine plastic spiral of loops that interlock.

Another innovative fastener is hook and loop tape, generally known by its trademark name, Velcro. Invented in 1951 by a Swiss inventor, George de Mestral, after he noticed how burrs stuck to his pants when out walking, it consists of two nylon tapes. The loop tape is soft and fuzzy, while the hook tape has stiff little hooks. De Mestral discovered that when nylon was molded under infrared light it formed indestructible hooks. When pressed together the two tapes mesh but can easily be ripped apart. Hook and loop tape has found a wide range of applications, from shoes and diapers to space suits, clothing, and blood pressure cuffs.

▼ The zipper's teeth are clamped to a tape and shaped to prevent them from pulling apart when parallel—the protrusion on the teeth of one side fit into the hollow of the teeth on the other. The slider curves the line of teeth so that they can join or separate. The working components of the zipper are made of metal or nylon.

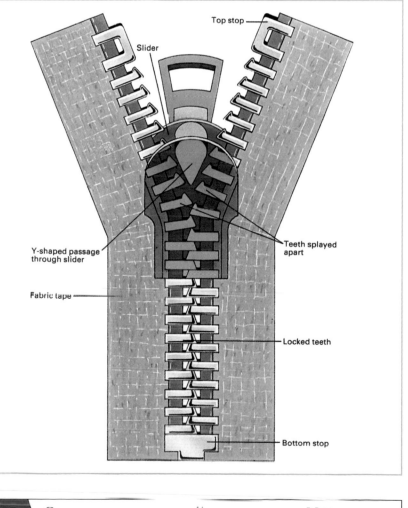

Top stop

Slider

Y-shaped passage through slider

Fabric tape

Teeth splayed apart

Locked teeth

Bottom stop

SEE ALSO: CLOTHING MANUFACTURE • FIBER, SYNTHETIC • METAL • PLASTICS • TEXTILE

Fat

◀ Dairy products are a major source of dietary fat. Although there has been a trend in recent years toward low-fat products, teenagers and young children need a certain amount of fat in their diet to help their bodies to grow. Removing fat from dairy products also removes some vitamins and trace elements that are fat soluble. Often, these are added back into the product after the fat has been removed.

Fats are an important part of a living organism's diet, providing twice as much usable energy, weight for weight, as glucose. They are found in many foods, notably meat, milk products (such as butter and cheese), nuts, and some fruits, such as olives, avocados, and bananas.

Chemical composition

Chemically, fats are compounds of one molecule of glycerol (glycerine) and three molecules of a fatty acid. The chemical formula for glycerol is $CH_2(OH)CH(OH)CH_2(OH)$.

Fats are formed when the three hydroxyl (OH) groups are replaced by fatty acids. The fat produced depends on the fatty acid that combines with the glycerol and whether all OHs are replaced by the same fatty acid. For example, in the fat tripalmitin—$C_3H_5(C_{15}H_{31}COO)_3$—the same palmitic acid radical ($C_{15}H_{31}COO$) replaced the hydroxyl groups. This fat is termed a simple glyceride. Most natural fats, however, are mixed glycerides, combining radicals from two or three acids.

Fats are often referred to as being saturated or unsaturated. Saturated fats have a greater proportion of hydrogen atoms than do unsaturated fats. Generally, fats that contain greater amounts of saturated fatty acids are solid at normal temperatures, whereas those with greater amounts of unsaturated fatty acids tend to be much softer or even liquid, as is olive oil. In fact, the distinction

between fats and oils is largely physical: glycerides are termed fats if they are solid at 68°F (20°C), and oils if they are liquid at this temperature.

Fat and energy

In the body, fats are digested with the aid of enzymes called lipases, which break them down into the component fatty acids and glycerol. Some of the fatty acids are used at once to provide the body with energy and others are reconverted into fats and stored in specialized fat cells. In warm-blooded animals, these fat cells accumulate around the major organs, particularly the heart and kidneys, and in the mesentery—the lining membrane that holds the intestines in place. Fat cells are also deposited in large quantities in the dermis (the deep layer of the skin) as adipose tissue, where it provides an effective insulator against heat loss.

In humans, skin fat can be responsible for up to one-fifth of body weight, particularly in females, who have a thicker, better-developed fat layer. Marine mammals, such as whales, have an enormously thick layer of adipose tissue (blubber) to protect them from the cold sea. Warm-blooded animals that hibernate lay down large reserves of fat while they are active, and this fat keeps their bodily functions working throughout their winter sleep.

In animals with a variable blood temperature (cold-blooded animals), body temperature is dependent on the ambient air or water temperature. The need for such animals to conserve body heat is not so great, so they store fat in the liver, rather than under the skin, and in the fat bodies or fingerlike structures in the abdomen.

Fats, particularly animal fats, are important sources of the fat-soluble vitamins A, D, E, and K. Vegetarians whose diet includes no animal products may need to take vitamin supplements.

Unsaturated fats

Unsaturated fats are not firm, so in the manufacture of margarine, refined vegetable oils are partly hydrogenated, or saturated (i.e., the number of hydrogen atoms is increased), to increase the solidity. Often cultured milk, vitamins A and D, yellow vegetable dye, and flavorings are added to make a product similar to butter. Some margarines have unsaturated vegetable oils whipped in to make them high in unsaturated fat.

Soaps

Fat is a basic ingredient in the manufacture of soap. The action of sodium hydroxide or potassium hydroxide on fats produces hydrolysis, or saponification, giving soap with glycerol as a by-product. Soaps made with potassium hydroxide and stearic, palmitic, and oleic fatty acids are highly soluble in water, producing soft soaps that are frequently sold as shaving creams.

Sodium-based soaps are harder and are sold as toilet soaps, usually with perfumes and germicides added. Some soaps used for scouring have an abrasive, such as pumice, added. Glycerol, the reaction by-product, is used to make explosives (glycerol trinitrate), plastics, pharmaceuticals, and antifreeze.

▲ Some scientists suspect that fatness may be inherited through a person's genes, though passing on family eating and exercise habits may also contribute.

◄ A giant mincer making soap noodles. Soaps are made by a reaction of fatty acids with caustic soda, and recirculated lye. The particular fatty acids used determine the soap's properties.

Obesity

The Western diet is typically high in animal fats and has been implicated as a major cause of heart disease. Excess intake of fat leads to obesity, which puts extra strain on the heart and increases the concentration of fats in the blood. High concentration causes deposition of fat on the inner lining of artery walls, causing a thickening of the walls and a consequent narrowing of the vessel—a condition called atherosclerosis. The consequent roughening of the normally smooth walls and reduction in blood flow can be dangerous, especially if it occurs in the coronary arteries, and can lead to a heart attack. Strongly implicated in the causes of this disease is a high level of cholesterol, a product of the breakdown of fat—especially saturated animal fats.

Fat-reducing plants

A study in 1999 by the U.S. Department of Agriculture suggested that people who adopt a low-fat diet to reduce cholesterol might lower it more by consuming a soybean extract with high levels of substances called plant sterols. Volunteers in the research study ate the soybean sterols as an ingredient in low- and reduced-fat salad dressings.

Although at an early stage, the research offered new evidence that soybean and other plant extracts containing sterols can increase the cholesterol-lowering benefits of a healthy low-fat diet. Cholesterol reductions nearly doubled in the Beltsville study's 53 volunteers, both male and female, when their low-fat diet included two daily servings (4 tablespoons total) of salad dressing containing soybean sterols. The volunteers consumed the sterols—2.2 grams, or about half a teaspoon—daily for three weeks of the six-week study period.

Plant sterols are ingredients in a number of fat-based foods on the market, including salad dressings and margarines. The potential dietary benefits of plant sterols, including cholesterol reduction, have been studied for decades. The Beltsville study was unique in being the first to examine plant sterols as an ingredient in low-fat foods and as part of a tightly controlled low-fat diet.

The soybean extracts used in the Beltsville study are compounds known as sterol esters. They have a molecular structure similar to that of cholesterol. It is believed by the researchers that sterol esters most likely lower cholesterol by limiting its intestinal absorption.

SEE ALSO: DIGESTIVE SYSTEM • HEART • METABOLISM • NUTRITION AND FOOD SCIENCE • SOAP MANUFACTURE

Feedback

Feedback is encountered in systems and devices that have an input to them and works by returning part of the output to the system to modify the input in some way. When one part of a process is coupled to an earlier stage in the same process, a feedback loop is established that can be used to monitor the process and make any adjustment that may be necessary.

Although of great importance in engineering systems and electronic circuits in particular, feedback is a word commonly used in social contexts to indicate this process of readjustment. For example, a broadcasting company may obtain "feedback" from viewers or listeners on a pro-gram it has transmitted that will affect the nature of future broadcasts. Also, a teacher obtains feedback from the children on teaching methods employed and may modify the curriculum accordingly. Consequently, feedback is an essential feature of teaching methods where the pupils must be informed of their progress.

A simple feedback mechanism

A thermostatically controlled heater is a simple feedback system used to control the temperature of the room to a predetermined level set on the thermostat. The thermostat turns the heater off, the room then cools down, and at a given temperature, the thermostat turns the heater back on again, and so on, maintaining the room temperature within required limits. The feedback loop in this situation is provided by the hot air traveling from the heater to the thermostat and by the thermostat connection to the switch controlling the fuel input to the heater.

Feedback in amplifiers

Feedback provides an extremely easy technique for controlling the gain (degree of amplification) of an electronic amplifier without altering any elements of the amplifier itself.

The amplifier alone has a certain fixed gain, called the open-loop gain (open loop because there is no connection from the output to the input). It is the ratio of the output amplitude to the input amplitude that caused it.

▼ The open-loop (no feedback) amplifier at the top has a gain of 60. In an amplifier that has negative feedback (bottom left), one-sixtieth of the output is subtracted from the input signal, and the overall gain is only 30. If there is positive feedback (bottom right), the overall gain is 100.

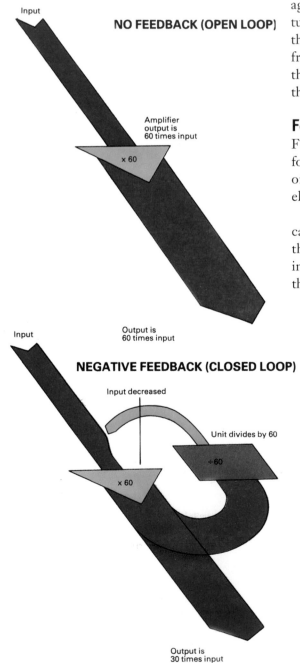

Input

NO FEEDBACK (OPEN LOOP)

Amplifier output is 60 times input

x 60

Input

Output is 60 times input

NEGATIVE FEEDBACK (CLOSED LOOP)

Input decreased

Unit divides by 60

÷60

x 60

Output is 30 times input

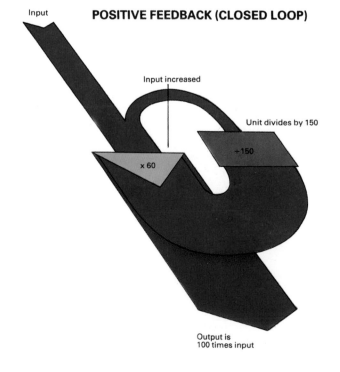

Input

POSITIVE FEEDBACK (CLOSED LOOP)

Input increased

Unit divides by 150

÷150

x 60

Output is 100 times input

When feedback is applied, a closed loop is created (from input to output back to input again). The feedback path includes an element that will allow only a certain fraction of the output amplitude back to the input. By controlling the size of this fraction, the feedback, and hence the closed-loop gain of the system, can be controlled.

Positive and negative feedback

When the feedback signal is subtracted from the original input signal, the resulting type of feedback is negative. Negative feedback systems are inherently stable because any increase in the input signal is automatically counteracted by the returning (negative) feedback signal. The closed-loop gain of such a system is therefore always less than the open-loop (no feedback) gain of the amplifier. By controlling the fraction of output to reach the input, this closed-loop gain can be controlled.

With positive feedback, the feedback signal is added to the original input. In such systems, the gain can be increased beyond the open-loop value, because the feedback signal increases the total input signal to the amplifier and a correspondingly larger output signal results.

There is, however, a limit to which the gain can be increased before the system becomes unstable. When the fraction of output reaching the input is the reciprocal of the open-loop amplifier gain (as 1/6 is the reciprocal of 6), the system "lifts itself by its own bootstraps." The output careers out of control from the size of the feedback signal alone, and no input signal is necessary. The system becomes unstable and oscillations occur—this is the principle of the oscillator.

Feedback theory played an important part in the development of radio for this very reason. Before 1913, high-frequency alternating voltages necessary for radio transmissions were impossible because alternators could not be driven at the required high speeds. Positive feedback applied to the triode valve amplifier overcame this problem and enabled medium, and shortwave frequencies to be used.

Care is needed when designing feedback loops to ensure that the feedback applied is of the desired polarity. If the signal being fed back is a regular waveform, a delay in the feedback path equal to half the period of the wave will be sufficient to turn negative feedback to positive and vice versa. Such delays may occur in circuits that contain capacitors or inductors. In some cases, the stray capacitances and inductances associated with the wires within the circuit may be enough to generate unwanted feedback.

When feedback is used for controlling large mechanical systems, it is normal to use varying amounts of three different types of feedback: proportional feedback is derived from the difference between the desired state of the output and its actual state, integral feedback is the time integral of proportional feedback, and differential feedback is derived from the rate of change of proportional feedback. While proportional control alone gives reasonably good performance, the addition of some differential feedback will increase the speed with which the output follows a change in input, and a little integral feedback will improve the accuracy of the output position when the input is static. Depending upon the relative magnitudes of these different types of feedback, the output may either approach its intended position ever more slowly, never actually achieving it (overdamped), move smoothly toward its intended position and remain there (critically damped), or overshoot and oscillate around its intended position (underdamped). When a large industrial process is being controlled, the oscillations may have a period of several days.

Atomic-force microscopy

Feedback may also be used on a minute scale in atomic-force microscopes. In this instance, feedback enables the tip of the microscope to respond to changes in force detected at the surface of the sample being scanned. The feedback helps to maintain a constant force between the tip and sample and results in topographical images of less than one angstrom resolution.

▶ When playing live, bands rely on sound engineers to monitor inputs from microphones and instruments and modify the output through feedback.

SEE ALSO: AMPLIFIER • ELECTRONICS • HI-FI SYSTEM • OSCILLATOR

Fermentation

Fermentation is a natural process used for thousands of years. Various alcoholic beverages, such as beer, wine, and whiskey, are the most well-known of fermented products. Liquids containing fruit juice, when left open to the air, might discolor and give off bubbles of gas. Milk becomes sour if left without preservative treatment, and dead organic matter changes its composition after a time. Modern science uses the life processes of yeasts, bacteria, and molds to produce chemicals and a large array of everyday products.

Microorganisms

The French microbiologist Louis Pasteur, in 1860, was the first to understand fermentation. He showed that it was directly caused by the life processes of microorganisms, including bacteria, yeasts, and molds, which feed on organic materials. Yeast and bacteria are microscopic unicellular organisms—yeasts are oval-shaped, bacteria are more diverse in shape.

When the conditions are right, yeast multiplies rapidly by a biochemical reaction that is used to advantage in the production of alcoholic beverages and bread. Bacteria multiply by binary fission—splitting apart—and are involved in a large number of different types of fermentation, including the production of cheese and vinegar. Molds are more complex microorganisms, consisting of multicellular filaments.

Organisms and energy

Usually, organisms obtain energy by breaking down sugar in the presence of oxygen into carbon dioxide and water. The reaction is

$$C_6H_{12}O_6 + 6O_2 \rightarrow 6CO_2 + 6H_2O + \text{energy}$$
glucose oxygen carbon dioxide water

Oxygen is essential for sugar to be broken down in this way. The process is called aerobic respiration. If oxygen is not available, the organisms normally suffocate and die. In some cases, however, sugar can be broken down and energy obtained without oxygen. Instead of being broken down into carbon dioxide and water, other products are made.

This kind of process without oxygen, anaerobic respiration, can occur in plants and animals. One type of anaerobic respiration breaks down sugar and produces ethanol and carbon dioxide:

$$C_6H_{12}O_6 \rightarrow 2C_2H_5OH + 2CO_2 + \text{energy}$$
glucose ethanol carbon dioxide

◀ Two antibiotic crystallization units. After fermentation, liquid antibiotic is chemically purified then concentrated and crystallized. The unit is sterilized before each batch is processed.

This process is called alcoholic fermentation or, more usually, fermentation.

Another form of anaerobic respiration is the production of lactic acid in the muscles of someone taking strenuous exercise. The process supplies energy when insufficient oxygen is taken into the body. Sugar is broken down into lactic acid and energy is released.

Anaerobic respiration does not produce as much energy as aerobic respiration. For example, fermentation does not break down sugar completely—a considerable amount of energy remains locked up in the alcohol, which may be released by burning. In aerobic respiration, the sugar is broken down completely. Though inefficient, anaerobic respiration is a way of surviving in oxygen-scarce environments.

Wine making

Fresh yeast looks like putty. In the wild, yeast grows on the surface of fruit and feeds on sugar. Essentially, sugar, water, and yeast are the only ingredients needed for making alcohol. In wine making, a process going back more than 4,000 years, the sugar is usually provided by the juice from crushed grapes. The juice contains sugar and wild yeast. As time progresses, the yeast feeds on the sugar, turning it gradually into alcohol.

The alcohol produced when making wine is always the same, but every wine has its own distinct flavor, depending on the type of grape and the exact conditions under which fermentation takes place. In most vineyards, grapes are harvested in traditional fashion, by hand, so that defective fruit can be discarded at once. However, the more reliable crops of the French Midi and California, where the climate is predictable, can be picked mechanically.

Vines require skillful pruning and training to make them suited to the latitude of the vineyard, the steepness of its hillside, and the microclimate involved. This process ensures the optimum number of high-quality grapes. Propagating wine-growing vines resembles the propagation of roses, by rooting cuttings and grafting and keeping young plants in the nursery before transfer out to the vineyard. Wine making is not just restricted to grape-derived sugar, however. Wines can be made from berries, fruits, or flowers.

Fermentation is usually carried out in a large, closed vessel fitted with a valve to allow carbon dioxide to escape and prevent air or airborne bacteria from entering and corrupting the wine. Traditionally these vessels were made of wood, but today they may also be made of steel or cement lined with epoxy resin, tile, or glass. To keep the yeast active, the vessel is maintained at temperatures between 40 and 50°F (5 and 10°C).

New methods of cultivation, harvesting, and fermentation are under constant research both in the traditional wine-making European countries—France, Germany, Italy, and Spain—and in the new world of wine—the Americas, South Africa, and Australia. The latest technology in wine making serves to adjust the natural process of production, frequently shortening the time involved. For example, in the carbon maceration of black grapes, the fruit is placed in a carbon dioxide atmosphere, which kills plant material in the grape skins and enables the color to dissolve into the juice, thus shortening the vinification process by several weeks.

Beer making

Beer making, or brewing, is a similar process to wine making. Various cereals are brewed with hops, which give the product a bitter taste. The important ingredient is barley. The grain is malted and mashed with water, then yeast is added, and the fermentation starts, converting the malt sugar into pure alcohol.

Alcohol is poisonous in large quantities. Beyond a certain concentration, it kills the yeast and stops the fermentation. For this reason, beer and wine never contain more than about 14 per-

cent alcohol. Spirits, such as whiskey, gin, and vodka need to be distilled after fermentation to achieve up to 60 percent alcohol.

Bread making

Alcohol is not the only useful product when yeast breaks down sugar. The carbon dioxide given off is an important ingredient in baking. A mixture of sugar and yeast is added to the dough, and the whole is left for about an hour in a warm place for the yeast to ferment the sugar. As the yeast cells multiply, they give off carbon dioxide gas, making the dough rise. During this period, alcohol is produced in the dough, but it evaporates when the bread is baked.

Enzymes

Enzymes are the active constituents in fermentation (the word enzyme means "in yeast"). Usually, they can be extracted from the host microorganism and work just as effectively when separated from the yeast cells. They can be thought of as biochemical catalysts—having a role in organic reactions similar to that of a catalyst in inorganic reactions. In common with inorganic catalysts, enzymes produce specific chemical changes, so the correct enzyme must be used in a particular fermentation reaction.

There are three main enzymes in yeast—zymase, invertase, and maltase. Zymase breaks up glucose and fructose; invertase breaks up cane sugar into invert sugar (a mixture of glucose and

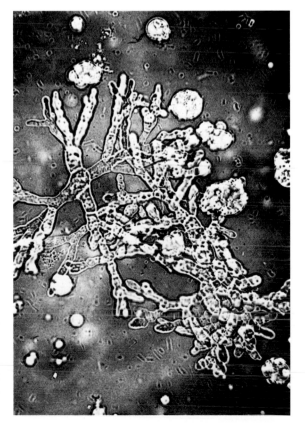

◀ The fermentation of *Penicillium chrysogenum* (magnified x750) yields penicillin G—effective in the treatment of previously resistant strains of staphylococci.

fructose); and maltase breaks up maltose into glucose. The effect of fermentation is to break up the sugar into alcohol and carbon dioxide:

$$C_6H_{12}O_6 \rightarrow 2C_2H_5O + 2CO_2$$
glucose   alcohol   carbon dioxide

The fermentation processes that produce beer are a little more complex. The cereals used are barley, flaked rice, oats, and corn. In Germany, wheat is used, and in China, rice and millet.

To make malt, barley is soaked in cold water, spread out on a floor and turned regularly for five to eight days. During this period, germination starts, and the enzyme diastase is formed. When rootlets appear, growth is stopped by heating the barley gently. Diastase converts the starch in the malt into dextrin and maltose. At a later stage, yeast is introduced. Maltose is converted into glucose by maltase, and zymase starts the alcoholic fermentation. The enzyme used to make vinegar

► In huge fermentation vats like these in a British brewery, yeast, which breaks down the malt sugars and turns them to alcohol and carbon dioxide, forms a thick, creamy layer on the surface.

◄ Mash tuns at a Guinness brewery in Dublin, Ireland, in which grain mash is heated and agitated to activate enzymes and convert starch to sugar.

is the same one that causes beer and wine to go sour when exposed to the air. The process is called acetic fermentation and is brought about by *Mycoderma aceti*. Generally, *Mycoderma aceti* finds its way from the air into weak alcoholic solutions. It lives on the nitrogenous matter in the solution and causes the alcohol to combine with oxygen from the air.

Fermentation and industry

By understanding how microorganisms function and how they interact with their environment, microbiologists can control fermentation for use in industrial processes. The production of lactic acid in 1880 was the beginning of industrial fermentation. During World War I, a fermentation process was developed to produce acetone for use in the manufacture of cordite. Today, most anti-

biotics and several important chemicals are produced by fermentation.

Industrial alcohol is an important solvent used in the synthesis of other chemicals. It can be manufactured from many different sources, including wood, wood wastes, corn, and molasses. Fermentation has been found to be an uneconomic process, but it is subsidized by some governments because of the products' importance.

Using fermentation to produce alcohol as motor fuel has been the subject of considerable controversy. Supporters argue that industrial alcohol, made from renewable biological materials, can be used to free the United States from dependence on foreign sources of petroleum. They also propose the use of surplus grain. Opponents claim that insufficient grain is available unless new technology is employed. Very pure alcohol will be needed if it is intended to mix with gasoline, requiring costly processing. Ethanol is used as an octane booster for gasoline, and, as petroleum prices rise, alcohol produced by fermentation will become economical.

Early fermentation processes yielded approximately two parts of butyl alcohol to one part of ethanol. This process used corn and the bacteria *Clostridium acetobutylicum*. Butyl alcohol became the most important product of the process, so there was a need to boost its production. Research has produced new cultures that feed on molasses, a by-product of sugar refining, producing three parts of butyl alcohol to one of acetone.

SEE ALSO: Alcohol • Beer and brewing • Biofuel • Catalyst • Enzyme • Gasoline, synthetic • Spirit • Wine making • Yeast

Fertilizer

Fertilizers are applied to the soil, or sometimes directly to the plant, to supply nutrients essential for plant growth. Fertilizer may replace these substances as they are used up by the plant or may be applied to mineral-deficient soils to make them more productive. Many nutrient chemical elements, such as the trace elements copper, boron, manganese, zinc, and silicon, are required only in minute quantities. Other elements are much more important and are needed by the plant in large quantities. These major nutrients are nitrogen, phosphorus, potassium, magnesium, calcium, iron, and sulfur, all of which are readily removed from the soil by plants, particularly under conditions of intensive cultivation. Most fertilizers are intended to replace these important nutrient elements, and their use has resulted in considerable increases in crop yields for farmers and gardeners.

Manures

Fertilizers are basically artificial mixtures of synthetic or naturally occurring substances. Manures, however, are composed of organic material, such as animal dung or various kinds of plant material. They often have the additional property of improving the texture of the soil, and giving it better water-retaining properties. Seaweed was formerly used for this purpose and is still often used to help break down heavy clay soils.

Manures contain a high proportion of nitrogen, which is essential for plant growth. Atmospheric nitrogen is normally "fixed" and made available to the plant by bacteria present either in the soil or sometimes in bacteria living in nodules on the plant roots. The plant can use the nitrogen only after it has been incorporated into a chemical compound. Most manures are produced by composting, which is a process designed to encourage bacterial breakdown of dung or plant material into a form readily used by the plant, and it is this process that results in the high nitrogen content of the manure. Composting also produces heat, which has the effect of killing weed seeds and pathogens contained within the compost material.

Modern livestock farming techniques produce huge quantities of waste material, mostly as semi-liquid cattle dung and poultry droppings, and the problem of disposal of this material without polluting the environment has led to renewed inter-

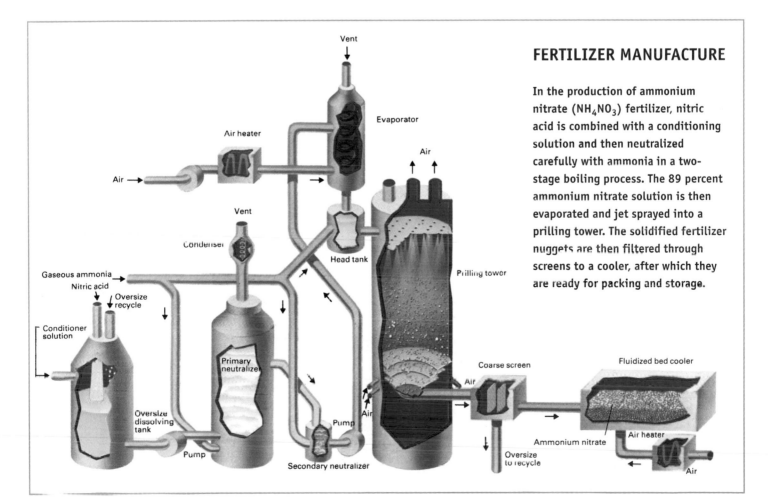

FERTILIZER MANUFACTURE

In the production of ammonium nitrate (NH_4NO_3) fertilizer, nitric acid is combined with a conditioning solution and then neutralized carefully with ammonia in a two-stage boiling process. The 89 percent ammonium nitrate solution is then evaporated and jet sprayed into a prilling tower. The solidified fertilizer nuggets are then filtered through screens to a cooler, after which they are ready for packing and storage.

est in large-scale manure production. Waste from intensive livestock operations is stored in artificial ponds or lagoons and the solid matter allowed to settle out while bacterial breakdown takes place. This nitrogen-rich solid material can then be used as agricultural manure. The sludge remaining after purification of sewage is also widely used as a manure. However, digested sludge may contain potentially harmful concentrations of lead, zinc, cadmium, arsenic, copper, mercury, nickel, selenium, and molybdenum if effluent from industrial processes has been treated at the same plant. For this reason, the use of sewage-derived fertilizers is regulated under the Clean Water Act. The U.S. Environmental Protection Agency also restricts the frequency of their application to particular times of the year.

Sometimes crops are grown especially to be plowed back into the soil as a manure. This practice is known as green manuring and is particularly effective when the manure crop is one that has nitrogen-fixing properties, such as legumes. The classic example of green manuring is the traditional European four-crop rotation method, where clover is grown every fourth year for plowing in. A further advantage is that the green manure crop acts as ground cover and can help prevent erosion.

▲ Liquid fertilizers and animal manures can be applied in a very similar manner. Here a cornfield is being treated with a diluted manure, which is sprayed out behind the tractor. However, farmers are restricted as to when and how often they can apply slurries to avoid polluting groundwater and nearby watercourses.

Manures contain variable amounts of nitrogen and may be deficient in other major nutrient elements. As a good supply of nitrogen is important to stimulate the growth of leaves, manures have been largely replaced by fertilizers in the agricultural industry, allowing the quantities of nitrogen and the other elements to be carefully and scientifically controlled by the farmer.

Fertilizers

Ammonium sulfate, $(NH_4)_2SO_4$, and ammonium nitrate, NH_4NO_3, are typical nitrogenous fertilizers. They can be prepared in large quantities quite cheaply and do not present problems in storage or applications to crops, in contrast to manures. Ammonium nitrate is produced by reacting ammonia gas with nitric acid. Ammonium sulfate can be made by reacting ammonia gas with sulfuric acid or by the reaction of calcium sulfate and a solution of ammonium carbonate.

Phosphorus is another very important element, often not present in the soil in sufficient quantities. It can be supplied in the form of bone meal, which is the powder remaining after crushing and grinding bones when other valuable chemicals have been extracted. Today phosphorus is usually applied in the form of superphosphate or triple superphosphate. Superphosphate is produced by treating naturally occurring rock phosphates with sulfuric acid and contains about 20 percent phosphorus. Triple superphosphate is manufactured by treating rock phosphate with phosphoric acid and contains nearly 50 percent phosphorus, while treatment with nitric acid produces nitrophosphates. The United States is a major producer of phosphate rocks with a production of over 35 million tons (31 million tonnes) per year. Basic slag, a by-product of steel manufacture, is another good source of phosphorus. Phosphorus is particularly important to establish good root growth and to encourage early maturity and ripening.

Potassium is necessary to encourage good growth and helps produce resistance to disease. It is usually obtained from natural potassium sulfate, K_2SO_4, or potassium chloride, KCl.

Availability to the plant

Fertilizers and manures are used by plants at different rates. Manure cannot be used by the plant until it is broken down into soluble chemicals that can be absorbed by the roots. Some liquid fertilizers, such as those used for horticultural purposes, contain only soluble nutrients, and these are absorbed and used very rapidly. Foliar, or leaf, feeds are applied to the leaves rather than the soil and are absorbed through the stomata, the tiny holes through which the plant breathes: 90 percent of a foliar feed is absorbed and used by the plant, as against only 10 percent when fertilizer is applied to the soil. Foliar feeds may also incorporate substances such as growth stimulants or trace elements that are not readily absorbed from the soil.

It is often desirable to use fertilizers in a slow-acting form so that frequent reapplication can be avoided. Like manure, most organic fertilizers containing nitrogen break down slowly in the soil and are available to the plant over a long period. Hoof and horn meal is a naturally occurring slow-acting nitrogenous fertilizer, and urea, $CO(NH_2)_2$, is a synthetic slow-acting source of nitrogen. It is often used today in the form of urea condensates, that is, combined with formaldehyde, crotonaldehyde, and isobutyraldehyde. These are, in fact, unstable resins (plastics) that break down in the soil, releasing urea.

If fertilizer is applied improperly or at the wrong time, it can be washed or leached out of the soil before it can be used by the plants. Such leaching contaminates groundwater, and the U.S. Environmental Protection Agency has been promoting the use of contaminated groundwater for irrigation in order to reduce the amount of extra fertilizer required. Leaching of fertilizers may also contaminate freshwater environments, leading to the rapid growth of algae, or algal blooms, which have the effect of deoxygenating water, resulting in the death of fish and other aquatic life.

Application to the soil or plant

Fertilizers are often compounded into granules or pellets, allowing a balanced mixture of essential nutrients to be supplied. Granules and pellets can be made that will break down at a predetermined rate to give a continuous supply of nutrients to the growing plants. Some crops need one or other of the major nutrients at different points in their growing cycles, so applications of fertilizers must be carefully timed to provide the correct nutrient balance when it is most needed.

Fertilizers and manures can be applied to the soil or plant by a wide variety of means, ranging from simple hand application to machine spreading. Manures are often scattered on the soil and then plowed in. Sometimes liquefied waste from intensive livestock units is sprayed or pumped onto the pasture as a source of nitrogen. It has been suggested that this practice may spread livestock disease and might also cause human infection with organisms and even some types of food poisoning.

Most mineral or synthetic fertilizers are applied by topdressing, or mechanical spreading on the soil, sometimes carried out on a very large scale. Such an application of superphosphate over huge areas of inaccessible land in New Zealand by means of crop-spraying aircraft resulted in a changed ecology throughout the area, making it suitable for sheep farming.

◄ The carrots on the left were fed with a liquid fertilizer containing nitrogen, phosphoric acid, potash, growth stimulants, and trace elements (including iron, boron, zinc, copper, cobalt, and magnesium). Those on the right were untreated.

SEE ALSO:

AGRICULTURAL MACHINERY • AGRICULTURE, INTENSIVE • AGRICULTURE, ORGANIC • NITROGEN • PHOSPHORUS • SOIL RESEARCH

Fiber, Mineral

Asbestos is widely used as a heat insulating, fireproof material. It is fibrous in nature, tending to disguise the fact that it is a mineral found in rock seams and obtained by mining. There are various types of asbestos, but they are all silicates of metals, such as magnesium, calcium, or sodium.

For most of its long history, asbestos has been used for making clothing, its fire resistance being regarded as a mysterious but fortunate property without being particularly well exploited. In ancient times, asbestos was used as wick material for lamps, thus accounting for its rather paradoxical derivation from the Greek word *asbeston*, which means unquenchable or inextinguishable.

The use of blue asbestos has been banned in many countries because of its danger to health. Other types of asbestos remain in use but will gradually be replaced by alternative materials when they become available.

Types of asbestos

There are two main types of asbestos. Chrysotile, or white asbestos, is the more widely used and historically longer-known variety. Its richest sources are in Canada (Quebec) and in the Ural Mountains of Russia. The other is a group known as amphibole asbestos, whose chief members are crocidolite (typically blue in color) and amosite (typically ash gray or fawn), both extensively mined in southern Africa. Chrysotile fibers tend to be shorter and softer than amphiboles and have a higher melting point (and so a greater fire resistance), which makes them particularly suit-

able for weaving into fireproof fabrics. The amphiboles, having high tensile strength, are useful as reinforcement fibers in the production of composite materials, such as asbestos cement and certain fiber-reinforced plastics.

Because research in the early 1960s revealed the health hazards associated with crocidolite (blue) asbestos, it has not been imported or used in many countries since then, and the use of amosite fiber is to a very large extent today obsolete.

Mining asbestos

Chrysotile fibers occur as seams in the soft rock serpentine, which is found close to Earth's surface. The asbestos ore is obtained by quarrying or by block caving. In the latter technique, a mass of rock is undermined so that it falls and breaks into pieces under its own weight while passing down a chute into haulage trucks below. Amphiboles, on the other hand, occur in rich but narrow seams lying at virtually any incline from horizontal to vertical, necessitating mines that may run deeper than 1,000 ft. (300 m) beneath the surface. Only about 10 percent of the ore is asbestos. In some cases, good long veins can be removed by hand, but usually the fibers have to be removed mechanically. A series of crushers deals with lumps of different sizes, the fibers being sucked out.

Uses of asbestos

Products consisting solely or chiefly of asbestos are usually made from asbestos yarn. The yarn is produced by weaving or plaiting the longer and better-quality fibers just as if they were wool or cotton. Typical products include insulating tapes, cloth, brake linings, gaskets, packings, rope, and gas filters. Fireproof gloves and clothing and theater safety curtains are also made in this way. In these applications, the material may sometimes be wire reinforced or impregnated with substances such as rubber, graphite, and resins.

The shorter fibers, shingles, are used in the production of composite materials, of which the oldest and best known is asbestos cement. It was invented in the late 19th century by the owner of a Viennese paper- and board-making plant. He found that mill board treated with a mixture of about 20 percent asbestos fiber and 80 percent cement produced a new material with many possible applications. The paper maker began to market asbestos cement in flat sheets 15 in. sq. (40 cm²) and this product more than anything created a market for asbestos.

Manufacture

The first stage in the manufacture of asbestos cement is to produce a slurry by mixing cement and asbestos fibers in water. A coating of slurry is then applied to a moving belt and the water drained off. The thin coating is transferred to a rotating cylinder where further layers are built up. When the coating is thick enough, the damp, flexible sheet can be removed and molded into the required shape. It is allowed to dry and mature for three weeks. Asbestos cement sheeting is fire resistant and weatherproof and remains one of the most widely used building materials, especially for the exterior siding of industrial and agricultural buildings. Other useful properties, such as thermal and acoustic insulation, can be improved by variations in composition, producing insulating sheet and tiles for internal wall and ceiling linings.

Pressure pipes, another important use for asbestos cement, followed quickly from the original development of the materials. Today they are commonly produced by feeding a thick asbestos slurry onto a revolving metal former, or mandrel. The slurry sticks to the outside of the mandrel, which may be up to 16 ft. (5 m) long, and is then slid off the end and oven dried.

Asbestos fibers are also used either alone or in conjunction with glass fiber for the production of reinforced plastics. Typical applications include

▶ Crocidolite, or "blue" asbestos, is no longer used because of its serious health risks.

corrosion-resistant lining in pipelines, storage vessels for chemical industry equipment, and shatterproof moldings for automobile components.

Health and safety

Despite its long history of use, especially on an increasing industrial scale since the mid-19th century, the potential health hazards associated with asbestos did not become seriously apparent until after World War II. The biggest problem in researching asbestos-related diseases is the long time lag between the first exposure through inhaling high levels of asbestos dust and the onset of disease. The time lag can range between 20 and 50 years.

The three principal diseases associated with asbestos are asbestosis, lung cancer, and mesothelioma. Asbestosis is a scarring of the lung tissue that progressively reduces the ability of the lungs to take in oxygen. Lung cancer is a malignant tumor that covers the bronchi and eventually invades the the air passages. Mesothelioma is a cancer of the pleural lining that is known to occur only after exposure to asbestos.

The rising incidence of lung disease (asbestosis) among workers who were working or had worked with asbestos from the early 1900s onward led to increasingly tougher regulations to control its use. In 1989, the U.S. Environmental Protection Agency banned many asbestos products, but in 1991, this ruling was largely overturned. Some uses of asbestos, however, remain banned, such as sprayed-on products that contain more than 1 percent asbestos, certain kinds of pipes and conduits, and various kinds of paper. In July 1999, the European Union decided to end almost all uses of asbestos in member states. This ban is expected to come into effect on January 1, 2005.

◀ In the case of protection for firefighters who are required to work in very high temperature conditions, such as oil well blowouts or aircraft accident fires, there is still little substitute for flameproof suits made of asbestos. It is still the cheapest and most durable fire-resistant material.

SEE ALSO: CEMENT MANUFACTURE • FIREFIGHTING • FLAME AND IGNITION • FLAME-RETARDING AGENT • INSULATION, THERMAL • PROTECTIVE CLOTHING

Fiber, Natural

Fibers are the raw material from which textiles are made for use in clothing, the household, floor coverings, and industry. For convenience, fibers are generally classified as being either natural or synthetic (formed by chemical processes, usually involving extrusion of the fiber).

Since 1971, world production of natural fibers has expanded only slightly, while production of synthetic fibers has increased at a slightly faster rate. While synthetic fibers have relied on petrochemical expansion, the expansion of natural fiber production relies on developments in agriculture and competition for land utilization. In 2000, the world production of cotton was estimated at 21 million tons (19 million tonnes). The estimate for jute, kenaf, and other similar fibers was a total of 2.8 million tons (2.5 million tonnes).

The use of natural fibers goes back to the Stone Age, when flax and hemp were exploited. Eventually wool, silk, and cotton fibers were utilized and were known to have been in use for several thousand years B.C.E. In medieval times, wool processing was a major occupation, but industrial processing, mainly of wool and cotton, dates from about 1750 C.E. Currently, textile fibers are made using animal, vegetable, and mineral sources.

Animal fibers

The hair of many mammals is potentially useful for producing textiles, but the principal fiber used is sheep's wool. Many different breeds of sheep are used to provide fibers differing in fineness. The products vary greatly—from lambswool (baby wool), Merino (fine and soft), crossbred (medium wool for mixing and for use in domestic fabrics) to upland and mountain wool (coarse and wiry for carpets).

Wool clipped or sheared from sheep or sliped wool, pulled from the skins of dead sheep, is not of constant quality from the same animal, and distinction is made between fine, coarse, outercoat, and kemp hairs, which are thick white fibers. The sorting of wool, usually at the country of origin, is programmed to separate the various grades of fiber to suit the intended use. Fibers are sorted according to their fineness, color, and length.

Each wool fiber consists of the protein keratin and is built up of spindle-shaped cells. The main cell material, or cortex, is covered by a layer of thin overlapping scales (cuticle) that is visible under a microscope and gives wool its characteristic ability to felt or mat. Pigment streaks in colored wools are distributed in the cortex. Wool

▲ Flax being harvested in the traditional way in Belgium. Today this work is often mechanized. Flax was one of the first fibers cultivated by humans and is used to make linen and linseed oil.

often has a crimp wave, which gives it springiness and warmth in finished products such as sweaters.

The principal producing areas are Australia, New Zealand, Russia, South Africa, China, and Argentina, although most countries with appreciable pasture produce wool. Clothing accounts for about 76 percent of the wool produced.

Other animal fibers in use include camel, llama, rabbit, horse, cow, and goat hairs—chiefly mohair from the Angora goat, cashmere from the cashmere goat, and common goat.

Silk is the extrudate, or spun thread, of the silkworm *Bombyx mori*. Silk is used by the worm to create a cocoon in which it will metamorphose into a silk moth. Cultivated silk is produced under factory conditions where the worms, fed on mulberry leaves, eventually grow to several inches in length. Each worm contains twin sacs of fibroin, or liquid silk protein. When it is ready to spin its cocoon, the worm attaches itself to a twig and extrudes the whole of its fibroin by muscular action through a small hole, or spinneret, forming a cocoon of endless thread several yards long. Since the emerging moth would break open the cocoon and spoil the thread continuity, the cocoons are stifled with heat, steam, or other gas. Next the cocoons are floated on water and reeled, several filaments being combined to form a fine and lustrous yarn. Japan and China are the main silk producing countries.

Wild silk, especially *tussah* and *anaphé*, is obtained from cocoons found in the open in Far Eastern countries. These cocoons are usually communal, and also broken, and cannot be reeled. The fiber is recovered by mechanical action and forms cut, or staple, fiber, which is made into yarn by twisting. A typical fabric made from this source is *shantung*.

Vegetable fibers

The many vegetable fibers can be divided into seed hairs, bast (inner bark), leaf, and fruit fibers.

Cotton is a seed hair, the plant producing numerous large seed pods from each of which radiate thousands of cotton fibers. These fiber clusters, or bolls, together with the seeds, are picked mechanically and processed in a cotton gin to separate the seeds from the hairs, which are subsequently spun into yarn.

The cotton fiber is a single cell, originally growing as a tube with a cell wall of nearly pure cellulose. When the boll bursts or opens, the fibers dry out and, when viewed under a microscope, resemble twisted flattened tubes. Cotton will spin into very fine yarns and is known for comfort and coolness. Mercerization is the treatment of cotton yarn or fabric with a concentrated sodium hydroxide solution, producing enhanced luster and smoothness.

Kapok, another seed hair, comes from a tree. It is used as a stuffing material; formerly it was used also as a flotation material in lifejackets.

Bast fibers, or soft fibers, are recovered from the stems (phloem and cortex) of various dicotyledonous plants, such as flax, jute, hemp, kenaf, sunn, and ramie (or China grass). Flax is made into the material called linen, which is used for clothing, but the others are mainly used for industrial textiles and floor coverings. Jute is the most widely used member of this group.

◀ Sisal is Kenya's third-largest export. It produces a coarse fiber that is used to make twine, rope, and other rough fabrics in which great strength is needed. The fiber is inexpensive.

WOOL PRODUCTION

Sheep are usually sheared in spring, though this varies in different parts of the world. The most common practice in the United States is to remove the fleece in one piece—an individual fleece may weigh from 7 to 18 lbs. (3–8 kg), and a skilled shearer may clip as many as 200 fleeces per day. After shearing, the fleece is sorted into different grades according to the color, fineness, and length of the fibers. Each grade of wool will be used for a different product. Carpet wool, for example, is made from coarse fibers, while lamb's wool is used to make garments such as fine sweaters. In the United States, wool is sorted into 16 grades using a system that measures the thickness of the fiber in microns (one micron is 0.00004 inch). This system helps to determine the price of wool.

After grading, any loose soil or sand is removed from the fleece by a machine called an opener that also separates the fleece into smaller pieces. The wool is then cleaned in a process called scouring. One such method is to wash the fibers in a mild alkaline solution. After scouring, the wet wool is dried using heat and a gentle flow of air, after which the fibers are straightened in a carding machine. Here, revolving cylinders with wire teeth comb the wool into a fuzzy sheet called a sliver that is then drawn out into a strand called a roving. The roving is wound around a bobbin for spinning, and the fibers are drawn out again into a single strand. Two, three, or four of these strands may be twisted together to form the final yarn.

Plant stems used for producing bast fibers need retting before the fiber can be used. Retting is a process of controlled rotting by soaking the stems in water where they are attacked by bacteria. The fibers are then separated mechanically by scutching (beating). Under a microscope, bast fibers are seen to consist of bundles of many overlapping cellulosic cells, which are much thicker, stiffer, and longer than those of cotton.

Jute is grown in Bangladesh and India. Flax, used to make fine linen cloth and formerly an important crop in Northern Ireland, is mainly grown in Russia, Poland, and Belgium.

Leaf fibers, or hard fibers, are similarly constructed but are obtained from the leaf, stem, or stalks of monocotyledonous plants. Mechanical separation only is necessary. Sisal and abaca (or Manila) are the main commercial examples. The main sources of sisal are Tanzania, Mexico, and the Philippines, the last being the source of Manila, which is very rot resistant.

Fruit fibers are mainly represented by coir or coconut fiber, which is obtained from between the outer husk and shell of the coconut. The fiber is reddish brown, stiff, and wiry and is used for matting. Countries producing coir include India and Sri Lanka.

▶ A silk factory. First, the cocoons are smothered to kill the worms inside, then the silk must be carefully unwound and reeled. Cocoons of wild silk are broken and cannot be wound; instead, strands are twisted to make a yarn.

| SEE ALSO: | Clothing manufacture • Cotton • Fiber, mineral • Fiber, synthetic • Floor covering • Textile |

Fiber, Synthetic

Synthetic fibers are of strands of polymeric materials, such as polyesters and nylons. Their principal use is in the manufacture of textiles. The earliest synthetic fibers were the regenerated fibers, produced by chemical modifications of natural sources of cellulose; newer fibers include fully synthetic materials, such as nylon.

Regenerated cellulose fibers

Modern processes for manufacturing regenerated cellulose, known since 1924 as rayon, all follow a similar pattern. First, wood pulp is treated with chemical reagents that dissolve its cellulose content and free it of impurities. Then, the dissolved and chemically modified cellulose is passed through a perforated disk called a spinneret. The fine streams of solution emerge from the spinneret and pass directly into a bath of chemicals that convert the dissolved cellulose derivative into insoluble cellulose, forming fibers of rayon.

The spinneret was patented in 1883, when a British chemist, Sir Joseph Swan, used such devices to make fibers of nitrocellulose. Swan subsequently converted the fibers into cellulose filaments for use in electric lamps. In 1889, the French chemist Comte Hilaire de Chardonnet used a similar process of nitration, extrusion, drying, and regeneration of cellulose to produce Chardonnet silk fibers. Commercial production of Chardonnet silk began two years later. The process was slow and dangerous, since nitrocellulose is chemically similar to explosive guncotton.

The cuprammonium process, patented in 1890 by the French chemist Louis-Henri Despeissis, overcame the problems of the Chardonnet process and is still in use. In this process, cellulose is dissolved in cuprammonium liquor—a mixture of copper salts and ammonia. Cellulose fibers are formed by extruding the resulting liquid into a bath of alkali solution.

In 1891, a third process developed using sodium hydroxide and carbon disulfide to convert cellulose into sodium cellulose xanthate, a soluble derivative of cellulose called viscose. In the 20th century, the viscose process became the predominant method for manufacturing rayon.

The modern viscose process starts by steeping wood pulp in a caustic soda solution (concentrated sodium hydroxide solution), which converts the pulp into soda cellulose and at the same time extracts certain impurities from the wood pulp. The alkali solution and soluble impurities are squeezed from the swollen pulp, which is then shredded into fine crumbs of soda cellulose.

◄ Syrupy orange viscose, prepared by the treatment of wood pulp with sodium hydroxide solution and carbon disulfide, is an intermediate in the manufacture of rayon. After ripening, this liquid will be extruded through a spinneret into a bath of chemicals, where it will form fibers of regenerated cellulose, or rayon.

After aging, the soda cellulose crumbs are treated with liquid carbon disulfide to form bright orange cellulose xanthate. The xanthate dissolves in dilute sodium hydroxide solution to give viscose—an orange-colored syrup. The viscose solution is stored for a while to allow further chemical changes to occur—a process called ripening—before it is extruded into a bath containing dilute sulfuric acid, sodium sulfate, and zinc sulfate. The fibers are stretched as they solidify to promote the alignment of cellulose chains in the fibers, which improves their physical properties.

The main disadvantage of the viscose process is that it generates a great deal of waste. In 1978, the British chemicals company Courtauld's initiated a project whose goal was to develop a rayon-manufacturing process that would be less wasteful and harmful to the environment. In the mid-1980s, the project succeeded in producing a cellulose fiber, trade name Tencel, whose manufacture generates no waste chemicals. In 1996, the U.S. Federal Trade Commission modified the definitions of textiles to include Tencel-type fibers, called *lyocells*, as a subclass of rayons.

The Tencel process differs from other rayon-manufacturing processes in that it it uses a solvent to dissolve cellulose directly rather than using chemicals to make a soluble derivative. The solvent is an amine oxide—N-methylmorpholine-N-oxide, $C_4H_8N(CH_3)(O)O$. In the first stage, wood pulp is heated with amine oxide until the cellulose dissolves. Extruding the amine oxide–cellulose solution into dilute amine oxide causes the cellulose to solidify and releases the amine oxide. The dilute amine oxide is concentrated by distillation and reused without waste.

Cellulose acetate and triacetate

Cellulose consists of long molecular chains of repeating sugar units. Each sugar unit has three hydroxyl groups (–OH), and each of those groups can be converted into an acetate group (ethanoate, –OCOCH$_3$) by treating cellulose with acetic anhydride, formula (CH$_3$CO)$_2$O.

Cellulose triacetate is formed by reacting all of the hydroxy groups in cellulose with acetic anhydride. Cellulose acetate is produced by reacting cellulose triacetate with water so that some of the acetate groups are converted back into hydroxy groups. This reaction, a form of hydrolysis, is stopped by diluting with an excess of water when approximately one in six of the acetyl groups have been converted into hydroxy groups.

Fibers are produced by dissolving the cellulose derivative in an organic solvent—acetone (propanone, CH$_3$COCH$_3$) for cellulose acetate; methylene chloride (dichloromethane CH$_2$Cl$_2$) for cellulose triacetate. The viscous solution is extruded into a stream of hot air, which causes the solvent to evaporate and the fibers to be formed. This is known as a dry spinning process, as opposed to the wet spinning method used in the viscose process for producing rayon.

Cellulose triacetate fibers were produced as long ago as 1914, when the only available solvent was chloroform (trichloromethane, CHCl$_3$), an expensive and harmful substance. Also, the fiber could not be dyed with the dyes then available, and as a result, the commercial introduction of this fiber was delayed for 40 years.

Cellulose acetate dissolved in acetone was used extensively in World War I for coating airplane wings. At the end of the war, a capacity for producing cellulose acetate, but no market existed. Cellulose acetate was easier to spin into fibers than the triacetate but was also very difficult to dye. The problem of dyeing was overcome with the introduction of disperse dyes in the 1920s. This development was important not only for acetate in the 1920s but also in later years for the fully synthetic fibers, such as nylons, polyesters, and acrylic, and for cellulose triacetate.

Cellulose acetate is currently sold under trade names, such as Estron. It has a silky sheen that makes it useful for furnishings and clothing. Cellulose triacetate, sold as Arnel and Tricel, can be durably pleated or set, and it has easy-care, quick-drying properties. In these respects, its properties are more similar to those of fully synthetic fibers, such as nylon, than are those of cellulose acetate. Cellulose triacetate is used to make dresses, knitwear, underwear, and linings for garments, and in household textile goods, such as bedspreads and bath mats.

▶ Dry spinning of acetate yarn by extruding cellulose acetate solution into a stream of hot air. The perforated metal disk, or spinneret, must be cleaned at regular intervals to prevent blockages.

Nylons and aramids

Nylons are examples of polyamides—polymeric materials characterized by the presence of amide linkages (–(CO)NH–) in their polymer chains. The first nylon was nylon 6,6, developed in 1934 by the U.S. chemist Wallace Carothers. Nylon 6,6 is so called because it forms by the reaction between two compounds that have six carbon atoms per molecule: hexamethylene diamine (1,6-diaminohexane, H$_2$NC$_6$H$_{12}$NH$_2$) and adipic acid (hexane-1,6-dioic acid, HOOCC$_6$H$_{12}$COOH).

The second common nylon is nylon 6, which is made by the polymerization of caprolactam (C$_5$H$_{10}$(CO)NH), whose ring-shaped molecules open as they join together in a chain. The raw materials for making nylons are products of petroleum refining and tar distillation.

Nylon is spun into fibers by melting polymer chips in an inert atmosphere, which hinders degradation of the polymer, and extruding the molten polymer through a spinneret. The fibers solidify as they cool and are then drawn to several times their original length. Drawing aligns the nylon polymer chains and greatly increases the strength of the resulting fiber.

The strength and fineness of nylon fibers made them ideal for their first major uses—for sheer stockings and hosiery and woven as textiles for parachute canopies. The thermoplasticity of nylons—their ability to soften when hot and harden again when cool—makes them useful in heat-setting fabrics for making easy-care garments that do not require ironing.

Aramids are polyamides in which the carbon blocks between the amide groups of the chains are rigid aromatic molecules. These blocks make such polyamides extremely tough. Kevlar, for example, is an aramid used for bulletproof vests.

Polyesters

The polyester used in textiles is polyethylene terephthalate, a polymer of terephthalic acid (benzene-1,4-dioic acid, $HOOCC_6H_6COOH$) and ethylene glycol (ethane-1,2-diol, HOC_2H_4OH), which are both made from oil refinery products. As with nylon, polyester fibers are melt spun and then drawn to increase their strength.

Polyester fibers are produced in larger quantities than any other synthetic fibers—16.5 million tons (15 million tonnes) of polyester were made in 1998 compared with 4 million tons (3.6 million tonnes) of nylon. Sold under trade names such as Dacron, Fortrel, and Trevira, polyester fabrics have set new standards of performance in textiles for easy-care suits, dresses, and shirts and for household items. Polyester is often used in blended fabrics, such as polyester-wool, polyester-cotton ("polycotton"), and polyester-rayon blends, and sometimes in all-polyester knitted fabrics.

Olefins

At the end of the 20th century, the olefin-derived fibers formed the fastest growing sector of the synthetic fibers market. The worldwide annual production of olefin fibers overtook that of nylon in the mid-1990s and reached 5.1 million tons (4.6 million tonnes) in 1998.

The olefin fibers are so called because they are made from polymers of alkenes, such as ethene (C_2H_4) and propene ($C_2H_3CH_3$), which were formerly called olefins. They are melt spun, often from molten mixtures of polymer and dye, since the fibers are difficult to dye using the techniques that can be used for other types of fibers.

Polyethene is mainly used to make cords and nets. Polypropene, which is tougher than polyethene, is used to make sacks, ropes, carpet backings, and finer fibers for carpet piles. Other olefin fibers are elastomeric—they stretch and recover just as rubber does. These fibers are used in support garments and swimwear under trade names such as Spanzelle and Lycra.

Acrylics

Acrylic fibers are polymers of acrylonitrile (propenonitrile, C_2H_3CN), a product of the petroleum-chemicals industry. They are sold under trade names such as Acrilan, Orlon, Courtelle, and Dralon. Acrylics, like other synthetic fibers, are ideal as easy-care fabrics, but they are characteristically warming and soft, which makes them useful in blankets and fake fur. Copolymers of acrylonitrile with vinyl chloride (chloroethene, CH_2CHCl) and vinylidene chloride (1,1-dichloroethene, CH_2CCl_2) have the added advantage of fire resistance.

An 85-times magnified photomicrograph of a lens-cleaning cloth. The integrity of the fibers in the cloth prevents the formation of lint, which would otherwise stick to lenses after cleaning, and the space between the individual fibers in the yarns readily absorbs cleaning fluids.

Yarn preparation

The individual strands that emerge from a spinneret are more accurately described as filaments. The properties of a synthetic fiber depend not only on its chemical composition but also on how the filament is prepared as a yarn.

Synthetic fibers can be prepared as simple continuous-filament yarn, or they can be chopped into short lengths of fiber and then twisted together to give a spun yarn that is rougher but warmer to the touch than single-filament yarn. The warm feel, which comes from the ability of the frayed spun yarn to trap air, contributes to the insulating properties of textiles made from such a yarn. Thicker fibers are produced in a monofilament form for applications where a single filament is strong and thick enough for use on its own, such as for fishing line.

The characteristics of a fiber can be modified by alterations in the extrusion and spinning processes. Filaments extruded to have a bone-shaped cross section produce fibers that have greater effective thickness and covering power than cylindrical fibers. Crimping the fiber—stamping it to form wavy staples—can improve the spinning qualities of a given fiber, while the characteristics of different fibers can be combined by spinning yarns from appropriate blends of fibers, which may be natural or synthetic.

SEE ALSO: CLOTHING MANUFACTURE • FIBER, NATURAL • FLAME-RETARDING AGENT • POLYMER AND POLYMERIZATION

Fiber Optics

Fiber optics use transparent strands, called optical fibers, as waveguides for light. Its applications are diverse, ranging from bundles of optical fibers that convey images through endoscopes to optical cables that carry telephone signals and other forms of information as pulses of infrared light.

Total internal reflection

If light were to escape through the walls of optical fibers, the intensity of the light passing along the cable would diminish rapidly. The phenomenon that channels light though an optical fiber with little loss of intensity—even when the cable is curved—is called total internal reflection.

Total internal reflection arises because of variations in the speed of light through different substances and is measured in terms of different values of refractive index. A substance's refractive index is defined as the speed of light in a vacuum divided by the speed of light through that substance; since the speed of light is greater through a vacuum than it is through any substance, refractive indices are always greater than one.

If a ray of light travels from one transparent medium to another, its direction changes in a process called refraction. If the ray passes from glass (refractive index 1.5) to water (refractive index 1.3), for example, the refracted ray strikes a shallower angle to the glass–water boundary than does the incident ray. At the so-called critical angle of the incident ray, the refracted ray is flat along the surface; at shallower incident angles, the light is reflected back into the glass. This phenomenon is total internal reflection.

Because of total internal reflection, a submerged diver in a perfectly calm pool would only be able to see the bottom of the pool reflected in the surface at angles less than 49 degrees to the horizontal—the critical angle for total internal reflection at a water–air interface is 48.8 degrees. In practice, however, ripples in the water's surface allow some light to enter from above at angles less than the critical angle by deforming the surface.

Another example of how surface imperfections disrupt total internal reflection occurs with a glass rod illuminated from one end by a light source. If the sides of the rod were perfectly clean and smooth, total internal reflection would occur at angles less than around 41 degrees to the sides of the rod. In fact, small scratches and other imperfections, appearing as bright patches on the rod's surface, allow light to escape at shallower angles.

▼ Optical fibers can be drawn from two concentric chambers in a tubular furnace (top left) or from a single preform (bottom left). The three main types of optical fiber are, from left to right, graded-index fibers, multimode step-index fibers, and single-mode step-index fibers.

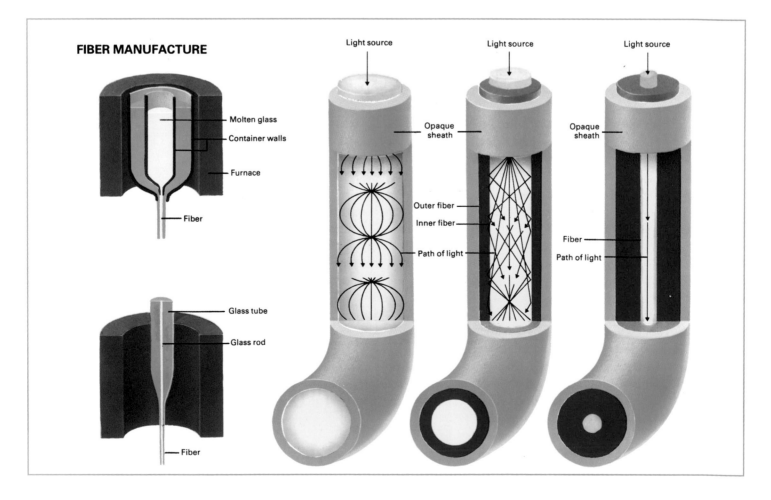

FIBER MANUFACTURE

Molten glass
Container walls
Furnace
Fiber

Glass tube
Glass rod
Fiber

Light source
Light source
Light source

Opaque sheath
Outer fiber
Inner fiber
Path of light

Opaque sheath
Fiber
Path of light

Optical fibers

The occasional leakages of light that occur along the walls of simple glass rods make them useless for carrying light over long distances, since there would be an unacceptable loss of light intensity. Furthermore, the rigidity of glass rods would make them awkward to lay in underground channels, as is usual for urban communications networks, and impossible to use in flexible endoscopes.

Optical fibers overcome the problem of surface imperfections by having their reflecting boundary at the junction between a cylindrical core, usually of glass but sometimes of plastic, and an outer cladding of low-refractive-index glass or plastic. The reflecting surface is protected from dirt and scratches by being on the inside of the cladding. The attenuation, or light loss, of such cables can be so low that silica-glass-cored optical fibers can carry infrared light signals over distances as great as 60 miles (around 100 km) between signal-boosting stations compared with a range of around 1 mile (1.6 km) between boosts for electrical signal cables.

By virtue of their fineness—they are typically 0.005 in. (0.125 mm) in diameter—optical fibers are much more flexible than thicker rods of the same materials would be. They are prone to snapping if individual fibers are handled roughly, but bundles of fibers are quite resilient, especially if they are encased in a flexible plastic sheath.

Types of optical fibers

The three basic types of optical fibers are graded-index fibers, multimode step-index fibers, and single-mode step-index fibers. In each case, "index" refers to the refractive index values of the glasses used to make the fibers.

Graded-index fibers typically consist of a 0.004 in. (0.1 mm) diameter silica-glass fiber clad in a plastic coating. The refractive index of the silica glass decreases radially from the center of the fiber, having the effect of bending light away from the edges and containing it in the fiber.

Multimode step-index fibers have a core of high-refractive-index silica glass, usually 0.002 to 0.004 in. (0.04–0.1 mm) in diameter, surrounded

▲ This bundle of optical fibers was part of an experimental telephone network to which all 1,500 homes in Biarritz, France, were connected during the summer of 1986.

by a layer of lower-refractive-index silica glass to a total diameter of 0.004 to 0.005 in. (0.1–0.125 mm). There is a 1 to 3 percent difference between the refractive indices of the two layers.

The core of a multimode fiber is wide enough to allow several signals—the modes—to be bounced inside the fibers at different angles. The modes are separated by equipment at the receiving end of the fiber.

Single-mode step-index fibers are of similar construction to the multimode fibers, but their core is narrower—typically 0.00004 to 0.0004 in. (0.001–0.01 mm). Also, the refractive index difference between the inner and outer layers is only 0.1 to 0.3 percent. Although they carry only one mode of signal, fibers of this type have lower attenuation values than do other types.

Optical fiber manufacture

The basic material in glass optical fibers is pure silica (silicon dioxide, SiO_2). The refractive index of silica can be increased by adding traces of germanium oxide (GeO_2) and decreased by adding traces of boric oxide (Be_2O_3).

The layers of an optical fiber can be assembled in a variety of ways. In one technique, glasses for the inner and outer layers are heated in concentric compartments within a tube furnace. Once molten, the two glasses are drawn through a die at the bottom of the furnace so that one glass surrounds the other. The united fiber is then coated with plastic and stored on drums.

More sophisticated manufacturing methods start with a preform—a cylindrical slug of glass whose radial composition matches that of the finished fiber. The preform is heated until molten, then drawn through a dye at such a speed that its diameter shrinks from around 1 in. (25 mm) to around 0.004 in. (0.1 mm).

Preforms for this manufacturing method can be prepared by fusing together a rod and sleeve of two different types of glass or by vapor deposition. In vapor deposition, one type of glass is vaporized and allowed to condense inside a sleeve of the other type of glass. Several layers can be built up by multiple vapor depositions on a sleeve followed by the insertion of a rod.

Lighting and imaging applications

When fiber optics were introduced in the 1950s, the relatively high losses of the fibers then available restricted them to short-range applications. One of the early applications of fiber optics was in endoscopes, which use fiber optics to illuminate an object and to carry its image to an eyepiece.

Illumination by fiber optics uses a bundle of many thousands of fibers to carry light from a source, such as a filament lamp, to the location that is to be illuminated. This type of bundle is called an incoherent bundle, since relative positions of the fibers at the two ends of the bundle do not have to be consistent to carry light. Incoherent bundles also carry light from laser sources to perform operations on tissue.

Image-carrying bundles, on the other hand, must be coherent to carry an accurate image. Each fiber must occupy the same position relative to the other fibers at both ends of the bundle. It is done by laying out all the fibers in parallel and then clamping the two ends in tight cylindrical sleeves that hold the fibers in place.

Fiber-optic communications

In combination with an appropriate laser-driven signal generator and a detector, a single optical fiber can carry many megabytes of information per second. Optical fibers also have the advantage over electrical cables that they are completely immune to electrical interference. Since the introduction of low-attenuation optical fibers in the mid-1980s, these properties have spawned the rapid development of long-distance networks to carry telephone calls and data. A more recent

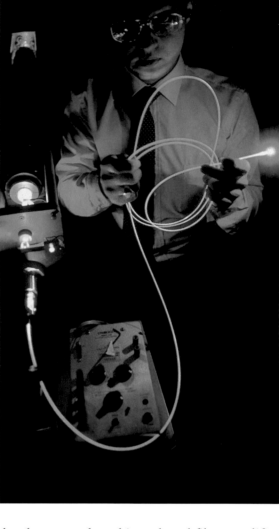

◀ The white flex in this picture is a bundle of optical fibers used to carry laser light for use in surgery. The flexibility of the bundle helps surgeons by making it possible to perform laser surgery in confined body cavities and through keyhole incisions.

development, the erbium-doped fiber amplifier (EDFA), promises to expand the scope of such networks even further. An EDFA is a stretch of fiber that, when illuminated by a semiconductor laser, boosts the signal in a fiber without having to detect, decode, and then regenerate it.

Cheap optical fibers based on polymers rather than glass are useful for local networks. A typical polymer cable will give an attenuation of 250 dB per mile (155 dB/km) compared with 8dB per mile (5 dB/km) for a typical glass cable, thus limiting the useful range of such cables. Nevertheless, polymer cables have the advantage that they can bend around curves up to five times tighter than glass-based fibers can without snapping. Furthermore, the terminations of polymer fibers are fitted by simply cutting the cable and pushing a plug on the end, whereas glass cables require special cutting and polishing tools. These properties make polymer fibers ideal for relatively easily installed local networks.

FACT FILE

- *When strain is applied to optical fibers, the way they transmit light is modified. Using this principle, researchers at Los Alamos National Laboratory in New Mexico have developed an optical-fiber sensor for detecting strains caused by earthquake activity. The laser-sourced sensor can detect strains as small as one part in ten billion.*

- *In October 1983, the Bell Telephone Laboratories succeeded in transmitting 420 million bits per second—the equivalent of 6,000 separate telephone signals—through an optical-fiber channel 100 miles (161 km) in length. It was achieved without the use of repeaters to boost the signal.*

SEE ALSO: ELECTRONICS IN MEDICINE • ENDOSCOPE • GLASS • GLASS FIBER • LASER AND MASER • LIGHT AND OPTICS • PLASTICS • TELECOMMUNICATIONS • TELEPHONE SYSTEM

Filter, Optical

Optical filters are used to eliminate or reduce the intensities of certain color components in a beam of light, by either passing the beam through or reflecting it off a material with the required color properties. Optical filters are used in a variety of applications including photography, color television, stage lighting, protective eyeglasses (goggles), and spectroscopy.

Just as electrical filters reject certain frequencies, so optical filters absorb or reflect particular wavelengths or frequencies of light. The spectrum of electromagnetic radiation ranges from red light through the colors of the rainbow to violet. Together, these colors produce white light. If a band of color is removed, the remaining colors will predominate—white light passed through a filter that absorbs blue and green light will then contain yellow, orange, and red light and will have an overall orange color.

Absorption filters

The most common type of filter uses the absorptive properties of various dyes and minerals. They are mixed with the transparent filter materials—glass, plastic, gelatin, or cellulose ester—or they may be coated onto a surface and then protected by being sandwiched in glass.

When light encounters molecules of certain materials, the photons, or packs of light energy, of particular wavelengths may force these molecules to resonate. The light is reemitted, but at a longer (infrared) wavelength, at which the photons have less energy. Thus, the beam of light has lost energy at one wavelength or, in practice, a band of wavelengths. Some wavelengths are more easily absorbed than others: it is particularly difficult, for example, to make a filter that will absorb only red

light, transmitting blue. Blue-colored filters tend to absorb a little of all colors.

The gelatin is extruded through a thin slit onto a very flat moving glass plate as a layer about 0.04 in. (1 mm) thick. It is then chilled to set the gelatin so that it can be peeled off the plate for drying. On drying, it shrinks to a thickness of only about 0.004 in. (0.1 mm).

If a more robust filter is required, the filter materials may be bonded onto optically polished glass and then sandwiched by another piece of the same type of glass. Alternatively, an extremely hard, durable resin may be used to make the filter, the surface of which will absorb the colored dye.

Dichroic filters

With normal filters, the light that is absorbed is lost, that is, unusable. However, there is another type, known as dichroic, or interference, filters, in

◄ Using white light, the transmitted ray appears blue, while the reflected ray appears yellowish. In color-television cameras, the image has to be split up into three colored components, red, blue, and green.

▼ These pictures show the effects of various gelatin dye filters on a spectrum projected onto a screen. The shots show the layout—the filter affects the lower half of the spectrum only. Here the color of the filter itself can be seen in the lower left-hand corner—magenta at left, cyan (peacock blue) at right. The magenta filter cuts out green and yellow light completely, while the cyan cuts out yellow, red, and some violet light.

which the nontransmitted light is reflected. They are so named (*dichroic*, from the root meaning two colored) because the light reflected off them contains every color that was present in the original (incident) beam except the color that is transmitted through the filter. And, by controlling their fabrication to within very fine limits, it is possible to allow a very narrow band of wavelengths through the filter. Dichroic filters are used, for example, in color television cameras, where the reflected part of the beam can be used rather than wasted.

Dichroic filters are also known as dielectric filters because of the particular electrical properties of the materials—usually ceramics— used in their construction. These materials are laid down in very thin and even layers on a glass base (called the substrate) by evaporating them in a vacuum chamber to make the filter.

The action of these filters depends on the interference effects of light waves reflecting from the surfaces of the various layers. The number of layers and the thickness of each determine the final properties of the filter. Generally, the layers are less than 0.00002 in. (0.0005 mm) thick. Three such layers will transmit about half the visible spectrum, about 180 nm, but with 17 layers, the transmitted bandwith is narrowed down to about 1 nm. Extremely narrow transmission bandwidth filters (less than 1 nm) have two sets of narrow layers separated by one thick one.

Filter descriptions

Filters tend to be given descriptions that vary with their purpose. The filter used to make red traffic lights is always called red, though it actually filters out blue, green, and yellow light. On the other hand, to make their photographs clearer, photographers often use filters that they call ultraviolet, to absorb the blue and ultraviolet wavelengths that tend to produce a haze on photographs of distant scenes, though these filters may actually be colored light yellow.

Materials

The types of filters that can be made depend on the materials. The earliest filters were made of glass, but now gelatin filters are more popular.

Colored glass can be made by simply adding various metal oxides to the molten glass. Iron oxide, for example, produces a green color and is present anyway in poor-quality window glass. Cobalt oxide produces a blue coloring, manganese produces purple, and so on. The range of oxides available is limited, but some of them have unique properties, such as didymium glass, which absorbs the yellow light of sodium streetlights while letting most other colors through.

The dyeing industry has produced a vast range of dyes, many of which can be mixed with gelatin, the material that is used to prepare the emulsion of photographic film. This gelatin is made very much thicker than photographic emulsions, since it will be used as a thin gelatin sheet and not coated on a flexible backing.

The different types of filters include band-pass filters, which selectively transmit desired ranges; long-pass filters, which block undesired shorter wavelengths; short-pass filters, which block undesired longer wavelengths; neutral-density filters, which exhibit nearly constant transmission, especially in the visible range; and conversion filters, which increase or decrease the color temperature or radiation sources based on their particular spectral curves. Polarizing filters allow the passage of light in one direction only and are often used in photography for controlling surface reflections and for darkening blue skies.

By combining different filters together, additional filter effects can be achieved, providing extra flexibility. Typical types of glass base material include cut filter glass, with or without machined edges, raw glass, block glass, and rolled sheet glass.

▼ A starburst filter— a type of diffraction grating—usually has a rotating mount that can be turned to position the spikes of the sun to help the photographer compose the picture.

SEE ALSO: CAMERA • DIFFRACTION • ELECTROMAGNETIC RADIATION • GLASS • LIGHT AND OPTICS • POLARIZATION • SPECTROSCOPY • STEREOSCOPY • TELEVISION CAMERA • THEATRICAL LIGHTING

Firefighting

◄ Firefighting vehicles at work. In the foreground is a tanker holding foam for the hoses. In front of it is the aerial ladder truck whose ladder can extend up to 100 ft. (30 m). Many different types of equipment are necessary to control a large fire.

Ever since the discovery of fire, humans have realized the importance of being able to control it, as an uncontrolled fire can cause widespread devastation. Throughout history there are examples of cities being devastated by fire, for example, Rome in 64 C.E., London in 1666, and Chicago in 1871.

Among the first organized firefighting forces were those established throughout the Roman Empire. Slaves were used as firefighters and were stationed on the walls and at the gates of cities. This organization, known as the Familia Publica, was later replaced by the corps of Vigiles, who had other duties including the capture of runaway slaves and policing the city at night.

After being in existence for more than 300 years the Vigiles were put on an equal footing with the imperial troops, although they were not classified as soldiers. They were also responsible for preventing fires, and they had powers to punish offenders responsible for starting fires.

After the decline of the Roman Empire, the countries that had been under Roman rule were left to make their own arrangements for fighting fires, and initially, they did not do very well. Centuries passed before any effective organizations evolved. In Europe, it became customary to ring a bell at night to order people to put out their fires and candles. This custom was known as the curfew, from the French *covrefeu* (to cover fire).

Small towns and villages usually kept a supply of buckets, hooks, and sometimes ladders available for fighting fires—basic items of equipment

◀ A Pathfinder heavy duty airport crash truck in action with a burning aircraft. Weighing 37 tons (33 tonnes), it can accelerate to 50 mph (80 km/h) in 50 seconds.

that can be found on even the most modern fire engine. As towns grew larger and more industrialized, the basic equipment supplied by the local parish authorities was soon found to be inadequate to meet the increased demands.

Portable pumps were introduced, usually operated by volunteers, but there were seldom any paid, responsible officials to look after the equipment. Contemporary records often mention instances of broken pumps and missing buckets, inadequacies that were unfortunately never discovered until it was too late.

Insurance companies

In the 18th century, the new business of insurance was gaining ground, and the early fire insurance companies took over the responsibility of providing professional firefighters and building fire stations. They also provided a fire mark, or badge, to identify the premises that they insured. When a fire occurred, several different fire engines would be summoned, and the first thing they did when they arrived was to look for the fire mark of their own company. If the mark was there, the fire would be dealt with; if not, the firefighters would often return to their stations.

It was inevitable that petty rivalries would occur. Sometimes the firefighters from one company would stand and watch the other putting out the fire, often jeering or even obstructing them. The hand-operated pumps were operated by volunteers who were often paid with beer, and fights were not uncommon.

Eventually the responsibility for firefighting was taken over by the local authorities. In Britain, there were about 2,000 separate fire brigades in operation when they were nationalized following the outbreak of World War II, and these were returned to local authority control in 1948.

Fire appliances

Today's fire appliances perform the same basic function as those used by the insurance company fire brigades in the early 19th century—that is, they carry the firefighters, equipment, and pumps to the scene of the fire as quickly as possible.

The equipment used by firefighters is more complicated these days and is as diverse as the types of fires they have to attend. In fact, there is so much equipment that fire appliances have become specialized units and broadly fall into one of several groups, each group having a particular role to play.

A firefighter's first responsibility is rescue, and actually fighting the fire must take second place to efforts to save life. The first group of appliances is therefore aimed first at lifesaving and second, at firefighting.

Typical of this type of appliance is the pump escape, widely used in Britain and many other countries. These machines have a powerful engine, usually with automatic transmission and a pump capable of delivering up to 1,000 gallons (4,550 l) of water per minute. They carry a wheeled ladder, which extends to about 50 ft. (15 m), equipment to break in through doors and windows, rescue lines to lower people from windows, lights to help penetrate the gloom of a smoke-laden building, breathing apparatus, hoses, and jets (hose nozzles). With its crew of five, this appliance is the basic rescue and firefighting unit of the modern fire service. Basically similar machines used in the United States are known as triple-combination pumpers. The most modern variant of the pump escape is the pump hydraulic platform, which is similar in most respects except that it carries a 50 ft. (15 m) hydraulically powered articulated boom and rescue cage in place of the wheeled escape ladder.

The second major category of appliance used in Britain is the water tender, which supports the rescue appliance and carries about 400 gallons (1,820 l) of water in addition to the basic firefighting equipment of breathing apparatus, hoses, jets and ladders. As well as the main pump, there is a portable pump so that the firefighters can take advantage of natural water supplies such as streams or ponds that are inaccessible to the tender.

Other basic appliances in use in the United States are the service-ladder truck, which carries a range of ladders; the combination pumper-ladder truck (the quad); the aerial-ladder truck, which carries a powered ladder (similar to the British turntable ladder) as well as a range of ordinary ladders; and a combined pumper- and aerial-ladder unit known as the quintuple truck.

The turntable ladder appliance enables the firefighter to work at a greater height. It carries a ladder capable of extending to 100 ft. (30 m) or more, mounted on a turret that enables it to rotate through 360 degrees. All the ladder movements are hydraulically operated and powered by the engine of the appliance, which is made into a stable working base by the use of axle locks to prevent the road springs from flexing and outrigger jacks to steady the vehicle. The firefighter at the top of the ladder has a telephone to enable communication with the driver below who is operating the controls.

This appliance is used for rescue purposes and to put large quantities of water onto a fire at a high level. When in use on a hill or on a road with a steep camber, the vertical plane of the ladder is maintained automatically throughout the rotation movement, thus assisting stability.

Many fire departments are now using the larger versions of the hydraulic platform (known as snorkels) for fighting fires in tall buildings. First introduced in Chicago in 1958, they can provide a stable working platform for several firefighters at heights of around 70 ft. (21 m), with a pivoted jet mounted on the platform supplied with water through built-in pipes.

Support vehicles

All the appliances mentioned so far are used for the actual fighting of fire, but at any large fire, the firefighting team requires additional facilities that are provided by a range of support vehicles. Hose-laying vehicles are used when long lines of hose are needed to provide large amounts of water. When special equipment, such as breathing apparatus, light, power tools, protective clothing, and radiation or gas monitoring meters are required, they are supplied by an emergency tender.

▲ An aircraft dumping fire extinguishing chemicals on a forest fire, often virtually inaccessible for land vehicles and hoses. Helicopters may also be used for survey and rescue work.

▶ Fireboats at a dock fire in warehouses in London. Fireboats can be used to reach inaccessible parts of a fire in buildings that border a waterfront and have the advantage that they can draw water directly from the waterway rather than use the main water supply.

The effects of smoke and water on the parts of a building not affected by the fire must be considered, and so a damage control unit or salvage tender is utilized, which carries equipment to help minimize any hazards and takes effective steps to control smoke and water damage.

At a large fire, communications will be centered on a control unit, thus enabling firefighters to maintain radio contact with their headquarters, other appliances and personnel, fireboats, rescue vessels, and helicopters.

Boats and aircraft

Fires do not always occur in places accessible to wheeled vehicles—for example, at ports one of the hazards to be faced is that of fire on board ship. To deal with this situation, firefighting is carried out from fireboats, powerful vessels fitted with pumps and all the equipment normally carried on land-based appliances. For work in harbors, docks and river estuaries, these boats are basically powerful motor launches, but larger versions based on tugboat designs are capable of dealing with fires on ships at sea.

Increasing use is being made of helicopters for survey, control, and rescue work in large cities. In Britain, the fire brigades often work in conjunction with Royal Air Force rescue helicopters, but in many large cities, such as Tokyo and Los Angeles, the fire departments have their own dedicated helicopters to help their work.

A further application for helicopters and light aircraft is in fighting forest and bush fires, where they can be used for reconnaissance, carrying firefighting personnel, or to dump water or fire suppressing chemicals onto the fire.

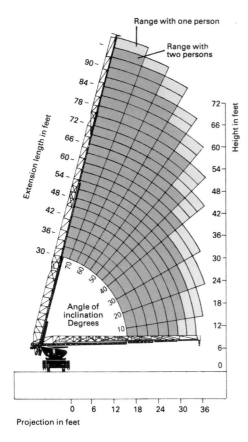

Range with one person

Range with two persons

Extension length in feet

90
84
78
72
66
60
54
48
42
36
30

Height in feet

72
66
60
54
48
42
36
30
24
18
12
6
0

70
60
50
40
30
20
10

Angle of
inclination
Degrees

0   6   12   18   24   30   36

Projection in feet

◄ This diagram shows the lateral and vertical extended reach of a typical rotating hydraulic ladder. The reach is greater with a single operator.

▼ Turntable (aerial) ladders being used at a paint factory fire in Maryland to extend fire hoses to reach the upper floors.

upon the surface of the burning liquid and thus smother the flames by excluding oxygen.

High-expansion foams are based on a type of stabilized liquid detergent and can have expansion ratios of as much as 1,000 to 1. They produce a very light foam that will cling to most surfaces, providing a very effective coating to extinguish the fire. In the case of a fire in a stack of tires, for example, water would put out the flames, but there may be enough residual burning within the tire to start the fire off again as the water drains away. Large amounts of water would therefore have to be sprayed onto the stack to prevent re-ignition. If high-expansion foam is used, however, it does not drain off so rapidly, and owing to this fact and to the high expansion ratio of the foam, considerably less water is needed.

Extinguishers and sprinklers

The main types of portable fire extinguishers are water, foam, and dry chemical. Halon bromo-chlorodifluoromethane (BCF) extinguishers were also commonly used, replacing the older carbon tetrachloride type, but halons have been found to destroy ozone, so restrictions in their use are planned despite their considerable effectiveness. In Britain, halon-based systems must be discontinued by 2003.

Every licensed airport has its own fire and rescue service, and the largest of all land-based fire appliances, the crash tenders, are to be found at big international airports. A typical example of this type of appliance is the Chubb Fire Pathfinder, weighing 37 tons (33 tonnes) and powered by a 635 brake-horsepower engine. It can produce, without replenishment, 24,000 gallons (109,000 l) of foam, enough to cover a Boeing 747 in a matter of seconds, sprayed from its remotely controlled monitor jet on the roof.

Foam generation

Foam is generated by mixing a foaming agent with water and aerating it. The foaming agent may be added to the water after it leaves the pump or circulated within the pump itself to mix it more effectively. The mixture is aerated at the hose nozzle by allowing air to be drawn in at the side by the vacuum created by the fast-moving stream of water and foaming agent.

Standard low-expansion foams have an expansion ratio of about 8 to 1 (the ratio of the volume of foam to the volume of the mixture before aeration), and the foaming agent traditionally was either a form of animal protein (usually hoof or horn meal) or soya protein. These foams, however, have been augmented in recent years by two new types: fluoroprotein and fluorochemical synthetic detergent foams.

Foams are particularly useful for dealing with liquid fires, such as oil fires, because they float

▶ Smoke detectors were first invented in 1969 and can now be found in most homes. Smoke alarms use either a photoelectric cell or an ionization detector to alert people to the presence of a fire. The ionization detector contains a small amount of radioactive material, which emits alpha particles that ionize the air molecules between two electrodes (left). The movement of the ions causes a current to flow. When smoke particles enter the alarm (grey spheres, right), they attach themselves to the ions and impede their movement. As a result, the current flow drops and triggers an alarm to sound.

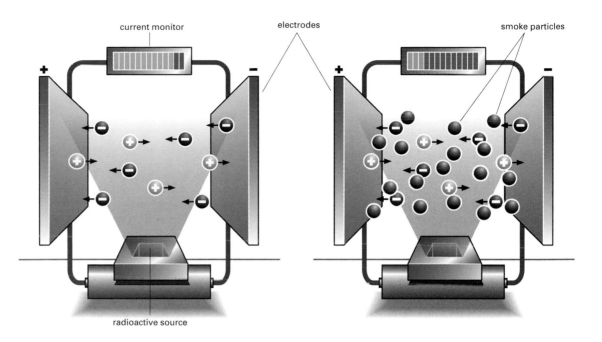

current monitor · electrodes · smoke particles · radioactive source

Water extinguishers are still widely used for fighting fires. They used to be operated by the interaction of a solution of sodium bicarbonate in water and a small quantity of sulfuric acid, which was released when the extinguisher was turned upside down. Today, all extinguishers are designed to be used upright. They work by simply withdrawing the safety pin and squeezing together two levers, releasing the firefighting agent, which may be continually pressurized by dry air or nitrogen (maintained-pressure type) or by carbon dioxide (CO_2) stored in a small pressure cylinder within the extinguisher shell.

Foam extinguishers use a stabilized protein or synthetic foam liquid mixed with water to be discharged as a solution to an aspirating nozzle, where air is entrained to form a firefighting foam. Dry-chemical types discharge a variety of special, easy-flow powders as high-velocity streams to inhibit a flame chain reaction.

The carbon dioxide extinguisher consists of a high-pressure gas container filled with liquid CO_2, which is discharged via a tapered horn to form a vaporized cloud of inert gas. Another type of extinguisher, the soda-acid type, mixes sulphuric acid with sodium bicarbonate when activated to produce carbon dioxide.

The most common halon extinguishers used Halon 1301 (bromotrifluoromethane). The agent interrupts chain reactions that propagate the combustion process and was regarded as safe for use with electrical equipment.

Detectors

Most of the calls dealt with by fire services are received by telephone, but increasing numbers of industrial, commercial, and public buildings are being protected by automatic fire detection systems, which locate the source of the fire and transmit the information to the nearest fire station. Many of these buildings also have automatic extinguishing systems that spray water, inert gas, or foam directly onto the fire.

The simplest types of fire detectors are heat detectors, which operate when a certain temperature is reached or the temperature rises abnormally quickly owing to the heat from the fire or when fusible links made of a soft metal alloy that melts at these temperatures activates the circuit.

FACT FILE

■ Caesar Augustus formed probably the first municipal fire department, in Rome. Seven squads of men were led by a fire chief, called a praefectus vigilum, with his own chariot.

■ On the morning of October 8, 1871, the Chicago Tribune carried an insurance advertisement urging citizens to "prepare now for fall and winter fires." The same day, the Great Chicago Fire broke out, which by October 10 had killed 120 people and destroyed 18,000 buildings.

■ As of August 31, 2000, nearly 6.5 million acres of forest had burned nationwide in the United States, more than double the ten-year average. States hardest hit included Alaska, California, Colorado, Idaho, Montana, New Mexico, Nevada, Oregon, Texas, and Utah.

Modern systems use photoelectric cells and other devices to detect the presence of smoke, and the newer detectors use infrared beams. A beam is transmitted across the area to be protected from transmitter to receiver. Some beam detectors use mirrors to reflect the beam to cover the area. The beam is aimed at a receiver having a grid of detectors; under stable conditions, the point of contact of the beam on the detectors remains stationary, but a variation in air temperature owing to a fire is enough to make the beam waver, and the detectors will react to this and trigger the alarm.

Sprinkler systems in buildings usually consist of pipes placed near the ceiling, with sprinkler heads placed at intervals along them. The heads are sealed off with fusible links or small glass bulbs filled with a liquid or solid material that expands readily when the temperature rises, breaking the bulb and opening the head.

The firefighting material is commonly water, but where this is ineffective and may be dangerous, such as in oil and fuel storage-tank fires, foam systems are used. In industrial plants that may contain flammable vapors, carbon dioxide flooding is used, and for electrical equipment, vaporizing liquids are used to create a nonflammable barrier. For some chemicals, only various dry powders can be used in the sprinkler systems.

Firefighting hazards

In addition to the obvious hazards of heat, flame, smoke, and falling debris, firefighters are increasingly being faced with new dangers that result from modern materials and technology. Typical of the hazards encountered even in small domestic fires are poisonous gases, which are given off by plastic tiles and insulating materials; fierce and rapid flame spread from modern furnishing materials; explosive liquids and gases, which are found in aerosol cans and portable gas cylinders; and radioactive materials.

Firefighters may also be faced with any one of the hundreds of dangerous chemicals now in use, many of which are transported in bulk by road and rail. In order to face these dangers safely, they need a system of communications that can bring them expert advice and information as quickly as possible. For instance, information on new firefighting techniques and equipment is commonly available on the Internet, and mobile telecommunications technology enables firefighters at the scene of a blaze to be put rapidly in contact with experts anywhere in the world.

The evolution of the present-day fire services has taken a long time, and it is one job that will always involve a degree of personal danger for the firefighters themselves.

SEARCHING THROUGH THE SMOKE

Thermal sensors use photo detectors that are sensitive to the direct contact of photons on their surface to detect thermal radiation emitted in the thermal infrared (3 to 15 mm) range. The detectors are cooled to close to absolute zero so that their own thermal emissions are limited. Thermal sensors measure the surface temperature and thermal properties of the area being scanned. They use one or more internal temperature references to enable a comparison with the detected radiation, so the information obtained by the sensors can be related to absolute radiant temperature. Thermal imaging can be achieved by day or night because this type of radiation is emitted, not reflected. It is used for a variety of applications, including finding hot areas or warm bodies in low-visibility environments such as smoke-filled buildings, forest fire mapping, and the monitoring of heat loss from various types of equipment.

 SEE ALSO: BREATHING APPARATUS • COMPRESSOR AND PUMP • FLAME AND IGNITION • FLAME-RETARDING AGENT • PROTECTIVE CLOTHING

Index

Page numbers in **bold** refer to main articles; those in *italics* refer to picture captions.